Becoming a Changemaker

Becoming a Changemaker

An Actionable, Inclusive
Guide to Leading Positive Change
at Any Level

ALEX BUDAK

balance

New York   Boston

Balance
Hachette Book Group
1290 Avenue of the Americas, New York, NY 10104
grandcentralpublishing.com
twitter.com/grandcentralpub

First Edition: September 2022

Balance is an imprint of Grand Central Publishing. The Balance name and logo are trademarks of Hachette Book Group, Inc.

The publisher is not responsible for websites (or their content) that are not owned by the publisher.

The Hachette Speakers Bureau provides a wide range of authors for speaking events. To find out more, go to www.hachettespeakersbureau.com or call (866) 376-6591.

Library of Congress Cataloging-in-Publication Data
Names: Budak, Alex, author.
Title: Becoming a changemaker : an actionable, inclusive guide to leading positive change at any level / Alex Budak.
Description: First edition. | New York : Balance, [2022] | Includes bibliographical references and index.
Identifiers: LCCN 2022004490 | ISBN 9781538707760 (hardcover) | ISBN 9781538707784 (ebook)
Subjects: LCSH: Leadership. | Change. | Organizational change. | Social change. | Motivation (Psychology)
Classification: LCC HD57.7 .B835 2022 | DDC 303.3/4—dc23/eng/20220318
LC record available at https://lccn.loc.gov/2022004490

ISBNs: 9781538707760 (hardcover), 9781538707784 (ebook)

Printed in the United States of America

LSC-C

Printing 1, 2022

For Asher and Bex,
my two favorite changemakers.
I love you.

Contents

Introduction   3

PART 1: CHANGEMAKER MINDSET

Chapter 1: Developing a Changemaker Mindset   17

Chapter 2: Question the Status Quo   39

Chapter 3: Confidence Without Attitude   63

Chapter 4: Beyond Yourself   84

Chapter 5: Students Always   105

PART 2: CHANGEMAKER LEADERSHIP

Chapter 6: Reinventing Leadership   133

Chapter 7: Microleadership   148

Chapter 8: Becoming the Leader You Wish You Had   169

PART 3: CHANGEMAKER ACTION

Chapter 9: Sparking Change: From Idea to Action   191

Chapter 10: Leading Change When Change Is Hard   210

Chapter 11: The Changemaker Canvas   227

Chapter 12: Catalyzing Your Changemaker Journey   258

Gratitude   265

Notes   269

Index   283

About the Author   295

THE WORLD HAS NEVER BEEN MORE READY FOR YOU.

Introduction

In 2012, I spent a day in Los Angeles, coworking at the offices of Tala, a startup based in Santa Monica, founded by Shivani Siroya. I was a young, scrappy entrepreneur, and as long as I had my laptop and access to coffee, I was content to work anywhere, but I was also grateful that Shivani, who was then a friend of a friend, had opened up a desk for me.

We took a morning walk together, coffees in hand, as the fog melted away and the Pacific Ocean gradually emerged from behind its mask. Shivani told me about her life and her work, and while she talked, it became clear to me that the labels we often use to identify people who are successful in business, like *entrepreneur*, *founder*, and *leader*, didn't entirely capture who she was. She was each of these, to be sure, but also more than these.

Shivani began her career working at the United Nations, partnering on microfinance initiatives, before switching careers to become a financial analyst on Wall Street. She had a career many would be envious of, but she found something lacking within the traditional finance sector. Although she was passionate about finance, she was also very interested in the over 2.5 billion people around the world who did not yet have a formal financial identity and were excluded from traditional markets. This inspired her to begin sketching out the idea that became Tala. In a half-page document, Shivani wrote that Tala would be an "online global investment fund...which enables everyday people to put their money to work in order to change the world." And she made the case for why her company was urgently needed, seeking to "bridge the gap [in the market] by providing smaller financial investments and training to ensure its entrepreneurs can achieve their goals and make a profound impact within their communities."[1]

It's an inspiring vision, but what truly impressed me about Shivani was not the *what* of her idea but rather the *how*. She had no formal experience as an entrepreneur, and she did not let that stop her. She began building her vision piece by piece; she reached out to contacts and strangers on LinkedIn (ultimately sending over fifteen hundred individual messages!), and she assembled a small part-time team. With some initial success, she faced a choice: continue the safe, prestigious, hard-earned Wall Street career she had coveted, or dedicate her full energy and time to Tala.

She found the courage and took the leap.

And she hasn't looked back, growing her startup's footprint to multiple continents, multiple products, and multiple offices. Hers has been an impressive journey, but what stays with me the most is not the scale of Shivani's venture or the impact she's had.

It's the personal qualities she possesses: Her willingness to question the status quo. Her inclusive leadership. Her service orientation.

I realized on that walk that we often ascribe the success of leaders whom we admire to their more tangible skills—such as Shivani's financial acumen—as we seek to replicate their success. But the personal qualities that truly make Shivani the impactful leader and founder she is are actually changemaker qualities. They are attributes of character, of hustle, of heart, of passion, and of persistence. And these changemaker qualities can be learned and practiced by anyone, no matter who we are or where we might have been.

During our walk, the concept of a "changemaker" came alive to me. Just as I saw these changemaker qualities in Shivani, I began recognizing how they also show up in so many other people all around me, even those who might not yet consider themselves changemakers.

In that moment, my perspective on the concept of change...well, changed. Up until that point in my life, I had always assumed that change came solely from one or two huge organizations—think the

Red Cross or the World Bank. What I came to realize was that positive change is actually made by each of us pursuing it in our own way, leading from wherever we are. Change isn't reserved for a special few. In fact, change calls out for all of us to lead from wherever we might be and in whatever form is true to who we are.

However, I also realized firsthand that there were simply too many barriers, both systemic and individual, getting in the way of all of these emerging leaders making their desired changes a reality.

I began imagining a world filled with, and led by, changemakers. Where positive change happens both in corporate boardrooms and at kitchen tables. Where changemakers spring to action both from behind a laptop and on the streets. Where changemakers of every possible background and experience, passion and interest, have the mindset, leadership, and tools they need to go make change happen.

Since that walk with Shivani, I've become obsessed with understanding what it takes to be a changemaker and studying what most often holds people back from becoming one. I've made it my life's mission to help others create their own personal versions of Shivani's story. To activate their innate ability to lead positive change from where they are, for themselves, their organizations, and their communities. To help all of us, and each of us, become changemakers.

Defining Changemaking

The first popular mention of the word *changemaker* dates back to 1981, when the social impact organization Ashoka used the term in its annual newsletter. Ashoka defines a changemaker as "someone who is taking creative action to solve a social problem."[2] While Ashoka deserves credit for beginning to bring the term into our collective parlance, I believe that the concept of a changemaker deserves a wider and more inclusive definition, far beyond the constraints of social challenges.

Put simply, I define a changemaker as someone who leads positive change from where they are.

I am deliberate in keeping the definition simple and radically inclusive. I believe that a middle manager at a technology company who comes up with a creative new feature has just as much claim to being a changemaker as a Nobel Prize winner. I'm not prescriptive here on the scale or scope of change, and I prefer an inclusive invitation to lead change from wherever we might be—whether that's as an intern, an individual contributor, or a CEO.

Ultimately, changemakers should not be defined by roles, sectors, or levels of impact. Instead, I believe what unites us is our mindset, our leadership skills, and our action in service of change.

Remember that we are talking here about a change*maker*, not a change*thinker*. Changemakers take action, believing that a brighter future, a better path forward, is possible and giving themselves permission to go create it.

In a world that is rapidly changing before our eyes, as you become a changemaker you will learn to navigate, shape, and lead positive change for yourself and others, and you will gain leadership skills to thrive amid uncertainty.

Being able to lead change begins with understanding it. And there has never been a better or more important time to be in the business of change than right now.

BEGINNINGS

January 24, 2019, 10:00 a.m.: I remember that moment vividly. I strode to the front of the classroom, the words THE WORLD HAS NEVER BEEN MORE READY FOR YOU leaping off the screen behind me in size 140 font, so that even students in the back row would feel their weight. "Welcome to Becoming a Changemaker," I said. "The world has never been more ready for you."

While it's not uncommon for students to feel first-day jitters as they begin a new semester, we rarely hear what that first teaching day is like for new faculty members.

I had just been hired by the University of California, Berkeley, and was about to deliver my very first college lecture; let's just say "jitters" didn't quite capture the intensity of the moment. I felt the vulnerability of putting myself out there for the first time as a brand-new faculty member, unsure of how students would react to this out-of-the-ordinary course, which I had built by bringing together all of my personal and professional experiences. It was the very class I'd wished I had been able to take in my final year of college, and now I was about to find out how many other students felt the same way.

If I'd looked ahead at age twenty-two, when I had graduated from college and was first embarking on my changemaker journey, it would have been impossible for me to imagine myself in front of a UC Berkeley classroom at age thirty-four, teaching the next generation of leaders. But this teaching opportunity was so in line with the work I had put my heart and soul into over the previous decade.

My professional career has been dedicated to creating platforms and opportunities to help changemakers of every possible kind succeed. I began by cofounding StartSomeGood.com, which helps changemakers all around the world take their first step from idea to action. The website and community my team and I built have empowered an incredible collection of over fifteen hundred changemakers to catalyze, fund, and create projects to make their positive-change initiatives a reality. I then had the privilege of leading an incubator for social innovators in Sweden, called Reach for Change. I coached and mentored many inspiring changemakers, helping them achieve their highest potential impact, all while I encouraged many other people all around Scandinavia to start seeing themselves as changemakers, too. Alongside some tremendously talented individuals, we helped raise over $30 million to scale Change .org into the world's largest platform for social change. Throughout it all, I've been fortunate to be able to run workshops and lead trainings for budding changemakers in dozens of countries, from Ukraine to

Cambodia, and in settings ranging from the World Bank to UN agencies, to leading corporations and universities around the world.

Looking back now and connecting the dots, it's exceedingly clear that all of these experiences led to a serendipitous meeting with Jay Stowsky, the senior assistant dean for instruction at UC Berkeley's Haas School of Business. Throughout my career as an entrepreneur, executive, and educator, there has been one common thread to all of my work: teaching and inspiring change. And yet I'd never considered teaching change at the college level to be an option. Jay has always been a mentor to me, and so I went to his office seeking some advice on a career transition. But then he asked me a question I will never forget: "But, Alex, what do you really want to do?"

"Well," I said, squirming a bit in my seat, "I really want to teach, but I know most faculty are decades older than me..."

To my shock, Jay wasn't fazed and, instead, directly asked me what I wanted to teach.

"Becoming a Changemaker," I said confidently, not a shred of hesitation or fear in my voice.

"Okay," Jay responded. "Go make a syllabus, show it to me, and we will go from there."

I shook his hand, my spirits leaping at the idea that someone else saw the possibility in my vision, and walked out of his office, where I pulled out my phone and immediately googled "how to write a syllabus." My initial confidence belied the fact that I had no idea what it actually took to create a course.

The process of developing the course allowed me to reflect on all the lessons I'd learned up until that time, particularly in my pursuit of positive change. The books I had read, the people from around the world whose stories have inspired me, the ideas about leading change from disciplines as wide-ranging as physics and music: All of these informed the course's syllabus, lectures, and hands-on experiences. Through this work, a clearer picture began to emerge, one that would help students harness their energy and enthusiasm and give them the real skills and mindsets to empower them to create positive change at an individual, organizational, and societal level.

I carried all of my experiences—the triumphs, the setbacks, and the insights—with me as I stood just outside the door to my classroom for the first time. I took a moment to collect myself and then opened the door. What I saw nearly moved me to tears: Not only was every single seat in the classroom filled, but students were sitting in the aisles, on the windowsills, and standing along the side walls, hoping for a spot in class. UC Berkeley students can select from over six thousand courses per semester, so to see my classroom bursting at the seams made my mission crystal clear: I would now put all of my efforts into making sure these students would not only become leaders but also the changemakers the world needs.

A World of Changemakers

I recently gave a talk to a group of seventh graders at a middle school in the Antelope Valley of California, as part of a project their teacher, Ally Benedetti, had created for them about changemaking.

The first question I received, which came from a soft-spoken girl, had the most profound implications. She asked, "Who can be a changemaker?"

To which I replied emphatically, "Everyone!"

We tend to think of people in leadership roles as changemakers: entrepreneurs, technologists, politicians. Most other people probably don't immediately self-identify as changemakers. In our polarized world, we spend much time crafting identities that are inherently exclusive, defining ourselves in some way to differentiate from others. To counter this, my definition of *changemaker* is deliberately and boldly inclusive. To reinforce this, I'll introduce you to changemakers of all types as you make your way through this book.

You'll meet introverts and extroverts, scientists and artists, Indigenous people and immigrants, men, women, and nonbinary individuals. You'll meet people who knew the change they wanted to create from back when they were children, and those who determined their mission only later in life, after their traditional career ended. You'll meet parents, children, college graduates, and high school dropouts.

This book focuses on what unites all of us: that we are *all* changemakers.

While you may not see yourself reflected in each story, my hope is that you absolutely will connect in a meaningful way with at least one. You can't be what you can't see, and I hope that discovering a bit of yourself in these pages will help you define yourself as a changemaker, too.

UNDERSTANDING CHANGE

We face two choices in dealing with today's pace and scale of change. Do we bury our heads and hope that we somehow emerge on the other side intact? Or do we recognize our own agency to not just survive change but to actively leverage, shape, and steer it, to create new opportunities for ourselves, our communities, and our world?

Changemakers choose the latter—the path of agency, of impact, of catalyzing change.

Before we are able to consciously choose that proactive path, we must first better understand change itself. To get comfortable with change, we need to appreciate two key aspects of it today: First, change is happening, and, second, change is challenging. Let's take a look at both.

If the world feels like it's changing faster and faster and faster . . . well, you're right! Let's look at the accelerating growth in technology over the last six hundred years.

Over 150 years passed between the time Johannes Gutenberg of Mainz, Germany, invented the printing press, in about 1440, and when the telescope was invented, in 1608. Ninety more years passed before the invention of the steam engine, and still decades more before the invention of the telegraph and then the light bulb.

Centuries ago, a single technological breakthrough of that magnitude was enough change for a person's lifetime!

In just the past five years, there have been incredible technological advancements: Consider self-driving cars, gene editing, artificial intelligence, and so much more. By the time this book finds its way to you, there will be even more world-changing discoveries.

This rapid technological growth is explained by Moore's law, an insight by the cofounder of Intel, Gordon Moore, in 1965. He predicted that the number of transistors on a microchip would double every two years while the cost would be halved. This would lead to exponential growth in computing power and therefore in technological change.

While many of us have come to take rapid change for granted when it comes to phones and computers, Thomas Friedman, in his book *Thank You for Being Late*, helps put Moore's law into context by applying it to automobiles: "If cars kept up with Moore's law, the 1971 VW Beetle would now travel at 300,000 miles per hour, cost 4 cents, and use one tank of gas in a lifetime."[3]

It may be helpful to extend our analysis of understanding exponential change through the lens of transportation. It wasn't very long ago that disruptive innovation in vehicles meant ditching your horse-drawn carriage for a motor carriage, with its oversized wheels and canopy.

Fast-forward to today, and we are preparing for a future of hyperloops and autonomous vehicles. While this will have many positive implications, from less exhaust to shorter commutes, as we think about change we must always also keep in mind the negative externalities. As of 2020, more than 3.3 million Americans were employed as truck drivers—a job almost certain to disappear as the changes to the transportation of the future take hold.

As we changemakers push forward with our efforts, we need to also remember that changes affect different people in different ways, and we have an ethical imperative to lead our change with empathy, recognizing that not all change is welcomed by all.

That perspective is helpful as we remember that change is challenging.

Wildfire seasons of increasing duration and intensity are a harrowing reminder of climate change, yet we struggle to take collective action to stop it even as our oceans rise and our glaciers melt right before our eyes.

The COVID-19 pandemic is a pathogenic reminder of how interconnected our entire world has become, through globalization, travel, and business, yet we struggled to change our daily lives and our community actions enough to immediately stop its spread.

The murder of George Floyd in 2020 is a visceral reminder of the systemic racism embedded in the US and, indeed, in nations around the world. His death and the protests following it generated a long-overdue awakening of the prevalence of racist systems and racial injustice. Yet it was also a reminder that change has not yet come, despite many efforts. Even, and often especially, on the most crucial issues, change is downright challenging, and sometimes paralyzing.

Our old ways of thinking, of leading, of acting will no longer work as we face this scale of change coming at us with so much speed and so much complexity.

While Moore's law helps explain the acceleration of change we are experiencing, Martec's law complements it, explaining why keeping up with that acceleration is so hard:[4] Technology, as we've seen, changes exponentially (increasing rapidly), while organizations change logarithmically (slowly). As time goes on, the gap between the changes occurring and our ability to match them grows and grows and grows.

The underlying concepts in Martec's law help us understand the growing chasm between the change occurring in the world and our ability as individuals, as leaders, as community members, as organizations, companies, and systems to keep pace. This is a huge challenge—perhaps the challenge of our lives.

But changemakers are defined by the ability to see opportunity where others only see challenge.

The world is, indeed, changing faster and faster than ever before. And it's becoming harder and harder for us to not fall behind.

Now is the time for changemakers.

Changemakers believe that the future can be better than today, and that we can ensure that it is.

Change is happening. Change is challenging. But with the changemaker mindset, leadership, and action skills you will learn in this book, you will not only be able to keep up with change, you will also be empowered to shape it and lead it. You are on a path of agency, and this is your first step.

YOUR CHANGEMAKER JOURNEY

This book follows the same structure as my UC Berkeley class (but luckily for you, this is the only reading assignment!). Just like the course, this book is composed of three parts.

Part 1, "Changemaker Mindset," introduces you to the attitudes and behaviors that successful changemakers share, irrespective of role, sector, or experience level. I build on the original research I've done with the Changemaker Index and share illuminating social science insights to help you apply key concepts to your own life and work. Anchored in principles like "Question the Status Quo" and "Beyond Yourself," this section introduces crucial traits like resilience, smart risk-taking, empathy, curiosity, and adaptability. And for the first time, I share with the outside world some of the original leadership exercises I have my Berkeley students do to help them develop and apply a changemaker mindset.

Part 2, "Changemaker Leadership," focuses on helping you become the type of leader our world needs. Anchored in key twenty-first-century leadership skills, including influencing without authority, leading through networks, and building trust in a virtual world, you are invited to reinvent your own approaches as you gain the confidence to lead others toward a vision for change. You will finish this section transformed from an individual contributor into a changemaker who does your best work through and with others, and with the courage and ability to go be a leader, even if you aren't the leader.

Part 3, "Changemaker Action," helps you take your newly developed mindset and leadership skills and apply them to turn an idea into action. Anchored in the Changemaker Canvas methodology I've developed, you will build your own changemaker toolkit for starting and realizing positive change. You will hear from diverse changemakers, including artists, nurses, engineers, and entrepreneurs, to learn how to take that crucial first step of action, and you'll discover key insights on sustaining change over time.

I'm deeply grateful for the opportunity to join with you on this journey and to help you find purpose, impact, and identity as you step into your leadership potential.

This is the moment. This is your moment.

The world has never been more ready for you.

PART 1

CHANGEMAKER MINDSET

Chapter 1

Developing a Changemaker Mindset

Hana was skeptical.

She sat in class, arms crossed, a dour look on her face. Her glare stood out among the sea of smiles.

Concerned, I sent her a note after class, to see how she was feeling about the course and if everything was okay. I know so many of my students are fighting all sorts of battles, which I'm not always privy to.

When Hana responded, I was surprised.

"I really want to be a changemaker," her email began. "I really do. But I just don't believe it's possible anymore. I've lost hope in being able to create change."

I felt, and even recognized, her despair, and my heart sank. Still, I saw this as an opportunity to better understand her experience and to perhaps support her to once again identify as a changemaker.

We met during my office hours, and Hana told me of a frustrating experience she'd had during a summer internship, where she'd attempted to lead a diversity-and-inclusion initiative. Although she had lots of support from her peers and her direct manager, and tons of passion for leading the initiative, her efforts were repeatedly blocked by more senior management. No matter how hard she tried, she just couldn't make change happen. As a result, Hana hit a wall. She stopped believing that change was possible, and that she could ever make any type of positive change happen.

I empathized with her. In fact, I had once been in a very similar situation myself. And we began working together to develop her change-maker mindset—a new way of seeing herself and her place in the world around her.

YOUR MINDSET

We start here because the beautiful thing about a changemaker mind-set is that it will help you no matter what passions you pursue or what disciplines you delve into. Entrepreneurs benefit from it just as much as artists; scientists, just as much as teachers, just as much as coders.

Before we can begin creating change for others, though, we must start from within. There are four reasons I'm passionate about helping others develop a changemaker mindset, which I'll discuss in this section:

- Each of us has incredible power over our mindset; it's based on an internal locus of control.
- Developing a changemaker mindset is practicable, learnable, and achievable by anyone. I've worked with all kinds of people on this, running the gamut from a formerly incarcerated person to the CEO of a big financial firm. They approached the process in different ways, to be sure, but the end result was the same.
- This change is a process, not a destination. It's not like there's ever a moment where we can clap our hands and go, "Okay, great, I'm done with my changemaker mindset!" Rather, it's like physical fitness—it's not something developed by one or two gym visits, but by a commitment to the process of regular training.
- Finally, it's a virtuous cycle for work and for life. While many folks are inspired to develop their changemaker mindset for work goals, this shift in mindset ends up being equally important for their other roles as parents, friends, and neighbors.

Mindset can be simply defined as the "established set of attitudes held by someone." The term came to prominence in the late 1990s. Much of the credit for this is due to Stanford University psychologist Carol Dweck, who later wrote an influential book on the topic, in which she differentiates between two types of mindsets: growth and fixed.[1]

A fixed mindset, according to Dweck, is the set of beliefs that one's basic qualities—say intelligence or talent—are unalterable and predetermined traits.

A growth mindset, on the other hand, emerges from the belief that one's abilities can be developed through dedication and hard work. Folks with a growth mindset embrace learning and practice resilience in support of their advancement.

Dweck teaches that each of us has the ability to develop a growth mindset—and that it's not completely binary. We might have some instances where we display more of a fixed mindset and some where we are more able to engage our growth mindset.

Someone with a fixed mindset might believe that intelligence is static, leading to a desire to simply appear smart. Meanwhile, someone with a growth mindset believes that intelligence can be developed, leading to a desire to learn.

We also see this when we look through the lens of challenges and obstacles. Someone with a fixed mindset will avoid challenges at all costs. Imagine that you believe that you have a certain natural skill in math and then you start reaching a point where it no longer comes easily to you; if you have a fixed mindset, you'll tend to walk away and give up, because that's a challenge to your belief about your natural intelligence. Meanwhile, someone with a growth mindset will persist. They'll embrace these challenges as a chance for learning and development.

And when it comes to criticism, if you have a fixed mindset, you'll tend to ignore criticism, because you see it as a fundamental challenge to who you are. Meanwhile, someone with a growth mindset will welcome that criticism and learn from it. Think about feedback you get on a test or an exam. Do you ignore that feedback because it feels painful, or do you take even harsh feedback and say, "Okay. This is a chance for me to get even better at my discipline and to strengthen my skills"?

How do you respond to seeing the success of others? With a fixed mindset, you will tend to be threatened by the success of others, seeing success as a zero-sum game; someone else wins, you lose. Meanwhile, with a growth mindset, you'll find lessons and inspiration in the success of others, believing that if someone else succeeds, it only means you might similarly succeed in the future as well.

While a growth mindset is a crucial base from which to work, simply having a growth mindset is not, in and of itself, enough to have a changemaker mindset. I'll introduce you to the key traits of a changemaker mindset in this chapter, and then you'll learn how to develop them in each of the following four chapters.

ILLUMINATING THE CHANGEMAKER MINDSET

Amanda Gorman captured the attention of the United States, and much of the world, when she delivered her powerful poem "The Hill We Climb" at the presidential inauguration of Joe Biden on January 20, 2021.[2] Her final lines incorporated the metaphor of light, speaking both to that moment in time and to something greater. Her inspiring call to find the courage to both see the light and be the light captured the essential components of a changemaker mindset and sparked new connections for how I think about developing one even when times are challenging.

In a world with so much pain and despair, our reflexes tell us to feel hopeless. But we must never forget that a better tomorrow is always possible.

In a world with so much inequity and injustice, our reflexes tell us to feel powerless. But we must never forget that we each have the power to be the change we desire.

A brighter future is possible, and we can each do our part to collectively illuminate our shared path forward.

Throughout this part of the book, I'll walk you through the key traits and characteristics that make up a changemaker mindset, all of which begin with three fundamental building blocks.

1. There's Always Another Way

Changemakers believe that a different way is always possible.

Which internet browser do you use? Would you believe me if I told you that the browser that you use can actually predict your success in a job? Sounds crazy, right? But researchers at HR software company Cornerstone OnDemand found a surprising, striking pattern.

In 2015, they were analyzing data about people who work in a customer service role, trying to figure out what made certain employees more successful than others, when they found a statistically significant correlation between success and the employees' browser of choice. People who used Firefox or Chrome were more likely to thrive in the role and were 15 percent more likely to stay longer at their job than people who used Safari or Internet Explorer.[3] Is it because one browser gives you superpowers or somehow makes you more efficient at your job? No, of course not. Despite any marketing spin, all are similar ways of accessing the internet. Here's the one crucial difference: Firefox and Chrome aren't the default. You have to consciously choose to download those browsers. You have to challenge the status quo, believe there's something better beyond what most people use, and give yourself permission to find it. Cornerstone found that employees who were willing to take that step to see that there is always a better way were more likely to do a better job and more likely to stay longer at their job.

As Cornerstone's chief analytics officer at the time, Michael Housman, told *Freakonomics Radio*: "My personal view is that the fact that you took the time to install Firefox on your computer shows us something about you... You've made an active choice to do something that wasn't default."[4]

A changemaker mindset begins with remembering that there is

always light, that the status quo isn't preordained but rather an invitation to imagine a different way forward.

2. *Existing at the Edges*

Changemakers innovate at the edges. If you think about the big meaningful problems that can potentially be solved in the twenty-first century—challenges like hunger, water access, climate change, racial justice, political polarization—these are all things that likely won't be solved by any one single discipline or one single approach. A changemaker mindset helps us recognize opportunities to create change by combining different perspectives, modalities, and ways of seeing the world. Changemakers use their mindset to identify where one discipline ends and another one begins, and to find the opportunities waiting at these edges.

The cofounders of Saathi are finding opportunities for change at the intersection of health and the environment. They set out to address two problems at once: the lack of access to sanitary pads among the majority of women in India and the terribly negative environmental impacts of traditional pads. They developed a new type of pad out of banana fibers, harvested from the stems of banana trees—a much more sustainable option compared with the plastic and bleached wood pulp most pads use. This means that not only are the pads chemical-free, more cost-effective, and widely accessible to local populations around Saathi's Gujarat headquarters, but the pads naturally degrade within just six months compared with five hundred years or more for traditional pads.

The team found an opportunity when it simultaneously applied lenses from women's health and sustainability together to address two systemic challenges at once. Cofounder Kristin Kagetsu explained to YourStory why innovation must occur at the edges: "Just a low cost sanitary pad isn't thinking through the entire life cycle of the product. If you're going to make a disposable product then you have to care about what happens to it and how it affects the environment. Otherwise, how would we be different from any other sanitary pad maker out there?"[5]

Saathi is different because it embraces the blurring of disciplines, where the contributions of each way of thinking generate brand-new possibilities. Thinking in traditional ways, within existing silos, might still have resulted in a solid product. But because Saathi's team innovated at the edges, bringing in multiple disciplines and approaches, it created a powerful building block for change.

3. Learned Hopefulness

Changemakers are inherently hopeful. Changemaking is optimism in action, but it's not hope alone. It's hope coupled with purposeful activity. As author Rebecca Solnit describes it, "Hope is not a lottery ticket you can sit on the sofa and clutch, feeling lucky...hope is an ax you break down doors with in an emergency."[6]

To be clear, I don't mean optimism in the traditional binary sense of pessimism versus optimism. Instead, I present this aspect of a changemaker mindset as an alternative to learned helplessness: what I call learned hopefulness. Through developing a way of seeing the world as changemakers and taking actions in service of it, we learn that even when we struggle—especially when we struggle!—we can still keep the candle of hope burning.

This more applied version of optimism is called learned optimism. Developed by the founder of the field of positive psychology, Martin Seligman of the University of Pennsylvania, learned optimism is learning to deal with setbacks in a new way. As my student Hana learned firsthand: Leading change is hard, and setbacks are inevitable. Learned optimism is a powerful aspect of our mindset that can keep us going—to keep us hopeful and keep us continuing to take action even when things don't initially go our way.

Many changemakers find that a setback—or even a tragedy—is the spark that ignites them. A changemaker mindset reminds them that no matter what happens, we can choose how we respond, including finding hope amid frustration or pain.

Dadarao Bilhore embodies learned hopefulness. His son, tragically, died from injuries while riding on the back of a motorbike through the pothole-filled streets of Mumbai in 2015. Because of heavy rain, the driver couldn't see the enormous pothole in front of him, resulting in the deadly crash. If anyone ever would have reason to feel helpless amid such an unimaginable loss, it would be Bilhore. But he consciously chose hope and then turned his hope into action. He's since dedicated his life to filling potholes throughout Mumbai. Not only has he filled hundreds of potholes himself, but he's also inspired many others to join him in his mission.[7] It couldn't have been easy to find reason to remain hopeful amid such loss, but in doing so he has shown what a changemaker mindset can make possible, both for his son's legacy and for the hundreds of other parents who—thanks to these fixed potholes—will never know the kind of pain Bilhore has felt.

Learned Optimism

In his famous 1991 book, *Learned Optimism,* Martin Seligman outlines the three P's of learned optimism—permanence, pervasiveness, and personalization—all of which help us learn to better process adversity.[8] Let's look at each and see how they applied to Hana's frustration in trying to create change in her organization.

Permanence. When you experience a setback, do you perceive it as temporary or the result of permanent causes? Here, Hana believed that because one change initiative—her very first—failed, she could no longer trust that any change was possible. By seeing setbacks as temporary, we build our mindset to see that bumps along the way are an inevitable aspect of leading change. Instead of dreading our stumbles, learned optimists remember that these challenges are a necessary aspect of the change process.

Pervasiveness. Do you compartmentalize bad events and radiate good events, or do you do the opposite? Learned optimists are able to experience something negative but isolate it from the other aspects of their work and life. Similarly, when something good happens, they can allow the glow from it to seep into other aspects of their existence. It's a fine line, but we should be mindful here of toxic positivity, which denies or minimizes the full range of human emotions. Learned optimism allows us to fully embrace negative events as they occur, while giving us a way of seeing them as a catalyst for change. Hana struggled with pervasiveness, as her frustrating experience completely took over other parts of her life, including her studies. But once she was able to isolate the discouragement she felt from the negative events at work, she could then find meaning and growth from her initial setbacks.

Personalization. Do you internalize or externalize blame? To be clear, this isn't about shirking responsibility but about recognizing that sometimes, despite our very best efforts, we are working in a complex system with many moving parts and many forces outside our immediate control. Here's where Hana really struggled. Because she wasn't able to make change happen, she believed it was her fault and she wasn't worthy of the title of changemaker. In reality, while change absolutely was possible, she was fighting a number of systemic challenges. She was as low on the power hierarchy as could be: an intern. She was in her job for only a couple of months, which made it less likely for senior leadership to invest in her idea. Who knows what else she may have faced—from sexism to a boss in a bad mood. This isn't to say that she couldn't have tried other approaches or eventually found a way to make change happen. But learned optimism reminds us that even despite our best intentions, sometimes we experience setbacks nonetheless. The key for a changemaker mindset is to remember we have the choice to reframe our setbacks: Experiencing setbacks doesn't suggest that we have a character flaw. Rather, they are feedback to remind us to practice courage: To learn and to try again. To continue to be brave enough to be the change.

THE THREE LEVERS OF CHANGE

There are three ways to rapidly accelerate your career and your impact:

The first is to <u>become a changemaker yourself</u>.

The second is to <u>surround yourself with changemakers</u>. You'll learn later on in the changemaker leadership section of the book (see page 131) how to identify fellow changemakers, how to collaborate with them, and how to inspire them to join you on your own changemaker journey.

The third and most trailblazing way is to <u>help others around you become changemakers</u>. This can be done formally as well as informally.

Formally, consider Laura Weidman Powers, the cofounder of the nonprofit Code2040. Created in 2012, Code2040's mission is to close the racial wealth gap by creating opportunities in technology for Black and Brown professionals. Along the way, it has built the largest racial equity community in technology. While many similar programs focus on teaching participants how to code, Weidman Powers thinks differently: The organization she started focuses on changemaker-mindset skills, like overcoming imposter syndrome, building confidence and courage, and making connections with other leaders. Code2040's focus isn't on building coders; it's on building changemakers, whose presence in the tech world will ripple change throughout what it calls the "innovation economy." "Leadership is not an end, but a means to achieving something beyond yourself," Weidman Powers has said.[9] Indeed, it's the ability to inspire and equip so many others to be effective changemakers at organizations around the country that will catalyze change simply otherwise unimaginable by a single person.

One of my mentors, Tony Carr, former president of Halloran Philanthropies, embodies informal changemaking. Beyond his traditional career, which also included stints as a hospital executive and an innovative impact investor, Carr has made supporting other changemakers his legacy. A true changemaker himself, Carr doesn't do anything the prescribed way. Following an introductory email from me, Carr rejected the norm of an email response and simply called me directly (waiting only about ten seconds from the moment I hit SEND, meaning he couldn't have possibly read my whole email)! Though we had never met, he told me to come visit him in Fresno, give a talk on changemaking to some students, and have lunch with him and a favorite school principal changemaker friend of his. Despite other commitments, I spontaneously said yes right on the spot, and two days later I made the four-hour drive to meet him. And since then, he's made a point of sending emails, making calls, and checking up on me regularly to make sure I'm continuing to make change and to see if there's anything I need. This would be exceptional, except that in the case of Tony Carr, this is ordinary—I learned that he supports dozens of changemakers in the same way. He opens his network, his creative brain, and his bottomless well of inspiration to each of us.

This third lever of change—helping others become changemakers—brings us back to Hana. She was still skeptical of ever becoming a changemaker herself, so I encouraged her to really reflect on someone who inspired her for my "Changemaker of the Week" assignment, to remind herself that change is possible. This was a challenge to her fixed mindset, as she would need to overcome the belief that someone else's success inevitably comes at her expense.

In class, Hana gave a presentation on a person who was completely unknown to the rest of the class, myself included. She chose this person not because she was famous but rather because of her resilience and her ability to persevere past trauma (aspects that especially resonated with Hana). Still questioning herself, Hana submitted her assignment with a note saying that she thought she could have done better. But I couldn't possibly see how. Her presentation was simultaneously deeply personal and impressively inspiring, deserving the great grade it had earned her.

Ultimately, though, the work of changemaking isn't graded. The real impacts often come later. This was true in Hana's case, when another student wrote me a note to specifically say how much Hana's presentation had inspired her. She, too, had been trying to find her own grounding as a changemaker—to connect her lofty aspirations to what she perceived as her lack of changemaker skills. She identified Hana and her leadership as the type of changemaker she hopes to one day embody.

I shared that note with Hana, and she responded: "I'm not sure how to begin but seeing this note was honestly completely overwhelming. It's just so incredibly fulfilling and I can't believe that someone else sees me as a changemaker and finds inspiration in what I did. I'm so moved and so grateful."

In that moment, Hana realized that, despite all of her resistance, all of her self-limiting beliefs, and all of her doubt and despair, she had just done something remarkable. She had just proven to herself that she, indeed, possessed a changemaker mindset and that no one could take that away from her. In that moment, she became a changemaker.

Changemaker of the Week Assignment

One of my favorite assignments in my Becoming a Changemaker class is called "Changemaker of the Week." Students prepare a presentation for the class where they select a person who inspires them, and make a persuasive case for why that person is a changemaker. The choice of person is completely up to them: Their changemaker can be famous or known only by a few. They can be alive or dead. They can lead change in any role or sector. It's up to students to tell us the story of their changemaker and show how this person embodies the traits, concepts, and characteristics they've learned in class.

I love this assignment because it means that each semester, every student is introduced to dozens of different changemakers and can see the diverse array of ways in which individuals lead positive change. Imagine you are in my class and have been asked to present on a favorite changemaker. Whom might you choose? What is it about their mindset, leadership, or action that you feel makes them a changemaker? I encourage you to keep this person in mind as you read this book and consider whether and how this person embodies the changemaker concepts we will explore together.

This is also an invitation to take on the extra-credit assignment I offer my students: Once you've thought about why this person is a changemaker, consider reaching out to them, via social media, email, or other form of communication. It's a huge compliment to tell someone why you think they are a changemaker, and students have found that it's a perfect opening line to begin connecting with individuals who inspire them. Job offers, phone calls, and long-term mentorships have all grown out of this extra-credit exercise. I know it might sound risky at first (if that's the case for you, keep reading: You'll learn frameworks in the next chapter to help you take smart risks). If nothing else, even if you don't get a response, you might just give your favorite changemaker the same magical feeling Hana received when she found out that she made a difference for someone else's changemaker journey.

The Changemaker Index

While I love a good inspirational story as much as anyone, I also live in the worlds of academia and traditional business, which are data-driven and empirical. From the very beginning of my changemaker work, I've believed in the importance of studying and measuring the results, relying on verifiable data and not just anecdotal evidence. As many data-focused leaders love to say, "You can't manage what you can't measure."

To date, no one has properly studied changemakers, and back in early 2019 I was puzzling over how to best do so.

Sometimes people show up in your life at just the right time, and such was the case for a fortuitous meeting with Calvin Chu Yee Ming, partner at Eden Strategy Institute, a Singapore-based innovation and consulting firm. He was in town for just twenty-four hours and, serendipitously, reached out to grab a coffee. During our chat, we connected over the importance of developing new leaders while also measuring results, and we began brainstorming how to do so in the unique landscape of developing changemakers.

I decided on the spot to collaborate with Calvin and his team. Together with his colleagues Jessica Kalip, Callysta Thony, and Angeline Seah, we created the Changemaker Index in early 2019, which is the first longitudinal study of changemakers ever attempted.

Although we are still early in our undertaking of this long-term study, we already have statistically significant results among students who have taken Becoming a Changemaker.

We went into this with an open mind, not trying to prove anything but rather leaning into our curiosity and simply asking the question: Is it possible for someone to become a changemaker?

We can now say conclusively that—yes!—becoming a changemaker is possible. And we have the data both to prove that it happens and to confidently trace the steps in effectively becoming one.

Changemaking, as a field and as an approach, might feel a bit soft or squishy to some. My hope is that these data are proof of concept that not only is becoming a changemaker possible but that it is measurable, quantifiable, and backed by the research-informed approach you will learn in this book.

The Assessment Tool

The Changemaker Index is a self-assessment instrument. Its key measures are attitudinal, behavioral, and situational. Participants complete the index at the beginning of the semester before the first class; at the end of the semester, after the final class; and annually thereafter. We seek to measure how individuals develop as changemakers throughout the course as well as how they are able to sustain—and even improve—their changemaker abilities in the years following. We correlate the annual post-course index with life events such as promotions, new careers, and even starting families, to look for interesting inflection points.

The index is made up of twenty-five quantitative questions that measure an individual's development as a changemaker. Individuals also provide demographic information and qualitative responses, to share more about their perceived development and their current needs to continue developing their skills. The five thematic dimensions of the index are:

- Changemaker Awareness. This area measures the extent to which a participant identifies with the changemaker concept in their life and work, and their self-awareness around current changemaker strengths, growth areas, and opportunities for impact.
- Changemaker Mindset. This area measures the extent to which a participant is able to navigate dynamic and rapidly changing environments, and

how readily they are able to identify new opportunities for change around them.

- <u>Changemaker Leadership.</u> This area measures the extent to which participants are able to develop a vision for change and then rally others to join them in their efforts—in ways both big and small—irrespective of the participant's leadership title or formal authority.

- <u>Changemaker Action.</u> This area measures the extent to which participants are able to take those crucial first steps of turning an idea into action, while being able to conceptualize how their idea might grow and scale beyond them.

- <u>Changemaker Effectiveness.</u> This area measures the extent to which participants are able to put the previous four areas into practice to effectively catalyze sustainable change and persevere through inevitable setbacks.

Results

The results of the Changemaker Index have surprised even me. In every single class, along every single dimension, class cohorts have developed as changemakers to a statistically significant degree. While there is an occasional student who stays essentially flat in their own changemaker development, at a population level the data are robust and clear. Not only is it possible to become a changemaker in as little as a few weeks, but, controlling for variables like age, gender, and race, the index conclusively shows that anyone can, to a statistically significant extent, successfully become a changemaker.

What follows are data from the Changemaker Index since its inception. These data are broken down by the five changemaker themes. Mean scores by theme are shown as measured before students took the class and after completing the course.

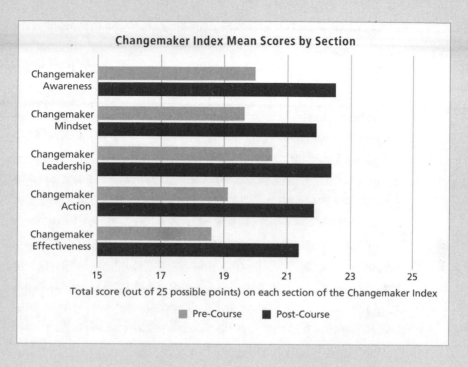

Changemaker Index Mean Scores by Section

Total score (out of 25 possible points) on each section of the Changemaker Index

■ Pre-Course   ■ Post-Course

Changemaker Theme	Pre-Course Mean per Question	Post-Course Mean per Question	Pre-Course Standard Deviation	Post-Course Standard Deviation
Changemaker Awareness*	3.99	4.51	0.80	0.69
Changemaker Mindset*	3.93	4.38	0.84	0.70
Changemaker Leadership*	4.10	4.48	0.78	0.69
Changemaker Action*	3.82	4.37	0.91	0.71
Changemaker Effectiveness*	3.73	4.27	0.99	0.84

*= statistically significant difference of means test at $p < .05$

Across all cohorts, from 2019 to 2021, with a total of 619 participants, there are a number of interesting highlights:

- In the baseline evaluation, Changemaker Effectiveness is by far the lowest scoring dimension before students take the course. This makes sense, as my class often attracts students who are eager to become changemakers but who are usually at the beginning of their changemaker journey. Connected to this, we see in the baseline evaluation that one of the highest mean scores out of any of the twenty-five questions is to a question that asks about how inspired they feel to develop personally and professionally as a changemaker (4.62/5). Excitement is high—as is the opportunity to become more effective in leading change.

- Perhaps not surprisingly, we see that the largest measured change in pre- and post-course surveys is in this Changemaker Effectiveness theme, but Changemaker Action is not far behind. This tracks with what I see both anecdotally and in the data among students at the beginning of the course. Responses to the prompt "I have the confidence in being able to turn an idea into action" bring in one of the lowest mean scores (3.55/5) out of any of the prompts. This figure rockets up over 20 percent in post-course surveys, showing that perhaps effectiveness as changemakers goes hand in hand with the ability to take action on ideas.

- My MBA students (median age: twenty-eight) improve at almost exactly the same rate as freshmen undergrads—with similar pre- and post-course scores across the total index. But there are noticeable differences in pre-course scores, especially in the Changemaker Leadership section. MBA students are much more likely to see themselves as leaders before taking the course compared with BA-level freshmen, but both see similarly remarkable jumps in their ability to influence without authority after taking the class. MBA students improve most on their ability to navigate and thrive in highly dynamic environments—likely a reflection of their previous work experience and their ability to apply learnings from class right away in their own professional work settings, which are certainly highly dynamic and rapidly changing!

- The greatest improvement on any single dimension is on students' awareness of real-world opportunities to become a changemaker (23.92 percent increase). I hope that you will find the same effect from reading this book. No matter whether your desired change efforts are big or small, or even if you don't yet know what they might be, the examples, stories, and advice in this book are meant to help you gain awareness and inspiration to go be an effective changemaker when you're done.

Though the data so far are encouraging, there is still a long way to go as we continue examining how changemakers develop and what enables their change-maker aspirations to become a measurable reality. It's a joy to share these results publicly with you for the very first time. But mostly I hope that seeing these statistical findings gives you confidence as you start your own becoming-a-changemaker journey, knowing that you are following a methodology that has worked for so many others.

The Changemaker Assessment

By reading this book, you are now part of our changemaker community! If you'd like to participate in the Changemaker Index yourself at the beginning of your changemaker journey, I would love for you to do so. You can access the exact same assessment tool my students take by going to changemaker.us/index.

Here is a special, shortened, ten-question version, so that you can get a feel for the types of questions you'll find online and also get a better understanding of both the index and your own changemaker development right away. Respond to each statement honestly, on a scale of 1 (strongly disagree) to 5 (strongly agree).

Changemaker Awareness

1. I consider myself a changemaker.
2. I personally know others whom I consider to be a changemaker.

Changemaker Mindset

3. I dare to step outside of my comfort zone and take smart risks.
4. I reframe setbacks as opportunities for growth.

Changemaker Leadership

5. I make it safe for those around me to be themselves and to try new things.
6. I can effectively influence others, even without formal authority.

Changemaker Action

7. Even if I start with leading smaller changes, I can see how they may lead to larger, systemic changes.

8. I have confidence in being able to turn an idea into action.

Changemaker Effectiveness

9. I am currently leading an initiative that results in positive change in some way.

10. I help others become changemakers.

DEFINING PRINCIPLES

UC Berkeley's Haas School of Business is my academic and professional home. I'm particularly appreciative of the school's commitment to its culture and values, with its explicit goal to "compete on culture" when it comes to differentiating among other business schools.

Haas has codified its four "Defining Leadership Principles," and these values are embedded into every imaginable aspect of the school.[10] I was asked about these principles during my very first job interview at Haas; course evaluations ask students whether faculty embody these principles in their teaching; and they are literally etched into the ground in the courtyard in front of the campus buildings, a tangible reminder of our culture whenever we enter and exit.

It's not only the import placed on values that matters to me; it's the principles themselves. The four principles are a terrific proxy for showing up in the world with a changemaker mindset. As an homage to Berkeley Haas's commitment to educating changemakers, I've organized the next four chapters around the Defining Leadership Principles.

- In "Question the Status Quo," we'll cover mindset traits like curiosity and smart risk-taking.
- In "Confidence Without Attitude," you'll learn how to bring humility, trust, and collaboration into your work and life.
- In "Beyond Yourself," we'll explore how to unlock service, ethics, vision, and long-term thinking in pursuit of your changemaker goals.
- In "Students Always," you'll develop adaptability, flexibility, and empathy to keep you curious, whether you are eight years old or eighty.

By the end of this part of the book, you'll have experienced each of the four Defining Leadership Principles that are central to Haas and to my Becoming a Changemaker course, and, like Hana, you will be ready to start applying your changemaker mindset everywhere you go.

BE THE CHANGE

Key Insights
- A changemaker mindset starts with a conscious choice, remembering that we have agency in how we respond to changes around us.
- We can all practice and develop a changemaker mindset, whether that's making positive change in the face of grief, like Dadarao Bilhore; challenging our fixed mindset, like Hana; or inspiring others to be changemakers, like Laura Weidman Powers.
- The Changemaker Index provides empirical evidence and confidence that each of us—no matter our background, experiences, personality, career, or title—can become a changemaker.

Changemaker Challenge
- Curious to see how you develop as a changemaker over the coming weeks and pages? Go to changemaker.us/index and take the Changemaker Index survey now! (And get a reminder to take it again after you complete the book.)

Chapter 2

Question the Status Quo

Bryan Stevenson is not your average Harvard Law School graduate.

When he started law school, he had never actually met a lawyer himself, having grown up in a poor, rural community in Delaware. His belief that everyone should receive justice, especially those most readily forgotten in our society, is what drove him to pursue the profession. He felt called, he says, to a "commitment to human rights and equal justice, which became a way for me to think about how I wanted to spend my time."[1]

But during law school, Stevenson observed that among his classmates "the conversations seemed, initially, very disconnected from issues like helping the poor or creating justice for those who were marginalized."[2]

When he graduated, he wasn't sure exactly what he wanted to do with his degree, but he had developed a world-class legal skill set and he knew he wouldn't be content to merely uphold the existing order with his career: "The rule of law was, for me, a very captivating forum in which to think about changing things," he said, "and I continue to believe it is a powerful space for reform."

An early experience during law school, working with the Southern Center for Human Rights, transformed him. There he met people who were desperately in need of legal help yet whose stories and sentences displayed the bias in the legal system against poor people and people of color. This experience brought him back to his own reflection on growing up in his small town: "There was this break in the world, and if you grew up on one side of that crack, it was definitely different than if you grew up on the other side of it."[3]

In 1989, with little money in his pocket but big ambitions for change, he began his life's work, founding the Equal Justice Initiative (EJI), which "works to end mass incarceration, excessive punishment, and racial inequality."[4] EJI began by guaranteeing legal representation to anyone in Alabama sentenced to the death penalty (the only state that did not provide legal support in such cases). EJI has helped overturn over 125 wrongful convictions—people who would have been executed otherwise—and Stevenson led a challenge that went to the US Supreme Court, which ultimately ruled that sentencing children seventeen or younger to life without parole was unconstitutional.

Stevenson has built his career and his impact by being willing to do what others would not. "Somebody has to stand when other people are sitting," he asserts. "Somebody has to speak when other people are quiet."[5]

With his intelligence, training, and talent, Stevenson could have found success in any traditional area of law he were to choose. Instead, he has made his mark by consistently questioning the status quo about everything from what it means to be a lawyer to whether our justice system truly serves all Americans. Stevenson has been able to deliver so much positive change throughout his life because he has embraced three bold principles of questioning the status quo:

He <u>dialed up his curiosity</u> in law school, regularly questioning why so many people in the United States were excluded from receiving the justice they deserved. He diverged from conventional ways of thinking about the concept of justice by centering the needs of the very least likely among us to receive justice and then actively advocating for their rights.

He <u>zigged when others zagged</u>, deciding to create his own legal justice organization in a part of the country far different from where he attended law school. Informed by his early experiences, he went all in to public-interest law, dedicating his life to advocating for the most vulnerable among us. He used his voice to speak for those individuals few others would take on as clients, including people sentenced to death. In doing so, he always championed the humanity in those readily ignored by most, reminding each of us that we're more than the worst thing we've ever done.

He <u>took smart risks</u> in supporting new clients—no matter how troubled or vulnerable they were. These were challenging cases, where the odds were stacked against his clients and where judgments in their favor would be that much more difficult to achieve. Further, he took on risk as an individual as well, putting his own success and well-being at stake, knowing the type of work he pursued likely wouldn't come with the financial payoff often found in other legal career routes. But the payoff—in many cases saving a person from a death sentence—meant that these risks came with a significant reward, ultimately making them smart risks worth taking.

"We cannot change the world if we aren't willing to do things that are uncomfortable and inconvenient," he advises fellow changemakers, balancing realism with hope. "Injustice prevails where hopelessness persists. Hope is your superpower. Don't let anybody or anything make you hopeless. Hope is the enemy of injustice."[6]

Stevenson's willingness to question the status quo—and to channel the aforementioned principles—has made him the changemaker he is today.

Effectively questioning the status quo requires two high-level capabilities working together. The first is learning to recognize an established convention worth confronting. The second is having the mindset and skills to take the risk to pursue the change and to bring others along with you. This chapter will cover both; let's start first by looking at how you can begin identifying areas ripe for change all around you. After all, being able to lead change begins with being able to find opportunities worthy of your efforts to go change them.

Why Question the Status Quo?

In the introduction, we discussed the two maxims around change: that it's happening, and that it's challenging. With so much change happening all around us, from technological advances to public health challenges to urbanization to shifting workplace cultures and beyond, we no longer have the luxury of attempting to insulate ourselves from these macro- and micro-level changes with inaction.

Even previous successes no longer guarantee future triumphs. Of the five hundred companies listed in the first-ever Fortune 500 list in 1955, only fifty-two (10.4 percent) still remain on that list, with the majority either merging with other firms or going out of business completely. This dynamism means that we can't rest on our laurels as individuals or as organizations—that we must consistently be challenging convention and finding new ways to evolve, change, and grow. Changemakers who can question the status quo are the ones who will find opportunities for positive change and then pursue them, even if that means shaking up existing norms and practices.

Think of all of the organizations that kept putting off creating a digital transformation strategy in the 2010s, assuming that there would always be an easier time to make these changes happen. They mistakenly took for granted that the status quo would hold for a while longer. In 2020, COVID-19's emergence disrupted everything and even the most conservative companies were faced with a harrowing choice: change, or risk no longer existing. The organizations and the individuals that did best amid this chaos and disruption were the ones who had regularly created a practice of challenging the status quo—even in seemingly good times.

Two Birds Brewing in Australia has always been an innovator; it was the first-ever female-owned brewery in the country. When COVID hit, its Melbourne-based tasting room and restaurant faced great peril, but it was prepared to nimbly innovate. It launched a "drive thru bottle shop" the very first weekend after mandatory restaurant closures hit, and launched food delivery and online ordering for its loyal customers. It was ready to adapt because its team had the "question the status quo" mindset active already.

Leaders who make big changes often face a lot of risk, but as we'll learn in this chapter, we can all learn how and when to take smart, calculated risks with buy-in from others, no matter our roles, power, or formal influence.

DIALING UP CURIOSITY

What does questioning the status quo look like in practice? For many changemakers, it begins with being willing to see the world—both as it is and how it might become—a bit differently from others.

Such was the case with Laila Ohlgren. Not many people can legitimately claim that their curiosity led to the creation of something used by billions of people. But Ohlgren, a Swedish engineer born in 1937, certainly can, because she was willing to question the status quo and imagine a different way forward.

Ohlgren was working for the national Swedish phone company in the 1970s, the only woman engineer on a team attempting to develop the earliest mobile phones and cellular infrastructure. The team had made some good progress, but it kept running into the same issue over and over. It was attempting to replicate the telephone experience that people were accustomed to in their homes and offices, even though the early mobile phones were to be used in cars. The engineering team believed that the mobile experience had to be exactly the same as the stationary experience: picking up a handset and dialing a number. This made sense, but in each trial, the connection would break.

"It was taking at least 15 seconds to dial a number," Ohlgren said. "During that time, a building or a tree could get in the way [of the signal], so you ended up in a radio shadow, which meant that not all the digits were getting through."[7] Fifteen seconds was a fairly long time to transmit information, and it felt like the team was running up against insurmountable challenges. By June of 1979, Ohlgren's team was running out of hope. Many started to wonder whether mobile phone technology would ever be technically possible.

At that inflection point, Ohlgren came up with a crucial insight that changed the trajectory of her team's tests and mobile telephony as we now know it. Why, she wondered, did they have to use the same process for mobile phones as for landlines? She proposed turning the entire process around, and in so doing, according to Swedish telecom giant Ericsson, "broke one of the commandments, which stated that the dialing procedure must be the same as in the fixed network."

Ohlgren dialed up her curiosity and reimagined how she could make mobile telephony work by questioning one of the core tenets of how telephones had always worked. "As each mobile telephone was going to have its own little microprocessor, you could let it store the numbers before it started the call. I thought it would make connections more reliable," she said. In other words, instead of dialing the numbers one at a time, Ohlgren invented a completely new way of dialing numbers—to store each entire phone number as it was entered on the phone and then connect to a cellular tower for signal only once the full number was ready.

That we now take it for granted that mobile telephones will easily connect to the network whenever we dial a number is thanks to this gutsy engineer who, when faced with the frustration of a problem that seemed intractable, believed that a better way was possible (even if it was not inevitable) and imagined an entirely new path forward. Indeed, many readers of this book will have never known of a time when Ohlgren's model of dialing phones was not the obvious way all phones work.

Perhaps the next time you call up a loved one, you can tell them the story of Laila Ohlgren, the changemaker who leaned into her curiosity, questioned the status quo, and forever changed the world of mobile phones.

Learning to Think Differently

What's the capital of France? Who was the twenty-sixth president of the United States? How much does a baby llama weigh?

These are all examples of questions that require "convergent think-ing," the process of coming up with a single well-established answer to a problem.

This type of thinking stresses speed, accuracy, and logic. When thinking convergently, we use cognitive approaches like recognizing familiar patterns, reapplying techniques we've used in the past, and accessing stored information. Creativity is therefore less important. We are looking for a single, objectively correct answer.

Oh, and for those of you who applied your convergent problem-solving to the questions I just posed, the answers are Paris, Theodore Roosevelt, and approximately twenty-five pounds (how adorable is that)?

Let's now contrast convergent thinking with its polar opposite: divergent thinking.

Whereas convergent thinking looks for a single right answer, divergent thinking attempts to generate creative ideas by exploring many possible solutions. It's free-flowing and nonlinear, and these ideas are often generated in an emergent cognitive fashion. Unlike convergent thinking, divergent thinking doesn't look for judgment right away. Instead, the focus is on generating lots of possible solutions. If you've ever done improvisational acting, it's the "yes, and" approach—building off possible ideas rather than applying specific probabilities or standards for analysis.

Both convergent and divergent thinking are incredibly valuable, and necessary, in your work as a changemaker. Unfortunately, we often speed through the divergent process on the way to finding a single answer. To embrace curiosity and be creative, status-quo-disrupting changemakers, we are well served to understand when to apply each type of thinking and to make sure we spend enough time and focus on the divergent process.

Divergent thinking is a brainstorming process where a single stimulus leads to many possible answers. To enable this process, you might try to write lists with as many ideas as possible or do free writing. You might spend time in meditation or use tools like bubble mapping, or even create artwork to tap into your creative side. If you think this sounds childlike, you are right! Psychologist J. Nina Lieberman studied kindergartners in 1965, and she found a link between playfulness and divergent thinking, and observed increases in "spontaneity, overtones of joy, and sense of humor,"[8] as well as curiosity and creativity.

It then becomes a dance between divergent thinking and convergent thinking: Coming up with lots of possible answers, then narrowing them down. Perhaps brainstorming again to find more possibilities, then again refining that list down, using critical thinking. Our schools and universities often value convergent thinking at the expense of divergent thinking, so as changemakers, it's helpful to create a deliberate divergent-thinking process, where you can be creative and curious.

A status-quo-disrupting opportunity will most likely emerge from a divergent-thinking approach. Rather than being confined by a single "right" answer, the divergent process welcomes a wide variety of ideas—holding off judgment at first. This generative process might yield some surprising insights—and it's those insights that are most likely to be the status quo disruptors. Of course, once you lean into your curiosity and identify many potential new approaches, then you can activate your convergent thinking to select the one worth taking a smart risk to implement.

I've quite often found in working with management teams that disagreements that feel personal or systemic during meetings are actually a misalignment on the type of thinking to apply at that moment. If half of the team is practicing divergent thinking and coming up with potential solutions while the other half is applying convergent thinking and trying to decide on a single best strategy, there will be inevitable conflict, no matter how good the intentions of everyone are. It's therefore helpful when you lead teams and meetings to clearly state when your team should be in divergent mode and when it should be in convergent mode. This helps unlock both creativity and status-quo-disruption potential—tapping into the full potential of the team to come up with ideas—as well as efficiency to ensure that divergent thinking happens concurrently for all to decide on a single approach.

Shaped to a T

Design firm IDEO is a global consultancy of designers, entrepreneurs, teachers, researchers, and many more types of changemakers. Founded in 1978 by designers David Kelley, Bill Moggridge, and Mike Nuttall, the company has worked with some of the biggest and most impactful companies in the world and has delivered innovations that have shaped our lives and work. In 1980, IDEO partnered with Apple cofounder Steve Jobs to develop a computer mouse for the yet-to-be-unveiled Lisa computer. The company also helped design the first-ever notebook-style computer, as well as innovations across industries as varied as financial services, toys, and medical products.

What's the secret to building such a diverse and infinitely curious and creative team to bring these innovations to life? A concept called a "T-shaped person." This is the backbone of IDEO's method of hiring.

T-shaped people have two crucial characteristics, which we can understand by visualizing the letter T. The vertical line represents depth in a specific skill. This might be expertise in engineering, architecture, social science, or finance. The horizontal line represents the "disposition for collaboration across disciplines."[9] This means that someone knows a little bit about a wide range of disciplines, topics, and approaches, and actively seeks to collaborate with others, integrating all of these perspectives. In other words, a T-shaped person, or a T-shaped leader, has not only a specific area of expertise but also insight on, and a propensity to engage with, the greater world around them. We'll discuss this in more depth in the next section.

Getting Curious About Change

How can you develop that horizontal line in your own T, that broad base of interests and disciplines? By practicing curiosity.

Ian Leslie, author of *Curious,* describes curiosity as being like a muscle. He says "you need to work it in order to keep it ... you've got to consciously cultivate the habit of curiosity in order to stay a curious person."[10]

So what gets in the way of us practicing and strengthening our curiosity, which will help us question the status quo? There are five specific obstacles I've observed, all of which you, as a changemaker, can address in order to unlock your own curiosity and creativity.

1. Stuffed-to-the-brim calendars and to-do lists. If we are bouncing from meeting to meeting and filling every waking hour with a list of items to be checked off, we remain in execution mode. In this state, we don't have the mental space or capacity to let our minds wander, to ask questions, and to simply observe the world around us. Amazon founder Jeff Bezos famously puts multiple hours of "thinking time" on his calendar every day. This is unstructured time, during which he won't be interrupted with meetings or emails and can just think, strategize, and...yes, be curious! While you likely don't have the privilege of the level of control over your schedule as Bezos does, you also aren't running one of the biggest companies in the world. So even if it's fifteen minutes per day, schedule that thinking time—or call it "curiosity time"—so that you have a chance to put your curiosity muscles to work.

2. Asking the wrong questions. To embrace your curiosity, consider approaching challenges in one of three ways. The first embraces your inner three-year-old: Approach a challenge with a childlike wonder and curiosity. Ask "Why?"—a lot. Practice a beginner's mind and try to see things in a fresh light. The second approach asks yourself: What would my replacement do? Sometimes we get so stuck in the way we've always done things that it's hard to zoom out and imagine that someone else might look at a challenge from a vastly different perspective. It's a wonderful and empowering question to ask, to put your ego aside for a second and look at a situation anew, through the eyes of someone else. Finally, consider leading with the question "How might we...?" This question, a foundational part of the "design thinking"

methodology, is a brilliant one. Notice that the question asks *might*, not *should*, which is an invitation for divergent thinking and new ideas and perspectives. Also note that it's about *we*, not *I* or *you*, so it's inherently an invitation for collaboration and for diverse ideas to be considered. Language matters, and these questions can help you tap into your own latent curiosity.

3. <u>Micromanagement.</u> I'll have more to say about this in coming chapters on changemaker leadership, but for now, suffice it to say, when individuals micromanage us—telling us exactly how to do every little aspect of a task—it robs us of our ability to be curious. It shifts our approach from a learning mindset to an achiever mindset and takes away the chance to ask "How might we...?" since we have no room for thinking here, only doing.

4. <u>Hyperspecialization.</u> Universities are especially guilty of this as they push students to declare a single major or take specific classes in order to graduate. So, too, are many of our models of working, which haven't fully evolved in centuries. Curious changemakers benefit from taking part in a diverse array of activities, even if they come at the expense of efficiency. The benefits of, say, reading a book on anthropology or having a conversation with a food scientist might not be clear in the moment, but they broaden our perspective and open up new possibilities for insight down the line. We need to give ourselves permission to think expansively, not just efficiently. As my grandmother would often say, "Nothing is ever wasted," meaning that every new experience we have and each new thing we learn might end up becoming valuable at some point in the future, helping us make new and interesting connections.

5. <u>Not taking time to play.</u> When psychiatrist Bruce D. Perry and colleagues studied the connection between curiosity, play, and brain development in children, they found a powerful, reinforcing loop: "A wonderful cycle of learning is driven by the pleasure in play...," they reported in a journal article.[11] "[A child] explores and discovers. The discovery brings pleasure; the

pleasure leads to repetition and practice. Practice brings mastery; mastery brings the pleasure and confidence to once again act on curiosity. All learnings—emotional, social, motor, and cognitive—are accelerated and facilitated by repetition fueled by the pleasure of play." Just because you go to work wearing a suit or you have an official-sounding title doesn't mean that play isn't for you. In fact, it may be that much more important for you to play! Play unlocks not just our curiosity but also our learning, begetting a virtuous cycle of more curiosity and more creativity.

Watching out for these obstacles will help you more readily spot opportunities for change and see situations where the status quo would benefit from a shake-up. We'll now take a look at some deliberate changemaker mindset practices and frameworks that will help you effectively catalyze change by questioning the status quo.

ZIGGING WHEN OTHERS ZAG

Yvon Chouinard, the founder of Patagonia, first fell in love with nature as a fourteen-year-old boy learning to rock climb in 1953. An unlikely entrepreneur, and an even more unlikely businessperson, Chouinard has created a company that from the very beginning has gone against nearly every bit of conventional business wisdom. Chouinard's first product, reusable steel climbing pitons, revolutionized rock climbing. However, the pitons also ended up having unforeseen negative impacts on environmental landscapes. His values trumped his desire for profits, and so he completely left that product and its revenue stream behind, as crazy as that might have been at the time.

He pivoted his focus to outdoor clothing, while ensuring that Patagonia was unlike any other company out there. Back in 1985—way before it became trendy—Patagonia started donating 10 percent of profits to environmental groups (later switching to 1 percent of total sales in 2002). Patagonia also gave free childcare to its staff and maintained open-plan offices, and strategically built the company's headquarters in Ventura, California, just steps from the beach, so that the staff could go surfing at lunch. This free-spirited ethos endures today as the company continues to consciously pursue its own path in line with its values and vision. Almost every piece of clothing it creates uses recycled materials, and it famously told customers, in a *New York Times* ad, "Don't Buy This Jacket," counterintuitively urging people to buy fewer things in order to reduce our collective environmental footprint.

Yet despite—or, more likely because of—always going his own way, Chouinard has built a beloved, sustainable, and impactful company. Chouinard zigs when others zag, a trait shared by many successful changemakers across roles and sectors. Other organizations, too, can reap the benefits of zigging when their entire industry is zagging if and when they take bold and principled action.

Beyond Black Friday

While living in Stockholm, I regularly took pleasure in seeing many American goods make their way to Scandinavia, from kombucha bottles on supermarket shelves to Yankees hats in department stores (though I would have much preferred Cubs hats). But there was one export that absolutely shocked me: Black Friday—the custom of big sales and bigger shopping anxiety the day after Thanksgiving. The craziest part? They don't even celebrate Thanksgiving in Sweden! Yet much to my chagrin, this uniquely American tradition had infiltrated both the malls and psyche of Stockholm.

Black Friday may have become a global cultural phenomenon, but the concept itself started innocuously enough. Stores—many of which depend on the holiday season to meet their yearly goals—would offer special sales the day after Thanksgiving, kicking off a month of Christmas shopping. Soon, stores felt pressure to one-up each other; they began to open up at six o'clock in the morning to maximize the duration of Black Friday. That trend soon spiraled out of control, with major retailers opening their doors earlier and earlier, first at the stroke of midnight on

Friday, then eventually creeping all the way back to six o'clock on Thursday evening—the very same time, ironically, that families were supposed to be sitting down to a meal to spend time together and give thanks. The push toward earlier and more aggressive Black Friday sales became a trend sweeping the entire American retail industry, and it seemed that stores had no choice but to participate, with increasing benefits to those that could open earlier than their competitors, no matter how destructive their actions would be to the underlying premise of the holiday.

While virtually every American company was going that direction, one company had the courage to forge its own path. In 2015, the outdoor retailer REI decided that it would completely close its stores on Black Friday and suggest that consumers spend the day in nature with family and friends. Its #OptOutside campaign was a huge risk. As REI's chief customer officer, Ben Steele, later said, "People thought we were crazy and retailers were saying, 'Why the hell would you give up one of the busiest shopping days of the year?' "[12]

The decision was indeed risky. But it was rooted in the company's mission, and it paid off for the retailer across all stakeholders. Employees appreciated it, because they wouldn't have to work on a holiday yet were still paid. Consumers loved it; the campaign had an impressive 91 percent positive sentiment on social media.[13] And investors loved it, as its first run in 2015 resulted in a 9.3 percent increase in sales compared to the previous year, when REI stores were open on Black Friday.[14]

You need not be a CEO or an influential leader to zig when others zag. Practicing this mindset is equally accessible to each of us when we begin with the curiosity to pay attention to macro-level trends. We can notice when entire sectors, groups, or teams tend to be thinking or acting a single way, and then identify opportunities for impact through bucking that trend. As the Asch conformity experiments (which I'll discuss in the following pages) show us, humans are wired to stick with the pack. If you can lean on your values, like REI, or connect your nonconformity to your mission and vision, like Chouinard, huge benefits and massive opportunities for positive change avail themselves. It might not mean zigging an entire company; it might be creating a new norm in your family or a new approach to volunteering at your child's school. Zigging is all about a mindset, and that mindset can be universal.

The Surprising Pull of Conformity

Have you ever seen a picture on Instagram and felt called to go re-create it yourself? Or traveled to a new city and found the decor of your Airbnb in Phoenix virtually the same as the one in Toronto? Have you been delighted to find a Google Maps pop-up that tells you that it has found a faster route for you, only to have every other car take the same off-ramp? We all crave originality, yet we find that there is often so much pressure to conform—a pressure only heightened by social media.

The pressure to conform is a deeply human instinct and one that goes back far beyond today's digital era. In the 1950s, psychologist Solomon Asch conducted his now famous "conformity experiments" at Swarthmore College, studying the extent to which individuals would yield to majority group behaviors and opinions.[15] A subject would enter a room alongside actors who were in on the study. They would be asked to answer some obvious perception questions—such as which lines on a card were the same length. Each participant would announce their answers in front of the group, with the subject always going last. While the correct answers were clear and unambiguous, the actors were scripted to purposefully answer incorrectly, with the study examining whether the subject would then conform to the group's opinions, even if obviously false. What do you think you would do in such an experiment?

While the control group—where actors answered correctly—resulted in an error rate of less than 1 percent, Asch found that 75 percent of subjects gave at least one incorrect answer across twelve trials in which the actors purposefully gave incorrect answers. This means that three out of four people purposefully answered an easy question with a response they almost certainly knew was false, all because of the pressure to conform, to not stand out. Of course, the results are nuanced; there have also been many variations of this run since, and a more detailed analysis shows only 5 percent were swayed by the crowd in every single test, with 25 percent never being swayed at all. But this still leaves about 70 percent of participants who could be influenced by the group to go against their own instincts and instead conform.

What does this mean for you as a changemaker? You will face pressure throughout your life to go with the majority, to do things the way everyone else does them. In some instances, this is harmless and perhaps even preferable, as we will learn later with the concept of "idiosyncrasy credits." To constantly challenge the status quo risks burnout, so we should be selective when we decide to go against convention. For instance, if you are helping plan an event with lots of complexity and a track record of success, it may not be worth your time to try and find a different caterer than in years past or redo a slightly imperfect seating chart. By letting these status quo decisions stand, you might then more effectively focus your energy on bolder changes—making the event zero-waste, inviting new speakers, or creating digital access, which are all areas with greater potential for impact. Changemakers can't change everything, and certainly not all at once; it's knowing when and where to question the status quo that makes the difference.

When we do find a status quo worth challenging, our ability to instigate and lead change requires having the courage to question norms—to face the pressure of peers, colleagues, and even family who expect us to go the "standard" route, yet still travel in a direction that is true to who we are. Remember the lessons from the Asch conformity experiments: that the pressure you feel to conform is normal and universal but you can develop the confidence, and apply the tools from this chapter, to find the courage and ability to lead positive change.

TAKING SMART RISKS

Are you a risk-taker? Or do you tend to be more cautious?

Is being a risk-taker baked into our DNA (nature) or a function of our environments (nurture)? Like so many aspects of our actions and our personalities, the answer is probably both. There are some relatively stable psychological characteristics that are correlated with individuals being more prone to taking risks. But the cultures in which we grow up, along with our everyday social groups, also influence our propensity toward risk.

Regardless of where you naturally fall on this spectrum, as a changemaker it's crucial to develop a more comfortable relationship with taking risks. After all, the act of leading change, of questioning the status quo, almost always has risk associated with it.

In my radically inclusive definition of changemaking, each of us can lead change in our own way. To that end, this section focuses on a more inclusive way of thinking about risk, teaching you not just to embrace risks, but also how to take smart risks. Through a counterintuitive case study of an entrepreneurial risk-taker and insights from economics and psychology, you'll gain the skills to be the sort of changemaker who can confidently take risks in order to make positive change.

Risk in Real Life

Along with protecting against the downsides of the risks we consider taking, we can also take time up front to understand just how risky a decision might be.

In my career dedicated to teaching, supporting, and advising changemakers of all kinds—from business executives to nonprofit program directors to entry-level product managers—I've seen that often it's not any one single risk that stresses them out; it's the sheer number of them, any of which might pay off handsomely or result in disaster. Knowing when to take a risk and when not to is an invaluable skill that differentiates the successful changemakers.

There's a deceptively simple and incredibly powerful tool developed by entrepreneur Tyler Tervooren called "the risk quotient" that helps aspiring leaders get perspective on which risks are worth taking.[16] Begin by identifying a risk and then quantify the potential rewards and potential losses on a 1-to-10 scale. The risk quotient is equal to the potential reward divided by the potential loss. If the risk quotient is greater than 3, then according to Tervooren, it's probably a risk worth taking. (I told you it's deceptively simple.) The concept can be applied to risks large and small, across the full spectrum of change efforts we seek to lead.

$$\text{risk quotient} = \frac{\text{potential reward}}{\text{potential loss}}$$

The risk quotient helps us gain clarity as to whether or not questioning the status quo is worth our time. Let's explore how this concept applies to Bryan Stevenson's work at the Equal Justice Initiative as the organization examined whether or not to take on and support a new client. We can't know for sure what Stevenson was thinking when deliberating on whether or not to take on this particular case. But looking back at it, we can see how applying a tool like the risk quotient can help us better understand the process for making high-stakes decisions.

In 1999, EJI attorneys considered representing Anthony Ray Hinton, an Alabama man who had been convicted of murdering two fast-food restaurant managers in 1985. Hinton was sentenced to death, despite scant evidence and the prosecutor's documented history of racial bias.

What were the potential losses to EJI in taking on such a case? Attempting to right these injustices, especially given lopsided power dynamics politically and judicially, would take a lot of resources—both financial and human capital. If attorneys were unsuccessful, it might be a blow to the reputation of EJI, which was just beginning to gain nationwide notoriety for its recent successes. There was even the chance that they would be fighting to free a man who had actually committed the crimes for which they sought to free him. How would you quantify these potential losses?

Now let's turn to the potential rewards from taking on Hinton's case. If EJI attorneys were successful, they would literally be saving this man's life. They would be restoring a sense of justice, and they could use this case to inspire change at a more systemic level. They would give hope to others unjustly convicted of crimes, they would build the reputation of EJI, and they would leave their mark in history books. How would you quantify these potential rewards?

The risk quotient helps us see that even though the potential losses were absolutely significant, the immense rewards that could come from taking on Hinton's case made this a fight worth pursuing.

EJI did, in fact, represent Hinton, and after more than fifteen years of fighting for justice, on Friday, April 3, 2015, at 9:30 a.m., Hinton walked out of the Jefferson County Jail as a free man, after being held on death row for nearly three decades.

"The sun does shine," he remarked as he gazed up at the blue sky.[17]

The reward for taking on his case, evident as Hinton was greeted by friends and family, far exceeded potential losses. Stevenson and EJI took a smart risk. And it paid off.

Getting Support

What's a risk that you are considering taking right now? How can the risk quotient help you make an informed decision and ensure that it's not just a risk but a smart, calculated risk? Take a minute to analyze it and calculate the risk quotient. Hopefully, you've determined it's a smart risk worth pursuing. Great! But what happens if you need someone else to go along with your new idea and that person tends to be more risk-averse?

Here, social science can teach us how to enroll others. By setting the stage to take action at just the right moment and with the ideal positioning, we can effectively convince even the most cautious among us to join in our change efforts.

You can take your first steps toward questioning the status quo even before you know where you want to zig. You can start developing what social psychologists refer to as "idiosyncrasy credits," which help you go against group norms. Idiosyncrasy credits, as conceived by psychologist Edwin Hollander, are earned through either conformity or competence. Hollander defines these credits as the "positively disposed impressions" an individual acquires from other group members.[18]

You can gain these credits in two ways. The first is by going with the majority on issues that you don't feel strongly about—so that you can then apply your credits toward leading change on issues that do matter to you. If you earn a reputation for questioning the status quo on anything and everything, you're more likely to be seen as a contrarian than a changemaker (remember the example earlier about identifying when and where to question the status quo in planning an event). This might mean going with the flow on what type of accounting software to use or where to post a job opening, so that when you do choose to deviate from the group and speak up about supply chain transparency, people will be more likely to listen because they know you don't always diverge.

The second way to earn credits is by developing and displaying expertise and clear abilities—for instance, by always doing high-level work. In other words, members of a group will be more accepting of someone taking a risk or pursuing a new path if they know that they generally are part of the group and that they are competent and talented. You can start building up these credits now so that when the time comes to zig while others are zagging, you can put all your idiosyncrasy-credit chips on the table to influence those around you to join you down this new path. Professional baseball manager Joe Maddon is eccentric; he drives a 1970s van, wears big glasses and bold hoodies, and has a penchant for talking philosophy instead of baseball tactics. But because of his reputation as a talented manager—especially being the one who helped the Chicago Cubs win their first World Series in 108 years—he's able to regularly question the status quo on everything from coaching style to demeanor. He has the idiosyncrasy credits to do so earned from his expertise and ability.

Yet even with idiosyncrasy credits to spend, you may still face a manager, for example, who is more interested in preserving the status quo than actively challenging it. In a terrific study titled "When Risk Seeking Becomes a Motivational Necessity," University of Waterloo professor Abigail Scholer and colleagues look at how we can motivate others, especially in decision-making positions, to pursue new ideas.[19]

Their findings show that we can reframe a new idea or a new change initiative by, instead of viewing it as a risk itself, flipping the narrative to view *not* pursuing it as the greater risk. In today's world, where everyone else is pursuing change, it's too risky for us to be the ones who don't. The insight from this study helps us gain confidence in communicating our vision for change and inspiring others to join us—even those who might find themselves more cautious around new ideas and less comfortable with change.

The Risk Quotient in Action

Jean Guo is truly indefatigable. She's an entrepreneurial force of nature, with a singular drive and vision to help refugees bridge the digital divide. To achieve that vision, she cofounded Paris-based Konexio to help immigrant communities receive crucial job training and compete in local job markets. In just the six years since its founding, Konexio has been recognized by the Google Impact Challenge and the World Economic Forum for its incredible impact throughout France and is now expanding into Malawi and elsewhere on the African continent.

As a board member of Konexio, I had the pleasure of working closely with Guo. Together, we put the risk quotient into action during one of our regular check-in calls. Using this tool, she gained crucial clarity on a big risk she was considering.

The measurable impact from Konexio's first pilot was undeniable. As a result, Guo was fielding calls from governments and organizations around Europe and Africa wanting to bring Konexio's programs to their locales. As a small startup, Konexio faced a challenge: In order to scale, Guo needed to hire many more teammates, but new staff would mean tapping into, and potentially exhausting, the limited financial reserves of her small social enterprise.

During one of our sessions, Guo asked for my advice on this potential risk, and I presented the risk quotient as a tool for her to make her own confident, informed decision about whether the risk of hiring more staff was worth pursuing.

We talked through and quantified the potential rewards: increasing the scale of Konexio, which would mean more refugees supported, more partners engaged, more geographies covered. It would mean building a more resilient and robust team to handle whatever new challenges would arise, and it would give her a chance to offload some of her least favorite tasks, like HR, to someone who would readily embrace the mission.

The potential losses, though, were significant: If partners fell through, or if the initial interest was all talk, Guo might be forced to lay off these new hires, implement pay cuts across the board, or even face the terrifying scenario of running out of cash and being forced to shut down. She would have to invest a lot of her own time to train and get new teammates up and running while simultaneously delivering on new projects for important partners, all with an unproven team.

Once we quantified each, Guo was able to see that her risk quotient was greater than three. She therefore recognized that while this was a risk with weighty potential losses, the huge potential rewards outweighed them. Now clear-eyed, she was able to make a decision with confidence, having identified and analyzed this decision through the risk quotient.

With boldness enabled through this analysis, she decided to take this smart risk—to hire staff and pursue more projects. And just as the tool suggested to her, it was worth it: She more than doubled her staff in mere months, launched a pilot program in Malawi, and opened up the doors to new fundraising avenues.

WALKING DOWN A NEW PATH

Muhammad Yunus has always been a personal hero of mine. The Nobel Peace Prize winner catalyzed the field of microfinance. His legacy is in recognizing that our greatest lever as changemakers is our willingness to see a status quo that is inefficient or unethical and then do something about it. He revolutionized the idea of providing small loans to many people, instead of huge loans to fewer people. He began in his home country of Bangladesh by giving small loans to mostly female entrepreneurs through the bank he founded, Grameen Bank. He showed that these individuals, who were so often excluded from traditional markets, not only would repay loans (the bank's clients have an astounding 99 percent repayment rate historically)[20] but they would do incredible things with the funds, from starting businesses to supporting their families. He refused to believe that traditional financial markets worked for the majority of people, and he made it his life's work to disrupt those systems.

Needless to say, I was absolutely pinching myself when he agreed to speak to my class in the fall of 2020. In his remarks to my students about preparing for a post-COVID world, he used an analogy that sums up a changemaker who questions the status quo. He asked why people were so eager to get back on the same roads we were traveling before the pandemic. He suggested instead that we seize this opportunity to build new roads instead of the old ones—new roads that would lead us to a more equitable, healthy, and connected future. The advice to get back to "normal" as quickly as possible was the wrong one, he said. Instead, we all need to question outdated structures and to find better ones to replace them. As changemakers who question the status quo, the new normal is in our hands, and it's up to us to create it.

BE THE CHANGE

Key Insights

- Curiosity can be learned, and being able and willing to see the world a bit differently, like engineer Laila Ohlgren did, can create so many new possibilities.
- Changemaking is not simply about taking more risks; it's about taking more smart risks.
- When everyone is headed in one direction, this is often a sign that it's worth thinking about what the opposite direction might make possible.
- We can identify when to use divergent thinking—coming up with lots of new ideas—and when to use convergent thinking to decide on a single course of action.

Changemaker Challenge

- Lean into your curiosity and practice some divergent thinking. Using Muhammad Yunus's analogy, think about a road you or your organization is walking down right now. What are some alternative roads you could build instead? Identify the risks it would take to pursue one of them, and then use the risk quotient to determine whether it's a smart risk worth pursuing.

Chapter 3

Confidence Without Attitude

Malaysia-based changemaker Gwen Yi Wong speaks with a confidence that belies her age. You can almost see how quickly the synapses in her brain fire as she gazes out from behind her wire-rimmed glasses. She has been an innovator from as early as she can remember, always with a strong desire to build meaningful projects and to connect, help, and inspire others.

Because of that, most people would assume she was thriving when an organization she cofounded, Tribeless, received worldwide attention for its first product, the Empathy Box. The Empathy Box, which has now been used in over thirty countries, is a facilitation and connection tool to help teams and groups practice empathy, respect, and mutual understanding, and she had become the face of it.

Wong built a strong founding team, and by all outside measures the organization was taking off under her leadership. But inside, as the company grew exponentially, she was struggling under the weight of it all. She was concerned by how her identity had become so wrapped up in this product, and she realized that there might be a mismatch between her strongest skills, as a visionary and change catalyst, and the traits Tribeless needed from a leader now in this growth stage, around product management and operations.

"I wasn't some brilliant, business-minded startup CEO," she said as she came to that conclusion, "and my baby was actually better off in someone else's hands."[1]

It took months of processing and having difficult conversations before she realized she needed to step down as CEO. "By learning to let go of this role," she said, "I was letting go of so much else—the emotional baggage I'd attached to Tribeless, the societal expectations I'd internalized, and most importantly, the idea that I'm some perfect, wise, irreproachable person." Her decision was rooted in humility and was made possible because of her confidence to do something really hard.

While mentoring and advising changemakers around the world, I've supported many leaders in Gwen's exact position, yet many of them lacked her self-awareness. Some also had overactive egos, which stopped them from recognizing what Gwen did: that the best thing for her organization at that point in time—and for her personally—was not to double down on something that wasn't working but to have the humility to step aside. She stayed on the leadership team in a position that better played to her many strengths, and her cofounder stepped up to become CEO.

"Leadership isn't about pretending you have it all together, or telling others what to do," she told me. "It's about humility and vulnerability and trust, and being willing to put yourself last."[2]

Gwen's embrace of both confidence and humility became her biggest strength as she set Tribeless up to soar to even greater heights.

Developing a changemaker mindset often requires holding two seemingly contradictory traits simultaneously: Having a strong personal vision yet being open to collaborating with others. Employing drive and determination to push through barrier after barrier yet knowing when to step back and recharge. And in this chapter, we explore the crucial polarity of confidence and humility.

As we'll learn throughout this chapter, changemakers don't find a muddled middle ground of semiconfident and semihumble; rather, they challenge themselves to do "both, and"—remain confident, courageous, and self-assured yet also humble, trusting, and open to working with and learning from others.

This chapter will teach you how to develop trust in yourself and others, how to loosen control without losing control, and how to display a confident, self-assured strength through practicing humility.

HUMILITY AS A STRENGTH

When I begin teaching executive audiences about the importance of humility, I'm used to seeing eye rolls. So I lead with a crucial message: Despite what you might think, humility is not weakness. "Humility is not the same as weakness," I often repeat for effect, challenging the assumption head-on. I do so with confidence (but not attitude!) because the data are on my side. Being humble is actually one of the greatest strengths a leader can have.

A powerful study conducted by Amy Ou, David Waldman, and Suzanne Peterson, titled "Do Humble CEOs Matter? An Examination of CEO Humility and Firm Outcomes," paints an exceedingly clear picture.[3] They examined 105 different companies after giving all of the CEOs a test to measure their level of humility. Ready for some spoilers? Here's what they discovered: Humble CEOs were found to have reduced pay disparity between themselves and their staff, they hired more diverse management teams, and they gave staff the ability to lead and innovate. Humble leaders have less employee turnover, higher employee satisfaction, and, most crucially for my dear skeptical executives, they improve the company's bottom-line performance.

Still not convinced? A study from two Canadian researchers shows that leaders low in humility are more likely to overreact during conflict.[4] And a study from Duke University shows that the more intellectually humble a subject is, the less likely they are to be susceptible to misinformation, the better they are at handling ambiguity, and the less likely they are to continue pushing forward on a path they know is wrong for fear of looking weak.[5]

Why does this matter in becoming a changemaker? The absence of humility is often the fatal flaw among leaders pursuing change initiatives. Two well-known examples: Elizabeth Holmes, the now-disgraced founder of Theranos, kept pushing forward a supposedly revolutionary blood-test product, only to watch her empire fall when consumers found out that there was no substance behind her claims. Lack of humility also helps us explain the viral failure that was the Fyre Festival, now forever enshrined in cultural lore due to a Netflix documentary, *Fyre: The Greatest Party That Never Happened.* What had been pitched as the greatest music festival of all time, leveraging Instagram influencers and famous musicians to help promote it, in reality became a debacle where participants shelled out thousands of dollars for a promised premier event but ended up receiving nothing more than premade sandwiches, accommodations in FEMA-style tents, and near riots when musicians dropped out. Festival organizer Billy McFarland faced multiple lawsuits, claiming hundreds of millions of dollars in fraud, and criminal investigations, all because of his inability to admit that his plan wasn't working until it was far too late.

These, of course, are famous examples memorialized in newspapers and movies, but I'll bet you can think of an example from your own life as well—where someone's lack of humility took an exciting project filled with promise down into an untimely demise.

Looking Out for Humility

Jim Collins, author of *Good to Great,* is notorious for his rigorous, data-driven analysis.[6] In 2001 he and his team used "matched-pair analysis," where they analyzed two very similar companies—think Wells Fargo and Bank of America—to examine why one company thrived while the other remained stagnant. In addition to findings on corporate strategy and market positioning, the data show that the leaders of "great" companies had two traits in common: fierce resolve and humility. It surprised many, including Collins himself, that one of the defining reasons a company became truly great is that the leader of the company was a humble one.

In explaining the concept of humility to a skeptical audience—often individuals working at leading companies like those he studied, who may not readily see humility as a strength—Collins uses the metaphor of a mirror and a window.

When a nonhumble leader receives praise, even if it's meant for their team, that leader will look in the mirror and take the praise for themselves.

And when a nonhumble leader receives blame, even if it is meant for them, they will look out the window and project the blame onto others.

A humble leader, meanwhile, does the opposite. When praise comes in, even if it's meant for them, they will look out the window and share that praise with their team. And, conversely, when blame comes in, even if it isn't meant for them, they will look in the mirror and take the blame themselves.

What is your default approach when you receive praise or blame? As we seek to develop our humility, think of this analogy: If you receive praise for a team that you led, will you find the humility to share that praise with others instead of taking it for yourself? And in the case that something goes wrong, even if it's not your fault, will you step up as the leader and take responsibility?

Now, of course, there are exceptions. For instance, as a marginalized person in the workforce, where your contributions might be less likely to be readily appreciated, there may be times where you need to have the confidence to accept the praise you deserve. But as a general rule, this analogy—as supported by Collins's rigorous data analysis—provides a simple but powerful framework to help you embrace your humility as a strength, not as a weakness.

TRUST AS A SUPERPOWER

In the early days of leading StartSomeGood, I used to judge my leadership ability based on how often my team would come to me with questions, how often my team would say, "Hey, Alex, what do you think about this? What should we do with our marketing strategy here?" And I used to think, "Wow, what an amazing leader I'm being. Look at how important I am to all of these people who need my advice."

In reality, though, I was failing myself and my team. I was a bottleneck; my employees weren't empowered, my self-importance stood in the way of growth for the company, and I was exhausted from working seventy-five-hour weeks.

By placing myself in the center of everything, my leadership was like the middle pole of a merry-go-round. There was plenty of action and excitement revolving around me, and the illusion of movement, but we were firmly planted in one spot the whole time, going around in circles.

How did I manage to get myself—and, more importantly, my team—off the merry-go-round? I learned how to lead with trust.

As a global society, we're facing a paradox. Think about all of the major trends that shape the world today: globalization, social media, online retailing, distributed and remote workforces. They all sit atop a bedrock of trust. The ability to trust—and be trusted—has never been more important.

But trust has never been more lacking.

According to Pew Research Center, from 1958 to 2021, the number of Americans who say they trust the federal government "always or most of the time" has plummeted from 73 percent in 1958 to under 25 percent today.[7] Meanwhile, 71 percent of Americans say trust in each other has been shrinking, with 70 percent saying that this decreased trust makes it harder to solve problems together. Sixty-two percent of respondents say that people are more likely to look out for themselves rather than help someone else, and over one-third of people don't trust their employer.[8] While there are variations by country—for instance, Swedes have much higher levels of trust[9]—overall the trend is clear: Trust in institutions, in organizations, and in each other is plunging.

Trust has never been more critical, yet trust has never been more absent.

But leading change requires the ability for you to trust others, and to get others to trust you back.

So the question for you as a changemaker is: How can you learn to use trust as a superpower to achieve your goals?

The next section will introduce you to the "trust leap," which will help you reframe how you think about trust, and I'll share advice on learning to trust yourself, trust others, and get others to trust you back.

Trust Leaps

In her TED talk, "We've Stopped Trusting Institutions and Started Trusting Strangers," Oxford University lecturer Rachel Botsman puts forward a provocative, but I believe correct, interpretation of what it means to trust.[10] She says trust is a "confident relationship with the unknown." We often try to conceive of trust as being fully rational, but ultimately, she teaches us, we have to make a "trust leap," recognizing that deciding to trust doesn't come with a guarantee of what's on the other side of the jump.

For instance, she talks about BlaBlaCar, a ridesharing service in Europe. Each time BlaBlaCar users ride with someone they've never met before, they take a trust leap. This trust leap is something absolutely unimaginable a couple of decades ago (can you imagine someone hopping into a random Chrysler pulling up next to you in the 1970s?), yet thanks to services like Uber and Lyft, getting in a complete stranger's car is now something that many of us do on a regular basis. We're constantly taking these trust leaps.

What I like about Botsman's definition is that she says when we try to make trust completely rational, it'll ultimately fail. At some point, we have to have that confident relationship with the unknown, be willing to trust, be willing to take that leap.

What's a trust leap that you have taken recently? What made you decide to go for it?

THE PILLARS OF TRUST

We tend to think of trust in binary terms; either it exists in a relationship or it does not. For changemakers, it's important to fully appreciate that trust is nuanced, in order to effectively apply it in service of our change efforts. Trust consists of three interrelated aspects, or pillars:

1. <u>Trusting ourselves.</u>
2. <u>Trusting others.</u>
3. <u>Earning the trust of others.</u>

Each one is important on its own, but to fully make trust a super-power, it's imperative that you are able to build upon all three pillars, which are mutually reinforcing. Having only two will leave the foundation of trust wobbly.

If you have the first and the second pillars without the third, you risk becoming isolated from your teams and your collaborators, remaining an individual contributor rather than a leader who regularly brings out the best in others.

If you have the first and third pillars without the second, you risk coming off as arrogant or aloof, potentially landing on the side of confidence *with* attitude.

Finally, if you have just the second and third pillars but not the first, you are never able to fully lean into your own talents, insights, and expertise, limiting your impact and contributions to your team's collective efforts.

Let's look at each of these pillars and see how we can build solid foundations on them.

Trusting Ourselves

The first pillar of trust—and one that so many people regularly struggle with—is learning to first trust ourselves.

How can you develop this self-trust?

My first suggestion is to develop trust-inducing habits.

Retired US Navy admiral William H. McRaven has led a distinguished career, including organizing and overseeing the strike that took out terrorist leader Osama bin Laden. A decorated leader with an esteemed career, what advice does he have for other budding leaders, military and otherwise, following in his footsteps? Complex theories of networked leadership? Tactical advice on executing multifaceted strategies? Nope. It's: Make your bed.

In his now-famous commencement address to the University of Texas in 2014, that was his advice to graduates about to start making their mark on the world: Make your bed.[11]

The concept here is as beautiful as it is simple. "If you make your bed every morning you will have accomplished the first task of the day," McRaven instructs. "It will give you a small sense of pride, and it will encourage you to do another task and another and another. By the end of the day, that one task completed will have turned into many tasks completed. Making your bed will also reinforce the fact that little things in life matter. If you can't do the little things right, you will never do the big things right.

"And, if by chance you have a miserable day, you will come home to a bed that is made—that you made—and a made bed gives you encouragement that tomorrow will be better."

Therefore, the first step to trusting yourself is to develop trust-inducing habits. Consistently accomplish small tasks to develop the trust in yourself that you can take on bigger, scarier tasks with confidence. A fun example: My StartSomeGood cofounder, Tom Dawkins, always begins his to-do lists with the same task at the top: Create a to-do list. That way, just as soon as he's created the list, he can check off his first accomplishment as done, creating a tiny bit of momentum to propel him forward.

My second suggestion to develop self-trust: Remember that imposter syndrome is totally normal and far more common than any of us realize. Originally called "imposter phenomenon," it was first theorized by psychologist Suzanne Imes and Georgia State University professor Pauline Rose Clance in 1978.[12] More recently, writers Ruchika Tulshyan and Jodi-Ann Burey defined imposter syndrome as "doubting your abilities and feeling like a fraud" in their crucially important article "Stop Telling Women They Have Imposter Syndrome."[13] Though we are often hard on ourselves for feeling this way, nearly all of us will experience imposter syndrome sometime in our lives. It's prevalent even among people whom we would consider unequivocally successful and the opposite of frauds—from Academy Award–winning actress Natalie Portman to former Starbucks CEO Howard Schultz, both of whom have talked about experiencing imposter syndrome.

While most of us feel it to some extent, I've found that it's especially common among the women, students of color, and first-generation college students I teach. This reinforces the argument that Tulshyan and Burey make that we need to see imposter syndrome not as an individual's problem but as the systemic issue it is. But the good news for those of us who feel imposter syndrome, myself included, is that research by MIT professor Basima Tewfik shows that we can learn to leverage these feelings for more productive outcomes.

Tewfik found that one of the main characteristics of imposter syndrome is a gap between how individuals perceive their own competence compared to how competent they actually are.[14] Learning to trust ourselves can help close this gap. In a study of medical students, Tewfik found that those experiencing imposter syndrome were "more empathetic, they were better listeners, they asked better questions," and they even made better eye contact and had more welcoming body language than those without. Instead of beating ourselves up because we feel imposter syndrome, we can remember that nearly all of us feel it, and that this can not only make us better at our job, but it can be used as a boost to remember that we probably are more competent in reality than we feel in our minds. This may not make imposter syndrome any less uncomfortable in the moment, but at least it can be a catalyst for us to remember to trust ourselves more, because we are more worthy of trust than we might otherwise give ourselves credit for.

Trusting Others

As the prevalence of imposter syndrome shows, learning to trust ourselves will be an important lifelong challenge for some of us. Developing trust in ourselves is necessary. It's not sufficient, however, to fully leverage trust as a superpower.

Learning to trust others is especially challenging for my high-achieving students, who put a lot of their success down to their own fastidiousness and dedication to doing things the "right" way—their way. One of these students came to my office hours to complain about his team in the final group project for my class, telling me that his group mates weren't doing the project to his standards and so he wanted to do the entire project himself. This student was the definition of a high achiever, pursuing a double major and a minor, and maintaining a nearly 4.0 GPA. In talking with him, I recognized that he had been trained to think going solo was the most efficient way to get work done. It was understandable that he preferred to work on his own. After all, in school, whether it's problem sets or standardized tests, we are graded on our own ability to learn for ourselves and by ourselves. Unfortunately, as this student was about to learn, what had been positively reinforced for him by his impressive academic achievements in school would not prepare him well for the collaborative environment that awaited him in the work world upon graduation, let alone his aspirations to be a changemaker, where trusting others is crucial.

I shared three specific approaches with him to help him become a changemaker who learned to trust others:

Start small. Many changemakers are overwhelmed by the idea of losing control over their projects and see trusting others as the first crack toward that loss. Instead of telling them to go all in, I advise changemakers to start with small trust leaps. Give collaborators room to contribute one small part of a project in their own way. Then, if that works well (it usually goes far better than expected), give them a slightly bigger project next time. Trust isn't binary. As the Russian proverb that was often quoted by Ronald Reagan during US–USSR nuclear disarmament talks advises, "Trust, but verify." Give a bit of trust, confirm that it was warranted, and then provide a bit more trust the next time.

Be clear on the "what" and flexible on the "how." Imagine you want to plan an event on the topic of sustainable cities and you want to delegate the planning to someone but you aren't sure how much control to cede. Outline the vision and the nonnegotiables, while giving lots of room for flexibility and creativity on how that plan is actually achieved. You might tell your collaborator that you want it to be held in a modern setting, featuring a panel with four speakers—two men and two women—and that you want at least fifty people in attendance. This is the "what," and this is crystal clear. But the "how" for achieving it is left up to the person you are learning to trust. Perhaps they will recruit speakers through their networks or perhaps through cold emails. Perhaps they will advertise through Facebook, or perhaps they will create an email campaign. Those details don't (and shouldn't!) matter to you. You have outlined what the end results will be, and in doing so, you are allowing yourself to trust someone else to execute on that vision in their own way—a way that might be even more effective than your suggested path.

Protect against the downside of risk. Even if you start small and remain clear on the what and flexible on the how, it can still feel really scary to take a trust leap, especially if it's an endeavor that means a lot to you. Here you can focus on protecting against the downside of risk. In other words, figure out what the worst-case scenario might be if someone were to flake on you and proactively plan ahead to overcome it. As you learn to trust people, you need not do so blindly. As you get more comfortable with trusting others, you'll get better at judging how and when to trust. But in the meantime, prepare for what will happen if your trust isn't warranted. For instance, if you delegate someone to plan that event on sustainable cities, perhaps you give them a deadline of completing all plans two weeks in advance. That way, in an absolute worst case, where your colleague falls through, you can still pull off the event on your own. Protecting against the downside allows you to take away your trust before it's too late, should things go wrong. (They probably won't.)

I'm proud to say that my student was willing to trust me with this advice and took it to heart in his group project. The final presentation was notable, because each member of the group played a speaking role, and the concept they presented had shifted significantly from the concept my student had initially pitched to me, suggesting that he took a leap and trusted his teammates. Not only was his team better off as a result of the trust he placed in them, but his own future potential as a changemaker improved as well.

Earning the Trust of Others

You're now feeling more ready and willing to trust others. But how do you get others to reciprocate?

Trust does not stand alone; it is forever intertwined with trustworthiness. As one party proves they are trustworthy, the other more easily trusts. As we trust, it comes easier to trust others, reinforcing our natural instincts to trust. It's a virtuous cycle.

This does not imply trusting blindly—my apologies to the folks flooding my spam folder offering urgent, secret cryptocurrency opportunities, which they promise will transform my life—but rather conveying that your first instinct is to trust, and that you are someone to whom trust can, and should, be granted.

This enables the virtuous cycle of trusting and trustworthiness to take hold, as it transforms potential adversaries into partners.

I can illustrate this better with a sharing-economy analogy. Consider entering your rideshare believing it will be a five-star ride, rather than a one-star ride. If you enter expecting a one-star ride, you'll find yourself more critical, more controlling, and more on edge. This, in return, will result in a driver who is less able to be their best, and thus even less likely to earn your trust. If you enter expecting a five-star ride, you'll meet your driver on terms where you both can be your best and where a great ride, or even a great relationship, can flourish. It's an amazing thing: When you trust others to be worthy of your trust, you'll find others working hard to show they deserve it.

My first recommendation, therefore, to get others to trust you is to offer your own trust first. This is the very definition of a trust leap, but its elegant simplicity gives you the agency to be someone who actively enters this virtuous cycle.

There are three more ways I advise changemakers to get others to trust them: transparency, vulnerability, and being hard on ideas but soft on people.

Let's start with transparency. When people lack information about what's going on, they tend to make up stories, trying to connect whatever dots they can discern. When people make up stories, they tend to make themselves both the heroes and the victims of their own stories. It's incumbent on you, as someone worthy of earning trust, to help people tell the right stories.

We often protect others from information, thinking it's in their best interest—think of a startup on the verge of running out of funding—but I would argue that in most cases we should bias toward sharing more information rather than less. A friend of mine loved the startup he was working for and was absolutely blindsided when the founder and CEO informed the team that the company was closing down that day. Little did the CEO know that my friend had been thinking of all kinds of new revenue opportunities and even had a few strong leads he was saving for a rainy day. Had the CEO let the team know about the dismal financial projections a few weeks back, the CEO could have engaged the full team, my friend included, in helping to brainstorm possible solutions. The lack of trust the CEO showed ultimately sped up the downfall of the startup, leaving my friend and me to wonder how different things could have been if the CEO had led with transparency.

From transparency, we move to vulnerability. Researcher and bestselling author Brené Brown does amazing work on this topic, and one of the most powerful insights I've gained from her is that we tend to see vulnerability as weakness in ourselves but as a strength in others.[15] Think about that paradox: We value vulnerability when we see it in others, yet we are loath to display it ourselves, thinking it's a weakness. As a changemaker looking to gain the trust of others, being vulnerable—being human, being our full selves, and being open and honest—is an incredible way to get others to feel comfortable around us and to trust us. As changemakers, we often think that we need to wear armor and appear invincible. Yet it's often that armor of invulnerability that repels others from being able to trust us. Of course, vulnerability is not a sympathy-seeking tool. Vulnerability must have boundaries. Just like changemaking requires humility and confidence, effective vulnerability requires openness and boundary setting. Having both helps catalyze trust.

Finally, I advise changemakers looking to develop trustworthiness to be hard on ideas but soft on people. Leading change often requires ruffling feathers and pushing forward ideas and visions that are uncomfortable to others. But while forging an agreement might not be easy, we need not be disagreeable in the process of pursuing it. The most trust-inducing conversations are ones where people can speak their minds and where teams can wrestle with ideas. But it's crucial to challenge the ideas—with new approaches, concepts, visions, possibilities—while separating those ideas from the people sharing them. We can value and respect the person behind an idea, even what we think is a terrible idea, while still challenging that idea.

What does that look like in practice? It's critiquing ideas but not people. It's respecting someone who has the courage to disagree with you and complimenting them for doing so, all the while keeping your focus on finding the best possible idea. As my UC Berkeley colleague Morten Hansen suggests in his book *Great at Work*, great teams "fight, then unite."[16] In other words, they fully grapple with finding the best approach, each individual passionately advocating for what they believe is best. But once a consensus is built, everyone unites around that idea to move forward in unison.

Trust can, indeed, become your superpower—as long as you are willing to take the trust leap yourself.

CHANGEMAKING AS A TEAM SPORT

You will do your most important changemaking work through and with others.

Your ability to effectively collaborate—to engage others and to balance your confidence and your humility in partnership—will determine much of your success as a changemaker.

Yuval Sharon has been called "opera's disrupter in residence"[17] by the *New York Times*, and indeed his work has created ripples of change throughout the most traditional of art forms. He's directed operas in moving vehicles, train stations, and elevator corridors. He's re-created old works of opera to critique colonial power structures within the opera itself. Yet Sharon is not some iconoclast working by himself to create these brilliant endeavors. His LA-based experimental opera group, The Industry, takes collaboration to the next level. Instead of one director, many of the group's works have two. Instead of a single lead writer, there are two cowriters and even two composers.[18] By creating structures that force dialogue between people, Sharon directs a collaboration filled with boundary-pushing creativity.

Are You a Collaborator or a Compromiser?

Whether large or small, artistic or not, collaboration requires working productively through conflict. Let's start our deeper look at collaboration with helping you understand what your default approach to conflict is, through understanding and applying the Thomas-Kilmann Conflict Mode Instrument, or the TKI model.[19] It's a simple but powerful tool to provide you with self-awareness about your default approach to conflict and disagreement.

Imagine a graph with two axes. On the vertical y-axis is "Assertiveness," defined as "the extent to which the person attempts to satisfy [their] own concerns," from low to high. On the horizontal x-axis is "Cooperativeness," defined as "the extent to which the person attempts to satisfy the other person's concerns," from low to high. Where would you place yourself on these two scales? Your answer will determine how you tend to react to conflict, and, as we'll see, there is a surprising place on the graph that yields the most effective collaborations.[20]

If you rated yourself low on both, your approach is "avoiding." You sidestep the conflict without trying to satisfy your concerns or those of your teammate.

If you rated yourself high on assertiveness but low on cooperativeness, your approach is "competing." You try to satisfy your own concerns at your teammate's expense.

If you rated yourself low on assertiveness but high on cooperativeness, your approach is "accommodating." You attempt to satisfy your teammate's concerns at the expense of your own.

Now, here is where it gets really interesting. Most people think that the best possible approach to conflict is being moderate on both assertiveness and cooperativeness. But this actually leaves us in a messy, uncomfortable middle ground called "compromising." You try to find an acceptable settlement that only partially satisfies your concerns and those of your teammate, meaning neither of you walk away from the work together feeling particularly happy.

Imagine you are designing an after-school program with a colleague. You want to create a hands-on science program for elementary school students, while your partner wants to create a video production initiative for high schoolers. Compromising in the middle might mean running a technology training program for middle schoolers, halfway between what both of you initially wanted but not playing to either of your strengths, interests, or passions. It's a compromise that doesn't serve anyone especially well—most notably, students.

It may seem paradoxical, but the very best collaboration happens when you are high on both assertiveness (looking out for your own needs) and also cooperativeness (looking out for your partner). This is "collaboration" on the TKI graph. You try to find a win-win solution that completely satisfies both your concerns and your teammate's concerns. Collaboration opens up all kinds of new possibilities. For instance, perhaps you create a program that engages high school students to teach elementary school students about science through directing and acting in creative educational videos.

This is the embodiment of the paradox with which we started this chapter. Just like having confidence without attitude means being both confident and humble, collaboration requires you to both pursue your own goals and, simultaneously, those of others, not to sulk away to some disappointing middle ground.

Collaboration is where confidence, humility, and trust all come together.

Collaboration in Action

When I teach collaboration, I share a few recommendations with my students, focusing on being the type of collaborator who does their best changemaker work while bringing out the very best in their partners. But first, let's check in with one of the boldest collaborators I know.

In a world that's becoming more and more polarized, Scott Shigeoka (they/he), whose story we will learn about in chapter 11, is a beautiful embodiment of a bridge builder. Shigeoka helped launch an initiative called Bridging Differences, which explores "the keys to positive dialogue and understanding across lines of race, religion, political ideology, and more."[21] Shigeoka regularly seeks opportunities to connect with others, even, and especially, those who might be openly antagonistic to their beliefs and values. They do so not with a desire to change minds but rather a desire to understand. In doing so, they support people who are on opposite ends of belief systems to build meaningful connections with one another. Scott's first advice on building bridges is to begin with "a recognition of common humanity." Scott reminds us—connecting back to our section on humility—that to meaningfully collaborate with others, we must remember we don't have a monopoly on the truth, though it does not mean abandoning one's beliefs or values.

While your collaborations might not be as potentially volatile as some of Shigeoka's are, a fantastic place to start your collaboration is finding an alignment on values. You might be trying to collaborate with someone who holds vastly different political beliefs from you. While those beliefs may manifest in different policy choices, the values underpinning those beliefs are most likely more similar than you think: values like safety, health, and well-being. Now, you might have a long bridge to build to connect those values to your common goal, but you can at least begin by recognizing that even in antagonistic collaborations, there likely are some shared values between all parties.

To be a great collaborator often means going slow at first so that you can go fast later. The initial steps of leading with values and focusing on alignment are not quick. Nor should they be if they are done well, where each party is fully engaged. But by spending time up front in a collaboration to align and discuss values first, you'll be able to make future decisions much more quickly.

I learned this firsthand while on a hike I took with my then girl-friend, now wife, Rebecca, just days after I proposed to her. What had started innocuously enough as a discussion about our upcoming wedding turned into a disagreement over what our "wedding colors" should be. We took a step back and realized we had gone straight into execution mode without first aligning on values. We spent some time sitting along a river, our feet dangling in the cold water, as we zoomed out and talked about what we actually wanted from our wedding, and which values we hoped it would embody. Much to our parents' surprise, we even created a mission statement for the event.

It read: "We are creating a wedding which is authentic to who we are as a couple; which values the contributions from our families; which enables us to celebrate with everyone important to us; and allows us to be fully present and enjoy the ride." It served as an anchor point for our entire wedding, and even for our marriage to come. It wasn't quick to make this mission statement, but by taking the time and space to fully engage in this process up front, it made so many future decisions quick and easy. (Yes, even our wedding colors!)

The final lesson on collaboration is that process matters. Sure, you can get lucky and get to the same outcome quickly through force of will or persuasion, but if your collaborators don't feel part of the process and bought-in as full participants, your change is unlikely to stick. Many changemakers prefer to be the first person to share their opinion or ideas; this is the confidence part, which is important. But equally so is the humility to hang back and to let others share their ideas first. Your collaborators are likely to suggest ideas you wouldn't have thought of. And if they suggest an idea that you would have raised yourself anyway, then that's even better. You can praise them for their terrific idea and let them take credit, while enjoying the fact that you'll still get the outcome you want.

As we close this chapter, are you curious about what happened for Gwen and her organization since she took her humble yet confident step back in late 2018? She once again had the freedom to experiment, to innovate, and to lean into her natural strengths around people, product, and design. The timing for this was important, because it allowed Gwen to play a key role in launching a new product. In April 2020, just as much of the world was shifting from in-person to remote work, Tribeless launched an online version of its Empathy Box, marking the shift of the company from producing a physical product to going completely digital. Wong had never imagined the path that would follow from that one decision to give up the CEO role, but she recounted to me, "Empowering, trusting, and investing in my team got us here."

Just like Gwen, you're now a changemaker who embraces the "both, and" concepts of leading change—confidence and humility, trust and trustworthiness, slow and fast. These will serve you well as we move to our next changemaker-mindset concept: going beyond yourself.

BE THE CHANGE

Key Insights

- Humility is a strength, not a weakness. Data show that humble leaders have much better outcomes on everything from revenue to team engagement.
- Gaining trust often requires offering your own trust first. Get off the leadership merry-go-round and see if there are ways you can step back and give your trust to others (while protecting against the downside).
- True collaboration happens at that sweet spot where both you and the others are all actively advocating for your own needs while also finding ways to meet others' interests, leading to win-win solutions for all.

Changemaker Challenge

- Start strengthening your humility muscles by putting the mirror-and-window concept into practice. The next time you receive praise, see if there are others whom you can share that praise with. The next time you see someone on your team receive blame, see if there are ways you might take responsibility. Then reflect: How do others respond when you show up with greater humility?

Chapter 4

Beyond Yourself

Perhaps it's my personality or my time spent in laid-back California, but throughout my entire career as an entrepreneur, executive, and academic, I can count on one hand the number of meetings I've taken with someone who dressed up in a three-piece suit. It's all the more remarkable that the three-piece-suit wearer I was about to meet on this particular day was only twenty-one years old. The poor guy was about to do a walking meeting with me, up and down the steep slopes of San Francisco's Potrero Hill neighborhood, and on an unseasonably warm day, at that.

We shook hands and set off, about to climb our way up a hill that would reward us with views of the shimmering San Francisco Bay and the Oakland Hills.

This young man had contacted me asking to have a mentoring conversation about becoming a changemaker—one of my favorite things to do. But from the very beginning, I could tell this wouldn't be a regular session for me. And it wasn't just because of his loafers.

The young man had ambition as high as the hills we would climb that day, but his sense of direction was as aimless as that of the visitors wandering around San Francisco's notoriously touristy Pier 39 neighborhood.

He told me he had one singular ambition: to make the Forbes 30 Under 30 list.

"What might you like to have accomplished in order to have earned that recognition?" I asked him.

The silence was deafening. He looked around as if a passerby might miraculously shout out an answer to my question.

But it never came.

He told me that he had no idea what he would do, but he reiterated that he wanted to be on that list.

Titrating a blend of candor and empathy in my response, I told him that he had it backward. He was mistaking the ends for the means.

"Flip the script," I told him without hesitation. "You can't control the impact you will have on others. But you can control your ability and decision to serve others."

"Whether or not you make that list will be up to some strangers in a conference room one day as they make their selections," I added. "You can't control that. But what you can control is deciding, right here and now, to find ways to serve others and make their lives better."

Become a changemaker who goes beyond yourself, I told him.

"I can't promise that *Forbes* will pick you," I said, "but what I can promise is that along the way you will improve a lot of lives. And that's much more meaningful, and gives you much more agency, than shooting for a top-thirty list."

As our walk continued, I spent our time together explaining what it means to have a mindset of going beyond yourself.

The four parts to this mindset are practicing servant leadership, practicing ethical leadership, engaging in long-term thinking, and developing and applying a vision.

Put another way, it's serving others (servant leadership) in the right way (ethical leadership) for the long run (long-term thinking) toward a meaningful goal (vision).

This formula doesn't guarantee fame or riches. But it does promise changemakers who apply it an opportunity to extend themselves and make a positive impact on those around them.

In this chapter, you'll learn how to understand and apply all four elements to become a changemaker who goes beyond yourself.

SERVING OTHERS

When you look around at the state of leadership in the world today and how it's most often portrayed in media, politics, and business, you might reasonably see it in unflattering and even dangerous terms. You might gravitate toward descriptors like *power-hungry* or *corrupt*, featuring individuals who ultimately serve only themselves. You might point to the growing wage gap between CEOs and their employees, or the grandstanding among political leaders who put their own self-interest ahead of constituents.

This may be the leadership we too often see. But that is absolutely not what leadership truly is.

While one might be able to get away with self-serving leadership for the short term, it's not a style that is effective for leading lasting positive change.

You can be self-serving and probably have some short-term success (perhaps even a good amount of ephemeral success), but putting yourself first ultimately catches up to you, and it certainly won't enable you to be a changemaker who leaves a lasting positive impact.

The mindset of a beyond-yourself leader starts with seeing yourself first as a servant leader.

A Timeless Approach

Servant leadership is simultaneously a concept that dates back millennia and a contemporary approach for leading in a fast-paced, rapidly changing world. It's equally applicable in formal structures and in informal ones, in big change efforts and in small groups.

The idea stretches back to philosopher Lao-tzu, who twenty-six hundred years ago taught: "The highest type of ruler is one of whose existence the people are barely aware... The Sage is self-effacing and scanty of words. When his task is accomplished and things have been completed, all the people say, 'We ourselves have achieved it!' "[1]

The notion has also found a home in the US military, albeit by a different name: Officers Eat Last. During mealtime, officers line up to eat in order from lowest to highest rank, meaning that the most senior officers eat only after those under their command have done so. It's not a formal rule; it's not codified anywhere and doesn't come with a punishment for those who violate it. Yet it's a powerful embodiment of servant leadership: Those who lead make sure the people under their watch eat before they themselves eat. It's putting the interests of those you serve ahead of your own.

Robert Greenleaf popularized the term *servant leadership* in 1970 in his essay *The Servant as Leader*, positing that "service ought to be the distinguishing characteristic of leadership."[2]

Servant leadership, he says, begins "with the natural feeling that one wants to serve," followed by "the conscious choice...to aspire to lead." Greenleaf helps show how my mentee in his three-piece suit had it backward. Instead of starting with a desire to lead, servant leadership teaches us to first start by serving others, then from there to consciously make the choice to lead.

Finally, Greenleaf tells us that the best test of a servant leader is asking: "Do those served grow as persons?" In other words, as we serve others, are they becoming stronger, more capable, and more willing to become servant leaders themselves?

What does servant leadership look like in practice? When I meet with direct reports, I consider my top priority to be doing whatever it takes to help them do their best work. I ask them what is getting in their way and how I might be able to intervene to help. Instead of thinking I know best, I actively look to serve others; I trust that they know best what they need, I listen to them, and then I take action. This means that my role as a manager could be anything from having a difficult conversation on my colleague's behalf, helping them strategize a big pitch, or even smaller actions like making sure that they have access to booking a conference room. It's being an offensive lineman to block whatever might be getting in the way of their growth, to allow them to become stronger and more capable in their work. It all starts with the conscious choice to serve others.

Servant Leadership in Action

If servant leadership is what we should all aspire to in our beyond-yourself mindset, what should we make of the realm of politics, where this notion seems all too rare? If you think that the current system for recruiting political talent is broken, you can be sure that Emily Cherniack would agree with you.

Cherniack has a long history of servant leadership, from participating in AmeriCorps to being one of the founding members of Be The Change, which engaged 250,000 people for a day of service action in their communities. She stumbled into politics when her mentor, Alan Khazei, ran for the US Senate in Massachusetts in 2009 and tapped Cherniack to be his deputy campaign manager. Although Khazei ultimately received only 13 percent of the vote in the Democratic primary, falling far short of the nomination for the Senate seat once held by Ted Kennedy, the experience opened Cherniack's eyes to just how broken our current political system is when it comes to spotting and supporting talent.

Cherniack believes that "the current talent pipeline is intentionally exclusive and has significant barriers that prevent transformational leaders from successfully running for office," and that "the only way to change that is to change the pipeline."[3]

To help remedy this, in 2013 she founded New Politics, a nonprofit and nonpartisan organization dedicated to revitalizing American democracy by recruiting servant leaders, especially those who have served the US in the military or in national service like the Peace Corps. The organization has said that servant leaders are some of our nation's best problem solvers and changemakers, and we need their leadership more than ever.

Instead of finding talented politicians and then helping them get elected, New Politics follows the servant-leadership script to a tee.

The organization finds individuals who have a committed history of consciously choosing to serve others, and focuses on that quality first, instead of on those individuals' particular political beliefs or electability. Then it trains these leaders, who already maintain a beyond-yourself mindset, on politics and policy, to help them get elected. In this way, New Politics prepares them to become the political leaders so many people on both sides of the aisle believe the US Congress so badly needs.

New Politics has already seen big wins getting servant leaders elected at the local, state, and national levels, proving that a mindset of servant leadership can help catalyze meaningful, systemic change.

The Five-Minute Favor

Servant leadership works across industries and sectors. Wharton professor Adam Grant's terrific book *Give and Take* explores servant leadership, albeit using different terms.[4] In it, he identifies three different personas: takers, matchers, and givers. Takers orient themselves to extract as much as they can from others. Matchers aim to perfectly balance how much they give and take. Givers contribute to others without expecting anything in return. Grant finds that givers are rarer and, perhaps not surprisingly, more likely to burn out. But he also finds, through rigorous data analysis, that givers are especially well positioned to be inspiring leaders and changemakers who achieve extraordinary impact.

If you're looking for a way to begin practicing servant leadership, consider starting with Grant's concept of the "five-minute favor." Ask yourself: "What is something I could do for someone else, with no expectation of reciprocation, in five minutes?" Perhaps it's making an email introduction between two people who you think would really enjoy meeting one another, or writing a note to a colleague, manager, or friend to thank them for their hard work. In just five minutes, you can begin becoming a servant leader by serving others.

ETHICAL CHANGE

Some leaders attempt to do the bare minimum and get away with simply not being bad. Sometimes that approach can work—at least for the short term.

As changemakers, though, we can and must aspire to a higher standard. There is now an imperative for leaders to go beyond simply "doing no harm," and instead to focus on actively making a positive impact.

According to a study conducted by Cone Communications, 85 percent of consumers (and 91 percent of millennials) would switch brands to one perceived as more ethical and values-aligned.[5] Further, 62 percent of millennials and a majority of all adults would be willing to take a pay cut to work for a "responsible" company.

Changemakers, as both leaders and consumers, believe that ethics aren't just a nice-to-have; they are a must-have. And the pressure is on CEOs, according to the 2020 Edelman Trust Barometer.[6] Seventy-six percent of respondents said that CEOs should take the lead on positive change rather than waiting for the government to impose it (an increase of 11 percentage points from the year before). A majority of respondents believe that CEOs can create positive change on issues ranging from equal pay to the environment, and 71 percent of employees said that it is "critically important" for their CEO to respond to challenges.

We are, rightly, expecting more from our leaders. And we are getting increasingly good as consumers at seeing through "purpose washing" or empty promises of positive impact, where rhetoric doesn't match the reality. We observed this on social media in the wake of the murder of George Floyd in 2020, when brands from Amazon to L'Oréal expressed support for the Black Lives Matter movement but were called out by everyday people who saw that the companies' actions—from the makeup of their executive teams to their workplace policies—did not reflect these statements.

Being a changemaker who goes beyond yourself means not seeing ethical leadership as a perfunctory minimum standard but rather embracing it as an opportunity to use your position to lead others, on your team and in your community, to join with you in aspiring toward greater aims.

The Three Steps of Ethical Leadership

There are three keys to becoming effective, ethical leaders today: authenticity, consistency, and inclusive engagement.

Many of us, especially digital native millennials and Gen Zers, are really good at seeing through empty promises of doing the right thing. So ethical leaders must start with authenticity. During social movements like #MeToo, many leaders made public statements supporting the cause when their own actions didn't reflect their impassioned calls for change in others. To be ethical, we must first be authentic and ensure that our own actions reflect those we would encourage in others. A beyond-yourself mindset requires more than words: It necessitates that our actions are first and foremost in line with our policies and rhetoric.

But it's not enough to simply do the right thing during one snapshot in time. Ethics are not ephemeral; they are enduring. And a legacy of consistency in doing the right thing will help you be a leader who inspires others toward meaningful change. Here, we can find inspiration from Apple CEO Tim Cook, who has been an advocate for LGBTQ+ rights for years and years. Personally, in his own philanthropy, and professionally, in both his own actions and his corporate policies, he has long been a champion for the cause of equality. When the landmark US Supreme Court case *Obergefell v. Hodges* made same-sex marriage a legally guaranteed right, we saw many—though certainly not all—leaders and companies begin to support the movement. While this is welcome, leaders like Cook, who have been consistently engaged in ethical leadership in this specific area (we aren't looking at all of Apple's policies here), truly embody a beyond-yourself mindset, doing so before there was a crowd. In fact, these early ethical leaders helped make it safe for others to follow their lead in pushing for ethical policies.

The third and final key is to inclusively engage all kinds of stakeholders in your ethical leadership. Ethical leadership is stronger when we engage more people of all kinds. REI proved this in its #OptOutside Black Friday campaign. Not only did it take an ethical stand for its consumers, but it also did so for its employees, giving them paid time off. Collectively, this led to a movement. Staff and customers alike were engaged in the same movement, instead of what could have easily become resentment from one set of stakeholders—for instance, if customers had benefited but employees had missed out on a day of pay.

We see all three play out at Ben & Jerry's, the popular ice cream company that often goes beyond itself, extending its impact far beyond the freezer aisle. Its advocacy work is the result of a long-term investment in living its values.

Christopher Miller, Ben & Jerry's head of global activism strategy, told *Harvard Business Review*: "We have this ongoing body of activism and advocacy that are rooted in our values. We have a team of social mission folks with an NGO or policy background paired with a world-class marketing team that knows how to connect with our fans and sell ideas. So when things happen, we have this privilege, power, and ability to communicate."[7] Matthew McCarthy, the company's CEO, then weighed in: "We do these things not to sell more ice cream but because we care about people and have values."

What makes Ben & Jerry's stand out in its corporate social responsibility is the way it authentically engages with its communities, from suppliers to consumers to community members. Miller described its response to the murder of George Floyd: "The team and I manage a pretty big constellation of friends and allies and partners, and so we make sure to gut check any response with them. In the BLM statement, we had four very specific policy recommendations. We don't make that up in a conference room at our corporate headquarters. We amplify the voices of those on the front lines, who know the solutions we need to bring to the table."

Sure, you might say, ethics and values are just as embedded in the DNA of Ben & Jerry's as the brownies and cookie dough are in its Half

Baked flavor (clearly, the best one), but what about companies that may not yet have articulated their values? "The reality is there's never a bad moment to start doing the right thing. And in fact, we need you," McCarthy argues. "You could decide that your thing will be The Humane Society. It could be packing lunches. It can be anything. What it can't be is nothing."

BE QUICK, BUT DON'T HURRY

Change takes time. Many changemakers with whom I work are naturally impatient, a trait that serves them well in many instances, because this restlessness leads to action. But forging real, lasting change is a marathon, not a sprint.

We see this in how we set goals for ourselves in developing new habits. How often have you committed to a new habit only to find yourself giving up on it in a week or two? While most people think a new habit can be formed in about three weeks, Phillippa Lally, a health psychology researcher at University College London (UCL), has researched habit formation, and in a study published in the *European Journal of Social Psychology*, she and her colleagues found that it takes sixty-six days for a new habit to form.[8] This reinforces why changemakers must commit to the long haul.

Perhaps following a pattern set by corporate America, which leaps from quarterly earnings call to quarterly earnings call, so many individuals and organizations have trouble going beyond themselves, and thinking long-term. Revenue is only one snapshot of organizational health. The management consulting firm McKinsey studied 615 firms over a fifteen-year period and compared long-term-oriented firms with short-term ones.[9] McKinsey found that even though the proportion of companies embracing short-term thinking and strategizing is growing, those companies that are focused on the long term exhibited 47 percent more revenue growth from 2001 to 2014 and were less volatile. Put simply by McKinsey, "Cumulatively, the earnings of long-term firms also grew 36 percent more on average over this period than those of other firms, and their economic profit grew by 81 percent more on average."

Many leaders feel pressure to focus on the short term, and many systems reinforce this shallow perspective. From Wall Street analysts pouncing on every quarterly earnings call to the pressure of social media to catch one viral moment—remember the Ice Bucket Challenge in 2014?—many leaders are thinking in shorter and shorter horizons. But this focus on only clearing the immediate hurdle in front of us without seeing and preparing for the full race often leaves leaders exhausted and unable to achieve lasting change.

Beyond-yourself changemakers, however, are able to zoom out and play the long game, recognizing that substantive and sustainable change is rarely a quick fix. Being able to see the bigger picture and practice patience is increasingly a differentiator for changemakers.

When Sid Espinosa came to speak to my class, I expected him to talk about how he had accomplished so much at such a young age. At the time, he was the senior director of philanthropy for Microsoft and had previously served as the first-ever Latino mayor of Palo Alto, California, and he was only in his thirties. Instead, his advice for students surprised me, and I was initially concerned that they might take it the wrong way. He talked about the changes required in companies and in communities, and told us to stop thinking of ourselves as individual sprinters and instead think of ourselves as runners in a relay race. It's quite possible that we may never see all of the changes we want to create become realized during our careers or our lives, he told the class.

I thought students' aspirations might be deflated upon hearing this, but actually they felt this advice was liberating. They saw Espinosa's advice as an invitation to continue pursuing the important work others before us have started and to leave things in a better place for those who will come after us. They felt a sense of connection and community to the changemakers before them and those who will come after.

Espinosa's advice applies equally well in corporate as well as social-change settings. We might be responsible for financial or other goals staring us down in the short term. But remembering that we can take care of what needs to be done in front of us right now, all while thinking about how we can hand off the baton to others in the future, can free us. We can heed the words of legendary UCLA basketball coach John Wooden: "Be quick, but don't hurry." We can take care of what needs to be done in the immediate time horizon while not hurrying the crucial changes that quite possibly will take much longer to realize.

Infinite Games

Simon Sinek lays this concept out beautifully in his book *The Infinite Game*.[10] Sinek builds off the original work done in the 1980s by NYU emeritus professor James P. Carse, which differentiates between two types of games we all play: finite and infinite.[11] Finite games, like Monopoly and basketball, feature fixed rules, agreed-upon objectives, and a clear point at which someone is declared the winner. Infinite games have no clear beginning and no clear ending, there are known and unknown players, and there are no exact rules. According to Sinek, business, politics, and even life are examples of infinite games. I would also add "leading change" as a quintessential example of an infinite game.

There are no clear winners in infinite games because players can join or drop out at any time—for instance, they can leave when they run out of resources or the will to keep going. When we are playing an infinite game, Sinek advises us to stop thinking about who wins and who loses and instead focus on building strong and healthy organizations that can stand the test of time. If we stop thinking of our infinite games—whether that's creating a healthier environment, better schools, safer neighborhoods, or better-informed citizens—as finite, we will be better positioned to serve others for the long term. By zooming out and playing an infinite game, our leadership and our organizations will become more resilient to external shocks and better able to navigate toward sustainable outcomes instead of quick fixes.

Working the Infinite Mindset

An infinite mindset can be helpful to us as individual changemakers as well. Students regularly come to me seeking advice about their first job out of college. Through these conversations, I've found a regular pattern: Students tend to overcontrol for short-term pain at the expense of long-term happiness and impact. They are showing up ready to play the finite game of landing what they hope and expect to be the single perfect job right away. I remind students that despite how it might feel in the moment, their first job doesn't define their career. While getting a job is "finite," one's career is "infinite," with countless opportunities to adjust along the way. With an infinite mindset, we can sit in the discomfort a bit longer if we choose to see our changemaker career in its entirety, where a year or two are merely a blip in a long career. This allows students to zoom out from that first job and see it as an opportunity for learning, for growth, and to further refine just what they might hope to do for the decades to come.

I regularly share with students advice from my friend Jocelyn Ling Malan, an expert in design and innovation, who says to think of your first jobs as a series of hypotheses to test that will inform your career: Do I like working in a small company? Do I prefer working in a fast-paced environment? Does a career in writing feel as fulfilling as the courses I took? This reframe of the job search from being finite to infinite helps students develop a new perspective on the decisions they then make in pursuit of that exciting first job.

Airbnb's Infinite Time Horizon

Airbnb is an example of a company that made the switch to an "infinite time horizon" and delivered many long-term benefits for itself as a company as well as for its stakeholders. In 2018, cofounder Brian Chesky penned an "Open Letter to the Airbnb Community About Building a 21st Century Company."[12] In it, he wrote: "Companies face pressures based on legacies from the 20th-century, and the convention is to focus on increasingly short-term financial interests, often at the expense of a company's vision, long-term value, and its impact on society. You could say that these are 20th-century companies living in a 21st-century world… We want Airbnb to be a 21st-century company with two defining characteristics: 1. We will have an infinite time horizon. 2. We will serve all of our stakeholders."

He continued the letter by outlining the importance of a long-term vision—very much in line with Sinek's concept of the infinite game—and provided crucial scaffolding to the vision:

"We must realize our vision and ensure our vision is good for society. This means that we must have the best interest of three stakeholders in mind: Airbnb the company (employees and shareholders), Airbnb the community (guests and hosts) and the world outside of Airbnb."

Airbnb has not experienced the smoothest ride. Its growth has been filled with plenty of understandably contentious disagreements with local policymakers and neighbors about crucial issues like gentrification and affordable housing. In telling the infinite-time-horizon part of Airbnb's story, I don't mean to suggest that the company is perfect, but in an environment where most companies can see only weeks ahead of them, if not days, as of this writing, Airbnb exemplifies long-term thinking.

It remains to be seen whether Airbnb will succeed in mitigating its negative externalities, living up to its ideals by delivering on its infinite vision and positive impact for all of its stakeholders. (As an infinite game, there's no end, after all!) But its ability to consciously move from a finite game, obsessing over quarterly results and short-term wins, to an infinite game, focused on vision and stakeholders, is a key step in having an impact beyond itself.

As an early indicator, we can look at how well Airbnb fared during the huge shocks to the travel industry brought on by COVID-19. While hotel business in the US was down over 50 percent in the first three quarters of 2020, Airbnb suffered only a 5 percent drop.[13] By playing the long game, leaders and organizations can be better suited to ride out the short-term shocks because they are aiming at a much-longer-term horizon. Of course, Airbnb still has challenges to address, both systemic and of its own making. But its positioning as an infinite-time-horizon company gives many people, from employees to investors, confidence in its ability to sustain itself long-term.

PAINTING THE PICTURE

The final part of a beyond-yourself mindset is developing and leading others toward a shared vision.

Rich Lyons, former dean of UC Berkeley's Haas School of Business, defines vision in a simple but powerful way: painting a picture of the future for others to follow.

Your ability to paint that picture and to articulate a future-oriented vision that is clear and compelling is crucial to your ability to lead. James Kouzes and Barry Posner, faculty members at Santa Clara University's Leavey School of Business, did a huge research study to understand which traits people look for in colleagues and which traits they specifically look for in leaders.[14] For both colleagues and leaders, the top characteristic was the same: honesty. But while just 27 percent of respondents said they wanted their colleagues to be forward-looking, a whopping 72 percent of people said they wanted it in a leader. This was by far the largest gap between leaders and colleagues. Your ability to see the future and paint a picture of it is one of the greatest differentiators in your ability to go beyond yourself from teammate to leader.

As a changemaker, how can you envision and then paint your picture to engage and inspire others? Two insights, one from the field of linguistics and one from marketing, are crucial.

When we first launched StartSomeGood, we asked would-be fundraisers using our site to answer two key questions that would inform whether or not potential supporters would pitch in financial support: "What is the problem you are solving?" and "How are you solving it?" To us, these seemed like necessary questions, and we didn't give it much thought.

We were fortunate to have help from Hildy Gottlieb, a social scientist and social entrepreneur. Gottlieb has dedicated her career to studying the questions we ask, and she works with leaders of all kinds to help them ask more powerful questions in service of leading change.

She helped us realize that the questions we were asking were not the ones that would bring out the best in either the funders or the fundraisers. Asking about a problem and then a solution to fix it limits the scope of potential solutions that could arise from such a vision. This only helps us go from –1 to 0. This binary confines us to metaphorically finding a hole in the ground and then merely filling it back up.

Gottlieb encouraged us to change the questions we ask to change the visions we enable. Instead of framing the questions as a problem/solution, we asked, "What is the future you are creating?" and "How are you creating this future?"

While the difference may seem like minute semantics, the impact of shifting these questions was huge. Not only did the stories and visions provided by the fundraisers grow exponentially more inspiring, but these new visions resulted in far higher amounts of funds raised on our site.

Changing the questions created an invitation to go from –1 to 1, and helped fundraisers paint a picture of the future that supporters couldn't help but be excited to join. Visions were no longer confined to fixing a problem. Instead, we were all invited to be part of creating the future. Those questions helped all of us paint a more engaging picture, and more people joined these visions as a result.

Articulating Your Vision

Now that we know the power of language in crafting a vision, how might we define and articulate it in an inclusive way that convinces others to join us? I encourage changemakers to think on a long-term, aspirational time horizon. For a vision to be truly compelling, you'll want to think well beyond one-year or even five-year aspirations and instead think in terms of decades.

Can you imagine the change you hope to create and paint a clear, compelling picture of what it will look like ten, twenty, or thirty years from now? Articulating a vision at this scale automatically helps all of us zoom out from the short term to embrace long-term thinking as we then orient our decisions and our actions toward this shared envisioned future.

The changes outlined in these visions, by definition, aren't quick fixes; they are initiatives that will require sustained effort over years, not weeks. In his book *The Long View*, author Matthew Kelly articulates why thinking in decades rather than years is a powerful reframe for leading change: "Most people overestimate what they can do in a day, and underestimate what they can do in a month. We overestimate what we can do in a year, and underestimate what we can accomplish in a decade."[15] These ambitious and collective visions help us reorient our energy toward making our decades matter.

Don't be afraid to be bold here! Paint a picture that helps you and those around you focus your energy with clarity and conviction. Some good examples of these inspirational futures come from SpaceX and Volvo. SpaceX's: "Enable human exploration and settlement of Mars."[16] Volvo's: "No one should be seriously injured or killed in a new Volvo car."[17] Volvo could have spoken about improved safety, and SpaceX could have listed aspirations on a certain number of missions. But instead, in both cases the companies paint a clear, compelling vision that inspires teammates to be part of it and help make it happen.

Not only are these visions differentiators for the companies, but they also serve to attract changemakers who want to help the organizations make these visions a reality.

Developing Your Own Vision

One of the most common questions I get from changemakers is how they can develop their own vision statement, whether for themselves or their team. A vision is both applicable and important to all types of people, and you don't have to be an entrepreneur or lead a big team or organization to find utility in having one. There are two tips I give changemakers struggling to identify and define a vision: Seek inspiration from others and get feedback on your vision.

<u>Seek inspiration.</u> When looking to define or refine a vision statement, I encourage you to look to others for inspiration, whether that's people you admire or organizations pursuing changes similar to your own. Vision statements work on both an organizational and a personal level. Microsoft's corporate vision at the beginning of the personal computer revolution is a great one: "A computer on every desk and in every home."[18] Then there are personal vision statements, like "A world filled with, and led by, changemakers." (Take a guess whose personal vision that is!) You might have a vision for your family, like Rebecca and I do: "Raising a child who is kind, healthy, and courageous." Or you might aspire to be a manager of a team of three, who ensures that your team "finds joy, fulfillment, and meaning in doing their best possible work each day." Look to other individuals, teams, and organizations who inspire you, and see if there are aspects of their visions that resonate with you. If so, consider incorporating parts into your own vision.

<u>Get feedback.</u> Don't be afraid to ask for feedback. The best way to see whether the vision you are presenting is truly painting a picture that others will want to follow is to actively share it with people and see how they respond. The most inspiring visions aren't created in an empty room; visions are fundamentally people-centric. So remember to include the human element in testing and refining your vision. For example, in working with the manager whose vision statement I mentioned above, I encouraged her to share drafts of her vision with her team. In doing so, she found that she originally had "excellence"

in her vision, but her colleagues gave her feedback that "fulfillment" mattered to them more, so she was able and willing to tweak her vision to be more inclusive of the people she managed. This made her vision resonate throughout her team, and also ensured that she positioned herself as a servant leader, supporting her colleagues in the way they wanted to be supported.

THINKING BIG, ASKING WHY

I encourage changemakers to always think big—even bigger than they might initially think achievable. It's important not to shy away from, and indeed to embrace, the aspirational in a vision statement. After all, this is what you use to rally partners, teammates, and funders. And it's where you look when the odds seem insurmountable (as they no doubt will on your changemaker journey), to remind you to ride it out in pursuit of something truly significant.

If you are inspired to lead with vision but you aren't sure where to start, here are a few more suggestions to help you identify and craft your own vision, whether for you as an individual or for the positive change you want to lead.

The first step is to proactively take time away from the day-to-day to just think. Maybe this means going for a walk in the woods, or maybe it's putting planned "thinking time" into your calendar. Whatever it takes, do it. It's difficult, if not impossible, to develop a big vision while simultaneously responding to every email that pops in your inbox.

From there, ask the question "Why?" to get at the root of your vision. I've used this approach intuitively in my coaching of changemakers for years, but I learned after the fact that my approach is quite similar to the "five whys" interrogative technique developed by inventor Sakichi Toyoda and used throughout Toyota Motor Corporation. But as a changemaker, I can tell you that sometimes five whys aren't enough. So I say go question the status quo, and use as many whys as you need to drill down to the essence of your vision! Here's a recent conversation I had with an edtech entrepreneur based in Los Angeles:

Entrepreneur: My vision is to give students in underresourced schools in LA a better education.

Me: Why do you want to do that?

Entrepreneur: So that they can do better in school.

Me: Why is that important?

Entrepreneur: So that they can learn more things.

Me: Why does that matter?

Entrepreneur: So that they can be better prepared for life after school, whether that's college or work.

Me: Why?

Entrepreneur: So that they can achieve more in life.

Me: Why?

[By this point, the entrepreneur is probably sick of my questions, but I smile and press on.]

Entrepreneur: So that they can attain the same levels of achievement as students who attend schools with more resources.

Me: And why is that important?

[Now we are almost there!]

Entrepreneur: So that anyone, anywhere, can pursue their dreams.

Me: Why?

Entrepreneur: So that we create a more just and equitable Los Angeles.

Me: Great! Now let's put it all together.

Entrepreneur: We create a more just and equitable Los Angeles, where anyone, anywhere, has the education and skills they need to pursue their dreams.

We ended up needing seven whys, all of which helped us dig and dig and dig until we got to the real vision the entrepreneur was seeking to make a reality.

*   *   *

By applying the mindset concepts you've learned throughout the chapter, you will be on your way to becoming a changemaker who serves others in the right way, for the long run, toward a meaningful goal—truly going beyond yourself.

BE THE CHANGE

Key Insights
- Servant leadership is simultaneously an ancient practice and a highly effective modern approach to management.
- It's never too late to embed a sense of ethics into the work you do.
- Changemaking requires a long-term mindset—it's a marathon, not a sprint— and the data show that being able to take a long-term view will improve your chances of realizing lasting change.
- Don't be afraid of having an ambitious vision. It will differentiate you from others and inspire people to join you on your change initiative.

Changemaker Challenge
- Identify a five-minute favor you can quickly and easily do—such as making an introduction between two friends who would benefit from knowing one another—and then go do it!
- Develop your own vision statement—whether for yourself, your team, your family, or your organization. Begin by finding inspiration from organizations you find compelling. Share your vision statement with at least three other people for early feedback and input.
- Reflect on and define two to three things you would do differently in your changemaker work if you began thinking on an infinite timeline.

Chapter 5

Students Always

"Yes we can!" This saying is probably familiar to you—it became the rallying cry of Barack Obama's 2008 presidential campaign. It's a stirring phrase, and one that goes far beyond an American election, although the genesis of this uplifting call for change was similarly political, just not in an electoral sense. It started with Dolores Huerta, an unlikely labor leader, who initially thought that Cesar Chavez was kidding when he suggested they team up to start a union for farm workers. She was a single mother of eleven children and had plenty of reasons to say no. But she drew upon her deep empathy from her time as an elementary school teacher to motivate her response. She recalled seeing children coming into her classroom without shoes and with empty stomachs, and knew that she needed to take action in support of farmers and their families. Farmers at the time made less than a dollar an hour and often lacked access to toilets, cold water, and breaks, despite working from sunrise to sunset.

Even though she didn't have any formal experience as a negotiator, she and Chavez led a nationwide grape boycott. The bold move eventually resulted in grape growers signing some of the first-ever contracts for farmworkers that the United States had seen, engaging millions of people in the process. Her work led to better pay and benefits for grape growers, alongside much-needed protections. And in response to aggressive pushback telling her "no you can't" create these changes, she coined the movement's slogan, "Sí se puede!" (Spanish for "Yes we can.")

While this was Huerta's start in changemaking, her legacy extends far beyond the fields. Throughout her career, she has displayed the key "student always" components of a changemaker mindset, which you will learn in this chapter.

Huerta embraced flexibility as a changemaking necessity, learning how to be an effective advocate. For instance, she championed bringing women and children into protests, recognizing that entire families stood to benefit from the changes she and Chavez championed, and that diversifying the participants would reinforce the nonviolent nature of their advocacy.

She leaned into empathy as a hallmark of her leadership, always putting herself in the shoes of those whom she fought for. She led efforts as wide-ranging as ensuring that the California DMV exam was made available in Spanish and fighting for disability insurance for farmworkers. She dedicated her life to giving voice to others who might not otherwise have one.

She also practiced resilience, accomplishing so much and regularly pursuing change in spite of racial, class, and gender bias, as detailed in Mario T. García's book *A Dolores Huerta Reader*.[1] She's even been arrested twenty-five times for participating in nonviolent civil disobedience actions and strikes, but she keeps showing up again and again to fight for change.

Even now, in her nineties, she continues to embrace self-renewal and be a student always, leading her own foundation for community organizing, which has supported many organizations and has continued the spirit of her earlier work. Doing so, she's remained clear on her why, and flexible on her how, in continuing to fight for changes in line with the work she did at the very start of her career, even if it's now less about being on the front lines and instead more about inspiring and supporting those who follow in her footsteps.

Could we all learn to be like Dolores Huerta and practice flexibility, empathy, and resilience in pursuit of being a changemaker who is a student always?

Sí se puede!

WHYS AND HOWS

Comedian Demetri Martin created a graphic, a version of which has gone viral in recent years, on the topic of success, brilliantly bursting the distorted bubble of what many of us conceive it takes to become successful.[2] It's titled "Success," and on the left is a graph any CFO would love to see—a straight arrow heading up and to the right. This graph is labeled "what people think it looks like." Immediately to the right appears another graph, labeled "what it really looks like," which looks more like a toddler's attempt at knitting. We see squiggly lines going up, down, back, and around. The endpoint in the second graph still reaches the same height as the one in the first—but the path to get there is messy, filled with false starts, backtracking, and many loops.

The takeaway is clear: While we often fantasize about success being perfectly linear (and give ourselves a hard time when our own projects don't fit perfectly into this unrealistic paradigm), any real success—and any change initiative—will inevitably have setbacks, course changes, and low points.

The key to achieving success, then, is not getting lucky with a single strategy at the outset but rather remaining adaptable when all of the inevitable surprises, challenges, and complications come our way. As boxer Mike Tyson succinctly put it: "Everybody has a plan until they get punched in the face."

Adaptability is how we roll with those punches and keep fighting for our change initiatives to reach a point of success.

To remain adaptable as we lead change, I advise changemakers to remain clear on their "why" but flexible on their "how." This means remaining steadfastly committed to the larger goal, the vision, the change, but being willing to pivot and adapt the methods for achieving it. We don't alter our goals or our values. We merely find a more effective path forward. As Dov Seidman, founder of the ethics and compliance company LRN, describes it, "A pivot, as in basketball, is a very deliberate action where I put one foot solidly in place and I then move the other foot in a better direction. In a political leader's case, in a company leader's case, in an education leader's case, that pivot will be anchored, hopefully in deep human values."[3] Remaining committed to our "why" helps us pivot with confidence (but, of course, not attitude!). Remaining clear on the why and flexible on the how works for both individuals and organizations.

Pivoting in Practice

Darius Graham has catalyzed change in a wide variety of contexts and conditions. Through it all, he's remained anchored to a single, compelling why, which has served him well across sectors and roles. Let's look at how his why came to be and how he decides whether and when to pivot to his next changemaker opportunity.

Fresh out of law school, Graham began his career in a corporate bankruptcy role. He realized fairly quickly that the job wasn't the right fit for him, but he still wanted to get all of the training and knowledge he could, so he stayed in the role for a year. While there, he began to see just how many resources the firm he worked for controlled and, simultaneously, how unequally the resources were distributed throughout Washington, DC. He also had a realization that would change his life and would form the basis of his personal why.

Graham told me his "why" is recognizing that there are all kinds of problems facing our communities and our world, and that all of the solutions and resources we need are out there waiting to be activated, but that there is a mismatch. He's made it his life's work to make connections between communities—especially traditionally marginalized groups—and the resources from larger institutions to efficiently and effectively solve the problems we collectively face.

The first time he put his why into action was in founding the DC Social Innovation Project, which provided small grants of a few hundred dollars to grassroots community initiatives throughout Washington, DC. He was inspired by all of the changemakers whom he met and realized the transformative power of even a small grant when backed by the belief that someone's solutions were worth supporting.

Though he wasn't actively looking for his next opportunity, a dream role came to him. He was offered a job at Johns Hopkins University in Baltimore as director of its Social Innovation Lab, where he'd support student-led social ventures. There, Graham leaned into his why and pushed Johns Hopkins to think even more expansively, convincing the university to also invite changemakers in the local community to be part of the program, working alongside students. He received a bit of pushback here, but ultimately he succeeded. It was his first career pivot, and it was firmly rooted in his why.

Graham later found himself with the chance to take another dream job—this time at the Harry and Jeanette Weinberg Foundation, as its first-ever program director for Baltimore.

It would require another pivot, from academia to philanthropy. But because Graham was able to remain rooted in his why, it was easy for him to say yes to the opportunity, which now finds him directing the resources of an influential foundation to support community-led solutions throughout the city.

Graham has brought his why into other areas of life, too, as a trustee of the Baltimore Museum of Art and cochair of its Public Engagement Committee. As an art lover, Graham has catalyzed change in the art world, helping to initiate the sale of three works that will create an endowment for the museum, the funds of which will support crucial initiatives like increasing evening hours to reach underserved demographics.

Graham has already made many pivots in his relatively short career. But each one not only makes sense individually; they build upon one another. Each successive pivot brings Graham closer and closer to his why, so that he can continue to find creative ways to connect individuals and their solutions with the resources needed to make change happen.

Starting Some Good

This adaptability is also crucial at the organizational level. When we first conceived of StartSomeGood, my cofounder, Tom, and I led with a crystal-clear why: to help changemakers all around the world start doing good. But when we first brainstormed how we would achieve it, we had a considerable menu of ideas of how to do so. We saw the need to democratize the way social ventures get funded, helping changemakers get the financial capital necessary to get started. We recognized a painful catch-22: that it's nearly impossible to get funding until an organization can prove its impact, but it's nearly impossible to prove an impact until you have the funding to launch a program. We also recognized that changemakers needed intellectual capital—advice and volunteers—to help scale programs. And we simultaneously saw the value in social capital: a network of advisors, community members, and others who would rally around the vision of the venture and help support its growth and development.

It was over a late-night coffee-fueled work session at Tom's San Francisco apartment that we finally had a realization. It was well after 2 a.m., and his eclectic mix of house music (I would have been okay with a "pivot" to jazz) was thumping in the background, when it became clear: If we tried to pursue all of these paths simultaneously, we would do none of them well and would eventually fail. Our why was clear, but we needed to refine our how.

We ultimately saw transforming access to early-stage capital as the greatest opportunity for helping ventures unlock their changemaker potential—the one most underserved by existing options and the one that we believed would most quickly enable more changemakers to get started. In that moment, we pivoted our how to focus exclusively on helping changemakers raise funds. And that became our goal for the first few years of StartSomeGood.

Then once the organization began to scale and our community had grown, we revisited our how and realized we could begin adding in some of the other types of capital to support our changemakers. We next added in programs to support changemakers' intellectual capital, including a podcast, a virtual online summit, and more, to help changemakers get the strategy and ideas they need to do good.

But it was only because of that late-night insight, to remain steadfastly committed to our why but to focus first on a single how, that any of this ever became possible. In order to have a future, we had to build adaptability into the DNA of the organization.

THRIVING IN DYNAMIC ENVIRONMENTS

Established in 1980, the HR company Right Management conducts over twelve million hiring interviews per year. Its most recent *Flux Report*, from 2014, paints a powerful picture of what it will take to succeed in today's rapidly changing environments.[4] Its survey found that 91 percent of HR directors in the United Kingdom and Ireland said that, in the years to come, people will be recruited specifically on their ability to deal with change and uncertainty.

This is great news for you as a changemaker. But how do you develop the flexibility needed to not just survive but to thrive in such highly dynamic environments?

Steve Zaccaro, professor of psychology at George Mason University, has dedicated his career to trying to answer the question "What is it that allows some leaders to adjust better to change than others?"[5] His work focuses on flexibility and shows that the concept is a nuanced one, that there are, in fact, three different kinds of flexibility: cognitive, emotional, and dispositional. All three of these are crucial for you as a changemaker, both for your own well-being and in support of the change projects you lead.

Cognitive flexibility. Zaccaro identifies cognitive flexibility as "the ability to use different thinking strategies and mental frameworks." Think of this as being able to hold multiple potentially conflicting strategies or scenarios in mind at the same time. This may look like the ability to consider two very different strategic paths (for instance, deciding whether to launch operations in Peru or in Ghana, different geographies with different strategic rationales). It's the ability to listen to, receive, and process conflicting strategies at the same time, and the ability to see and leverage new connections. You might also think of this type of flexibility as "strategic" flexibility. In the StartSomeGood example, this concept is akin to our keeping several different hows in mind at the same time, even though we decided to pursue only a single one.

Emotional flexibility. Per Zaccaro, this is "the ability to vary one's approach to dealing with emotions and those of others." It allows you to support a wide variety of emotional responses. Imagine, for instance, that you are in the unenviable position of needing to fire people from your team. Some people might respond in a heart-centered, emotional way—crying, asking for support and comfort. Others might respond more analytically—asking for details on severance packages or a justi-fication for their termination. An emotionally flexible leader is able to modulate their response to these different individuals, meeting them where they are. Rather than a one-size-fits-all approach, it's adjusting our emotional cues and disposition to better support others. If we connect this back to the concept of servant leadership (see page 86), it's being able to put your own emotions aside to better serve others in matching their emotions. It's not easy, but it's a powerful mode of flexibility to support the emotional side of leading change.

Dispositional flexibility. This is "the ability to remain optimistic and, at the same time, realistic." Put simply, dispositional flexibility is the ability to find optimism while being grounded in reality. Two paths are most common when people face overwhelmingly scary and uncertain futures: fear-based pessimism or blind optimism. Applying dispositional flexibility allows us to survive amid ambiguity. It enables us to honestly recognize that, yes, this situation is scary, while simultaneously believing in a brighter tomorrow (which we can help create). It means taking the necessary precautions while remembering that there is still lots of good in the world and that our actions are the antidote to despair. It's looking for opportunities to help others instead of reasons to admit defeat. While we will all experience a crisis in different ways based on our identities and situations, we can also all nurture this changemaker trait. Dispositional flexibility helps us learn to lean into the ambiguity and find a balance between optimism and the current set of challenges.

All three are necessary for changemakers, but the dispositional type is absolutely critical as we lead positive change. As changemakers, we identify and proactively choose to engage with some of the most taxing situations and scenarios out there, and we do so in the face of numerous obstacles and detractors. Practicing dispositional flexibility will help us remain grounded in the seriousness of the situation while enabling us to effectively put our "optimism into action."

EMPATHY IN ACTION

In 2014, Rosie Linder founded the app Peppy Pals with a single goal in mind: to teach children empathy. From her own experience as an executive and a mother, she observed that emotional intelligence, or EQ (of which empathy is a crucial component), is at least as important as, if not more important than, traditional IQ measures. The Peppy Pals app introduces children as young as three to cute animal characters as they work through word-free scenarios, learning to recognize and name emotions and connect with the feelings of others. Developed in partnership with psychologists and researchers, the app helps children recognize and respond to emotions and microexpressions. A study conducted by Gunnar Bohné of Uppsala University in Sweden showed that preschool children can indeed perceive and use emotions through the app.[6]

This sets students up well to be changemakers as they grow up, since empathy is an essential aspect to a changemaker mindset. We'll revisit Rosie Linder's story in chapter 11 (page 242) as we learn about how she helps children develop empathy at scale.

Visualizing Other Perspectives

The Greater Good Science Center at UC Berkeley defines empathy as "the ability to sense other people's emotions, coupled with the ability to imagine what someone else might be thinking or feeling."[7] Crucial here is that empathy is not the same as sympathy. Practicing empathy does not require that you change your mind or compromise on your beliefs. Rather, it means that you are able to put yourself in someone else's shoes and see things from their perspective.

Being able to see things from others' perspectives—especially those who might disagree with you—is a fundamental building block of leading change.

At a bare minimum, we must be able to understand how our change initiatives will impact others (and, as research will show, this is far too often overlooked). But beyond a baseline level, practicing empathy will help us create a culture where our changes are more likely to be well received.

The Empathetic Leader

In a 2018 *Harvard Business Review* article, Patti Sanchez, chief strategy officer at Duarte, makes a compelling case that "the secret to leading organizational change is empathy,"[8] that before we can innovate and create new paths forward, we must first practice empathy with those who will be affected by the change. But Sanchez found that 50 percent of executives fail to consider their team's feelings when it comes to change! One in two executives who lead change do so without stopping to think about what it will mean for others. To be truly effective changemakers, however, we must regularly practice empathy.

When I work with executives at global companies, I coach them to be aware of biases and blind spots. Culture and context matter greatly, so if their communications are read and vetted only by people in a single office or a single managerial level before being sent out, they will almost certainly be missing crucial nuances and perspectives. I advise these leaders to build an employee advisory board that is representative of their entire organization—including different levels of seniority, geography, length of tenure at the company, and more—and to regularly ask them for advice and input. I help executives make communication with their team two-way: asking employees to share feedback and to raise issues that executives might not yet be aware of but that are important to employees.

This is hard to do. And it takes more time, effort, and energy to practice this level of empathy. But as changemakers, we must rise above our own stresses and pressures and take time to think about how others will perceive our change. How would we respond if we were them?

If we don't first start with empathy, our change efforts will stop in their tracks.

Empathy Is Contagious

Princeton psychologist Erik Nook and colleagues prove in the five-part study "Prosocial Conformity" that when individuals observe empathetic behavior in others, they shift their own empathetic feelings.[9] In other words, group empathy norms influence an individual's empathetic behavior. Therefore, as changemakers, we should practice empathy ourselves, which will also encourage it among those around us, for a virtuous cycle of empathy to take hold.

I saw firsthand the power of empathy being transferred from person to person as I got to know one of my outstanding students, Aurora Lopez. Aurora admitted to me that as a kid she never imagined she would go to an institution like UC Berkeley, let alone graduate—especially at the moment as a high school sophomore that she heard a knock at her door.

A police officer informed her that the department had been conducting an investigation and had found that Aurora was using her uncle's address to attend Henry M. Gunn High School in Palo Alto, instead of the high school to which she was assigned based on her home residence. Raised by her mom, who was fifteen at the time Aurora was born, as well as her aunts and grandparents, Aurora would wake up at 6 a.m. to get to school on time. But everything was about to change for her.

In 2015, she was made to start going to her local school, Woodside High. She reflected, "During my first semester, I was like, 'I'm not going to succeed or do anything well in life because I'm here.' "[10] Her feelings began to change, though, when she met Pablo Aguilera, a history teacher at her new school, who had a similar background to hers; he was Latino, he was from the same city, and he had gone to Woodside High himself. He made a point of telling his students that he graduated from Stanford. He did this not to brag, but to show his students of color that people like him—and them—can attend college and that they deserve to be there.

Aguilera invested time in Aurora, seeing the potential—and perhaps a bit of himself—in her, and he made her promise she would submit an application to at least one college, even though she didn't believe college was for her. "He actually sent me to a classroom with an application to San Jose State and closed the door and said, 'Don't come out until you have applied,'" she said.

Aurora was admitted to San Jose State, and after a year there and at a local community college, she transferred to Berkeley. She signed up for Becoming a Changemaker during her first semester. "It revolutionized my perspective of leadership," she told *Berkeley News* when asked about her experience. "I took these concepts to heart and tried implementing them every day."

Aurora went on to work as a teaching assistant for me for the next three semesters, and she did something absolutely remarkable. As I reviewed the grading she did, I noticed that she had reached out to many of the students, sharing personal notes of encouragement and belief in them. I'd never asked her to do so; she did so based purely on her own sense of agency and empathy, especially for fellow first-generation college students. She'd leave notes like "I'm so proud of you for this paper you wrote. I know how hard it is to be a first-gen college student, and I'd love to support you however I can," before providing her contact information and social media handles. Her personal outreach was so exceptional that I even once found a proud parent posting on Instagram sharing how touched they were by Aurora's comments to their son! Aurora took the baton of empathy that was passed to her by Pablo Aguilera when she was in high school, and then as a college student she spread that empathy far and wide to even more students.

This concept can also be applied to specific changemaker endeavors.

Take, for instance, bullying in schools. Research by Princeton University psychology professor Elizabeth Levy Paluck and colleagues from Rutgers and Yale shows that when they empowered a small group of middle school students to take a public stand against bullying in their school, an empathetic culture spread through social connections. This study demonstrates "the power of peer influence for changing climates of conflict."[11]

A culture of empathy creates a culture of positive change.

The Empathy Exercise

I have my students do an experiential exercise to tap into and cultivate their empathy through a counterintuitive process: challenging them to empathize with their archnemesis. I draw inspiration for this exercise from Byron Katie's brilliant work on mindfulness and especially her guided reflection called "The Work Is a Practice."[12]

I start by asking them to write down a person and situation that has most annoyed or upset them in the last year. It could be a roommate who refuses to clean up their mess, a campus group that rejected them, or teammates in a group project who don't listen to their ideas.

Once they have that person and moment written down, I invite them to let their most judgmental sides run wild and extrapolate what that behavior says about the person. As we discussed regarding transparency (see page 76), when we lack complete information, people make themselves both the heroes and the victims of their own stories. And here, I let students run wild with both sides of the narrative as they make judgments based on observable behavior. A colleague who never does her share of the work? She must be entitled. A driver who cut them off with a last-minute merge? He must be an inconsiderate jerk who thinks he's more important. (Students seem to really enjoy this part.)

From there, I ask them to sit with a simple question: "Is that true?"

I let the silence hang in the air until it verges just past the tipping point into uncomfortable.

Then I offer the next question: "Can you absolutely, one hundred percent know that your judgment is true, without a single doubt?"

Some nervous laughter pierces the silence.

I ask the next question: "If you can't be one hundred percent sure in your judgments, what might the other person be thinking and feeling?" I invite them to use their "students always" curiosity here, putting themselves in the other person's shoes and playing out the scenario from their perspective.

Once they've imagined the situation from the other person's point of view, I invite them to answer the second-to-last question: "What values might this person be using to inform their behavior?"

For instance, if someone isn't giving you the time to speak and rushing you, perhaps their value is efficiency. We aren't making good or bad judgments here, but isolating the values allows us to speak about the situation at a much higher level. And students often realize that even though someone's observable behavior is disagreeable, the values underlying their actions likely are not.

Then comes the final question as we cement this empathy lesson: "With this newfound perspective, how might you approach this in the future?"

I've seen students on the verge of tears as they realize that what seemed like an intractable problem, including a roommate on the verge of moving out due to growing resentment and a student group leadership team on the brink of disbanding due to recurring disagreement, is actually solvable once they practice empathy. I've seen them take brand-new approaches in their life and work once they saw how putting themselves in the shoes of someone else—even the most disagreeable person—unlocked new perspectives and solutions. Empathy, combined with the curiosity, adaptability, and flexibility to implement it, helps changemakers of all kinds become and remain students always.

RESILIENCE

Although the concept of self-care has become increasingly popular, it often gets a bad rap; the term may make you think of things like bubble baths or massages. While those things are part of self-care, the idea is a deep one. The practice of caring for ourselves, for investing in our most valuable resources—our minds, our bodies, our energy, our well-being—is one of the most crucial practices we changemakers can cultivate.

We all need to remember that leading change is hard. Really hard. It's easy to get burned-out, especially if we are trying to address systemic, long-standing problems that are far bigger than any one person. It's especially important for changemakers of color, who are likely to face high levels of daily toxic stress, especially while leading change. Scholars Danielle D. King, Abdifatah A. Ali, Courtney L. McCluney, and Courtney Bryant powerfully show this in their *Harvard Business Review* article, "Give Black Employees Time to Rest and Recover."[13] We changemakers put so much heart into our work, yet we must also put that same love into ensuring we stay strong for the long haul. As poet and activist Audre Lorde says, "Caring for myself is not self-indulgence, it is self-preservation."[14]

Educator and author Stephen Covey might not use the word *self-care*, but he's created the best analogy I know to explain why it matters; he calls it "sharpening the saw."[15] Imagine that you are sawing down a huge tree. It's likely you would just keep sawing and sawing and sawing until the tree finally falls. That's how most of us approach change; we keep going and going without stopping to think too much until the job is done. But Covey teaches us to question the status quo and think differently: "We must never become too busy sawing to take time to sharpen the saw," he advises us. A saw's blade dulls over time. The more it is used, the weaker it gets.

As changemakers, it's easy to feel guilty about taking any time for ourselves when we are so motivated to lead change, especially for others.

But if you don't care for yourself, if you don't establish these crucial self-care practices, you will end up like I did during my time with Start-SomeGood: sawing and sawing and sawing, becoming both less effective and more exhausted with each passing day. The practice of sharpening the saw encourages us to take a break from the work, metaphorically sharpening our saw through self-renewal, so that we can get back to sawing much more effectively.

SELF-RENEWAL

In his book *The 7 Habits of Highly Effective People*, Covey identifies four areas of self-renewal, four aspects of our life where a deliberate practice of self-care can help us sharpen our own saw. As changemakers, we must invest in each of these to ensure that we are positioned to lead change effectively for the long haul. It's totally normal for the focus we put on each of these areas to evolve and change over time. Crucially, this model helps us care for ourselves holistically and in a way that is true to who we are as agents of change. Covey's four areas of self-renewal are:[16]

Physical: Beneficial eating, exercising, and resting

Social/Emotional: Making social and meaningful connections with others

Mental: Learning, reading, writing, and teaching

Spiritual: Spending time in nature, expanding spiritual self through meditation, music, art, prayer, or service

What I love about reframing self-renewal in terms of these buckets is that while these categories are universal, the way we apply them is personal and infinitely customizable. To help you think about developing your own practices for staying strong for the long haul, I'll share what I do to fill up each bucket. I've also asked two other changemakers to share what they do: Cynthia, a product manager in her twenties, and Javier, a consultant in his forties.

Physical

- Alex: Exercise is the single biggest catalyst for me, so I prioritize at least thirty minutes of weights or interval training each day. I've also started running...slowly. (Proof that not all changes come easily to me!)
- Cynthia: I used to only sleep a couple of hours each night, especially in college. Now I am hard-core about getting eight hours of sleep, meaning I am in bed every night by 10 p.m. to make sure I wake up rested.
- Javier: For me, it's a balance of physical exercise and nutrition. I find that eating a healthy breakfast every day is key to starting my physical well-being off right, and I also try to exercise each morning before work.

Social/Emotional

- Alex: Catching up with friends is key for me, but it's really hard to do, so I approach this in two ways. First, I have regular monthly calls with buddies of mine, and at the end of each call we put our next one in the calendar. I've also started being more spontaneous and randomly calling friends when I have twenty minutes free: If they are around, that's great. If not, I leave a long message and encourage them to do the same with an update.
- Cynthia: Connecting with my coworkers is crucial. Instead of working through lunch, I try every day to have lunch away from my computer, where I spend time with these wonderful teammates.
- Javier: Family dinners with extended family every Sunday night, and getting involved with my child's school through volunteering.

Mental

- Alex: This one comes most easily to me (so I spend more time deliberately cultivating the others). Here I devote time to lots of audiobooks and podcasts to introduce myself to new ideas and regularly take time to synthesize these ideas in the form of newsletters.

- Cynthia: I take a lot of free online classes and watch a lot of YouTube videos to embrace my curiosity and learn new things whenever I feel like it.

- Javier: I mentor people from my church and my community so I can always feel like I'm learning new things and then teaching them to others.

Spiritual

- Alex: This is the biggest challenge for me of the four. I continue trying meditation and yoga, though so far haven't found a routine that sticks. I do find great joy and spiritual release when out in nature, so this is my main approach here.

- Cynthia: Definitely meditation. I was so skeptical at first about all of the benefits, but I've found that even a few minutes in the morning and at night makes a huge difference in my spiritual openness.

- Javier: I'm involved in my church, so I embrace my spirituality in community with others and also try to make time to play piano and guitar to find connection musically as well.

In which of these areas are you sharpening the saw best right now? Which areas could deliver the greatest impact with a bit more intention? What practices might you try to help you sharpen your saw across these four areas? To be a student always, you must keep yourself strong for the long haul. Creating a deliberate practice around resilience and renewal will ensure that you continue your changemaker efforts for years and years to come.

FALLING DOWN, GETTING BACK UP

Feeling doubt and fear, particularly when we're really invested in pursuing something we deeply care about, is not uncommon. While visiting my Changemaker class, entrepreneur and investor Kalsoom Lakhani—who speaks quickly and assertively and generally exudes confidence—was not shy about admitting this.

"You seem so confident!" Shannon, one of my students, said to her. "Did you ever struggle with your confidence or fearing failure, because it really doesn't—"

"Oh my god," Lakhani started to answer before Shannon could even finish the question. "I experienced it this morning!" she said, much to the surprise of every student in the classroom.

While she speaks with a general American accent, Lakhani was born in Dubai, raised in Dhaka, Bangladesh, and lived in Islamabad, Pakistan, before moving to the US for college.

Upon graduation from the University of Virginia, she began working for a defense contractor, putting her foreign affairs degree to use. However, she quickly realized that this was not her calling. It didn't fully resonate with her values or ideals. And as one of the only female analysts in the more male-dominated military environment, she didn't feel fully included or respected.

In 2007, while Lakhani was working in this job, she saw that Pakistan was on the cover of *Newsweek* magazine, which had labeled it "the most dangerous nation in the world." Having spent formative years there, she felt it was an injustice to use such a pejorative term, especially when she knew that there was much more nuance to Pakistan than most Americans often see.

So in early 2008, she started a blog about Pakistan, covering the news and insights people might not otherwise see. Contrasted with her day job, this role felt empowering, and as she started to write about the artists, the founders—indeed, the changemakers—in Pakistan, raising up their stories, she realized how much potential young people in Pakistan had, a perspective those outside the country just weren't hearing about.

This led her to establish Invest2Innovate in 2011, which became Pakistan's first startup accelerator program. Believing that the next great innovations won't come only from Silicon Valley but rather from all kinds of frontier markets, Lakhani has continued to scale this model to other countries, including Cambodia, Vietnam, Bangladesh, and Nepal.

Most recently, she cofounded Pakistan's first-ever female-led venture capital fund, i2i Ventures, an opportunity for her to put financial resources behind the same types of people she first started lifting up with her writing a decade earlier.

By leading with her values and bringing her changemaker mindset into all of her entrepreneurial and financial endeavors, Lakhani has already achieved an impressive amount. So Shannon's question was a poignant one. Certainly, it would seem someone so accomplished simply didn't feel fear or doubt herself.

This, of course, was completely to the contrary.

Lakhani grew up in a family of entrepreneurs. Her dad made his first million dollars before he turned thirty and then lost it all when she and her siblings were small children. Her mom taught aerobics in Dubai to keep the family's lights on for a while until he launched his next successful venture.

It was a hard way to learn this lesson, but Lakhani discussed with my class that seeing her father's struggles firsthand helped her realize that failure is just part of the diet of doing anything meaningful.

When she was first learning to ride a horse as a little kid, she told the students, she almost immediately fell off and cried out. She was so embarrassed.

"My dad didn't even blink," she said. "He dusted me off and was like, all right, now you're a real horse rider."

Lakhani said she rarely has days where she doesn't feel self-doubt or fear, even as she leads these nationwide efforts. But it's those lessons that she learned from an early age that remind her to keep going—even, and especially, when leading change is hard.

Lakhani doesn't fear failure; she embraces it as an opportunity to challenge herself, to learn and grow, and to further her change efforts.

Science Says Failure Is Meaningful

Mia Brunell, a leading Swedish executive and investor, once told me, "Failing simply means that you are trying something meaningful; without failure, there is no progress." Brunell's insight is backed up by data both at an individual and a collective level.

In the paper "A Scientific Approach to Entrepreneurial Decision Making: Evidence from a Randomized Control Trial," researchers Arnaldo Camuffo, Alessandro Cordova, Alfonso Gambardella, and Chiara Spina put forth the most compelling data I've seen on how entrepreneurial success is determined by our ability to learn from failure.[17] They did a study with founding teams of different Italian startups, where a group of entrepreneurs learned to apply the scientific method of hypothesis testing to their startups, and then compared results to a control group that did not. They found that those trained in the scientific method generated higher revenues in their startups and were more likely to make more pivots along the way.

Scientists in a lab don't consider an experiment a failure; rather, they test hypotheses and see whether or not the data backs their initial guesses of what would happen. What a healthy way to think about failure! By leveraging the scientific method in their work as innovators, and therefore leaning into curiosity and away from any possible sting of failure, these entrepreneurs were able to more quickly learn from their mistakes and more successfully apply those learnings to improve their companies.

The Privilege of Failure

One's willingness and ability to readily fail is inherently tied up in privilege. Some of us have a wider and stronger safety net than others when it comes to recovering from failure. As changemakers, we have an opportunity to create a collective culture where failure is appreciated, not feared, where having the courage to try and fail is valued over never failing but also never trying. And on an individual level, we can use the risk quotient to understand just how risky a potential failure could be and whether it's worth the risk. Our mindset also plays a key role in our response to failures. Can we turn them into good failures—ones that result in learning and growth, not undesired setbacks?

As leaders, can we also help others learn to gracefully "fail forward"? A first step is to recognize power imbalances and remember that for a variety of reasons, both personal and systemic, not everyone will be able to embrace failure in the same way. Systemic biases, from race to class to ability and beyond, mean that changemakers from traditionally marginalized backgrounds often face greater repercussions from failure as a result. While all of us will fail, not all of us have the same support and acceptance when we do.

An entry-level teammate I managed made the mistake of using cc instead of bcc on a really important email she sent to hundreds of recipients, resulting in Reply All messages clogging up their inboxes. She came to me mortified, on the brink of tears, fearing that her mistake was irreparable. I reminded her that while this, of course, was not the ideal situation, we'd find ways to follow up and fix any potential harm. We discussed that each of us has made mistakes like this, and that a single setback should never define us. In fact, it's not whether we make mistakes that counts—because each of us inevitably will—it's how we respond to them that makes the difference. And, more importantly, I reinforced that she had just learned a lesson she'd never forget: to double-check the bcc line going forward. A simple mistake, powered by the mindset to embrace failure, resulted in learning and growth. That's what good failures make possible.

FAILING ON PURPOSE

Developing a healthy relationship with failure—learning to see it as a catalyst for change, not an inhibitor—is a central theme running throughout the Becoming a Changemaker course. And the way my students learn it in class has now become legendary on the UC Berkeley campus. As we near the end of my lecture on failure, after students have heard the perspectives of changemakers like Kalsoom Lakhani and I've regaled them with empirical studies on smart risk-taking and insights from Silicon Valley's culture of failing forward, I put up a slide with just two words:

Go fail.

Students giggle with nervous excitement, but their smiles quickly turn to looks of panic when I flash the next slide with instructions, as they realize I'm not kidding.

I tell them they have fifteen minutes to leave the classroom and to ask for something and get rejected. They have to go set out to purposefully get rejected—to proactively fail. If they ask for something, no matter how ridiculous it is, and the person agrees to it, that doesn't count. They have to try again, and again and again, until they get someone to flat-out tell them no. They can ask for anything they want. There are only two rules: They cannot ask for anything illegal or dangerous, and they can't tell the other person it's for a class.

The image of my students' reactions is memorable. The notion of failing, of purposefully getting rejected, for these supersuccessful UC Berkeley students can be overwhelming to them, and I see them react somatically. Faces turn bright red. Beads of sweat form on foreheads. And I've heard from numerous students that they feel their heart begin to race uncontrollably.

That very response is the reason I give them this hands-on failure assignment. These students have achieved so much at such a young age, yet the prospect of rejection and failure absolutely terrifies them.

I give them some words of encouragement, remind them of the concepts they just learned in lecture, and wish them luck as they nervously leave the classroom, unsure of what the next fifteen minutes will bring.

When they stream back in, having completed the assignment, there's been a monumental shift in the feeling in the room. Students return with

smiles from ear to ear, their tense departing shuffle replaced with buoy-
ant, bouncing steps, laughs, giggles, and stories so boisterous that I once
had a professor in a nearby classroom come over and ask me to keep the
noise down.

These students are ebullient because they realize they've just learned
an important, life-changing lesson. They've developed a new, healthy
relationship with failure. Instead of fearing it, they've started to learn to
embrace it as a means toward achieving their changemaker aspirations.

We spend the remaining part of class giving everyone a chance to
recap their rejections and share their lessons. Their stories are epic, and
there are two key lessons that always emerge.

The first lesson is that our fear of failure often holds us back from
asking for something we clearly want, sure that we will be rejected, when
in reality it's refusing to ask in the first place that is the actual failure.

Approximately 40 percent of my students ask for something they
think is completely ridiculous, only to have their ask granted. There
was the student who, on a rainy day, asked a fellow student carrying
an umbrella if he would walk him across campus to his next class. To
his shock and amazement, this kind student agreed. He was willing to
walk thirty minutes out of his way to make sure my student didn't get
wet! One student went to a café and asked for a free orange juice. When
her request was granted and knowing she couldn't come back until she
failed, she kept asking for another one, and then another one, until the
café finally said no and she came back to class carrying six juices. I've
had students who got everyone in the campus gym to sing them happy
birthday (despite proactively telling them that it was not actually their
birthday), and I've had others who—to their absolute shock—ended up
getting someone's phone number for a possible date.

As students recount these stories, I help them see the first takeaway
of the exercise: that we are often so sure we will get rejected that we fail
to ask for something we want. This means that we are setting ourselves
up for failure at the start by simply expecting failure. Imagine if Lakhani
had embraced this mindset and had never summoned the courage to risk

falling off her metaphorical horse again and again. We can't get something we don't ask for, and students realize through this exercise that we are bad predictors of what actions will actually lead to a rejection, that the only way to know for sure is to try.

The second lesson from this exercise is that the sting of failure is nowhere near as painful as we make it out to be in our head.[18] Here, I consider the student who asked a construction worker if he could use his bulldozer. The request—thankfully!—was quickly and resoundingly rejected. But it led to a conversation about real estate development and a connection that resulted in the student getting an internship with the construction company. There's the shy student who nervously paced the hallway for the first fourteen minutes of the failure exercise, trying to summon the courage to make her ask. With the clock ticking, she nervously asked another woman if she could try on her shoes. "No, I'd rather not. I hope you understand," the woman responded reasonably. My student, who told me she had expected to burst into tears the moment she was rejected, felt a weight lift off her chest. She hadn't been scolded. She hadn't been laughed at. This woman took even a ridiculous ask with kindness and good humor. My student, readying herself for a spiral of shame, took a deep breath, smiled, thanked the woman, and came back to the classroom. She went on to run for student government at UC Berkeley and won her election. Can you imagine this path ever being possible had she not found the courage to learn that crucial lesson that failure isn't fatal?

I've had students in other classes refer to me as "the failure professor." I presume that this is because of the mythology of this exercise throughout campus and not a subtle dig at my many setbacks in entrepreneurship and academia! But no matter why, while many professors would loathe having the concept of failure so intimately tied to their reputation, I wear it as a badge of honor. No meaningful change has ever happened without many failures along the way. To lead change is to fail, and to be a changemaker is to embrace failure. The more comfortable we get with failure, the more effectively and quickly we can learn and grow, allowing us to be changemakers who remain students always.

BE THE CHANGE

Key Insights

- Remain clear on your why but flexible on the how of achieving it.
- Changemakers practice three kinds of adaptability: cognitive, emotional, and dispositional, with dispositional being especially important for leading change initiatives.
- Resilience is staying strong for the long haul, and your deliberate practices across the physical, social/emotional, mental, and spiritual dimensions will help you thrive when facing challenges.

Changemaker Challenge

- Try the failure exercise. Go ask for something with the specific goal of getting rejected. Keep going until you get your rejection, and then reflect on what emotions the exercise brought up for you and what insights you've gleaned about how you can get more comfortable failing forward.

PART 2

CHANGEMAKER LEADERSHIP

Chapter 6

Reinventing Leadership

If it weren't for a great stroke of luck, I never would have been hired at UC Berkeley's Haas School of Business.

UC Berkeley had already rejected me twice—once for my undergraduate studies, and once for my graduate studies—so it wasn't a big shock when I got rejected by the university again, albeit this time professionally. (I have somehow found myself on a regular cadence of getting turned down by Berkeley every seven years; I wonder what might be waiting for me next!) But this rejection hurt more than others because it was for an absolute dream job: to become the founding executive director of a brand-new leadership center on campus. The opportunity would bring together all of my experiences as a changemaker and would leverage all I had learned about leadership from the Reach for Change incubator in Stockholm. So, although it wasn't a complete shock, it hurt when I received the rejection letter.

"I'm sorry to say that you were not selected," the email began, with more sympathy than in my previous two Berkeley rejections combined. "But you should feel very proud as you finished in second place among many outstanding candidates." While those words should have comforted me, there is no second place in a gunfight, or, apparently, in leadership centers, since a silver medal doesn't come with a job. But I thanked the folks at Haas for their time and said I looked forward to staying in touch.

Much to my surprise, they got back in touch far sooner than I had expected, mere days later. I received an email (with the dramatic subject line "Development...") that informed me that the first-place applicant had withdrawn, and the job was now mine. Perhaps it was the cocktail I had just enjoyed, or my Pavlovian response to notifications from Berkeley, but it was hard to break the pattern and believe that I had just been offered this job. I accepted on the spot.

The role was a stretch for me, having never before worked in academia and with a daunting fundraising target for the center already set, which I would immediately inherit, but it was a meaningful and welcome challenge.

The job allowed me to connect with many leaders whom I deeply admired but did not previously have access to. I cherished these conversations. I got to speak with some of my heroes in the leadership space and talk with them about their own development as leaders and what they believe leadership looks like today.

My favorite question to ask was: "How did you develop your own model of leadership?"

There was one most common answer from respondents (by a landslide, probably 75 percent), and that was that at some point in their career they had experienced a bad leader and made the conscious choice to be a different kind of leader. Most of these leadership heroes of mine learned how to become great leaders by observing bad leadership and deciding as a result to purposefully do things differently.

I found this infinitely inspiring, because we all have experienced bad leadership in one form or another. But these leaders had found a sense of agency, a belief that they could chart a new course. They gave themselves permission to lead differently.

In this chapter, you will learn how you, too, can reinvent your leadership.

My definition of leadership makes no mention of roles or titles. It's intentionally egalitarian, and it's equally accessible to all. It's not prescriptive, except in the sense that it's an invitation to embrace leadership as an act, as a conscious choice to serve others.

I define *leadership* as "the ability to make meaningful things happen through and with other people."

This definition focuses on the act of leadership. Sometimes leadership happens *through* others. Sometimes it happens *with* others. Sometimes it's a combination. But it's always a meaningful act, and it's always done in cooperation and concert with others. (Leadership does not happen alone in a vacuum.)

This definition sets the stage for us to reinvent leadership. It's a chance for us to break free from the twentieth-century models and relegate them to the past.

There are four important twenty-first-century leadership skills, all of which are accessible to changemakers no matter their age, title, or experience. These skills are inclusive, and you can begin putting them into action right away.

LEADING WITHOUT WAITING
FOR PERMISSION

The first step in reinventing leadership is to stop waiting for permission.

London Business School professor Herminia Ibarra's book *Act Like a Leader, Think Like a Leader* is perhaps my most often recommended book to new and emerging leaders.[1]

She writes, "The paradox of change is that the only way to alter the way we think is by doing the very things our habitual thinking keeps us from doing." In other words, as leaders and changemakers, we must act, not just think. This fits in well with my model of changemaking—after all, it's not change*thinking*.

Ibarra presents us with a counterintuitive model for thinking about our own leadership. The traditional model of leadership, she teaches, is that we focus first on thinking: We change the way we think. Then based on that thinking, we act: We change what we do. She makes a compelling case that this model is backward in today's world. Instead of thinking and then acting, we should act and then think. First, we should change the way we show up in the world (for instance, trying out a new approach or style of leadership). Once we've taken action, we can stop, think, and reflect on whether or not it was effective, which will then inform our next action we take. It's a reinforcing cycle.

"Experimentation," she tells us, "not introspection is the secret to leadership development."[2]

Acting like a leader, not merely thinking like one, happens when we stop waiting for permission and instead give ourselves permission to be changemakers and leaders.

Key Leadership Abilities

Let's look at why Ibarra's insights matter for us as changemakers. Today, organizations, roles, and opportunities are constantly evolving, and the pace of change will only increase. Opportunities to lead in today's world are seized, not given. Sure, you can wait until you have the CEO title to finally believe that you are a leader, but it's unlikely that you will ever reach that position if you don't first give yourself permission to start leading along the way.

Ibarra conducted research on the most important leadership competencies, and based on surveys and analysis, she identified the six most crucial skills. They are:

- Collaborating across organizational units and functions
- Inspiring and motivating others
- Getting buy-in/support
- Providing strategic direction
- Making decisions under conditions of uncertainty/ambiguity
- Influencing without authority

I love this list, because every single one of these—except perhaps, in some cases, making decisions under conditions of ambiguity—are leadership skills you can do regardless of your title. Collaborating, inspiring others, providing direction, influencing without authority: These are all things that you can start doing right now. You don't need anyone's permission to do them; you simply need to give yourself permission to lead.

While others sit back and wait for permission, once you give it to yourself, you can begin separating from the pack. Suzanne McKechnie Klahr is the founder of BUILD.org, an inspiring nonprofit organization that uses "entrepreneurship to ignite the potential of youth from under-resourced communities and propel them to high school, college & career success."[3] She scaled the organization from the small basement of a house in East Palo Alto, California, to a nationally recognized organization working from coast to coast. She's raised tens of millions of dollars for BUILD, and along the way she's relentlessly built a collection of Silicon Valley contacts that would put even the most connected venture capitalist to shame.

I asked her how she convinced one of the busiest and most influential leaders in technology, Jack Dorsey, then the CEO of both Twitter and Square, to join her board. She told me her secret in three words: "I asked him." She also told me she later asked Dorsey why he decided to say yes and he said that she was the very first person who ever asked him to join a nonprofit board. While every other nonprofit leader figured that Dorsey would be too busy, McKechnie Klahr gave herself permission to ask. She ran the risk quotient and found that there were tons of upsides and virtually no downsides. By choosing action and not waiting around for permission, she unlocked an influential ally and a powerful new board member.

Breaking Bad Habits

In class as we start our Changemaker Leadership module, I have students get into groups and brainstorm (using the divergent-thinking approach we learned in chapter 2; see page 45) all of the bad leadership traits they have observed throughout their lives. They share examples they've experienced, or even practiced themselves, and they come up with a specific illustration of each.

Once they've generated their lists, I have them break into pairs and discuss their list with someone from another group. And it's amazing how many of these traits are similar across classes, no matter their makeup.

I ask students to raise their hands if they identified five bad leadership traits. Then to keep their hands raised if they came up with ten. Fifteen? Twenty? Until a single student with the most traits— usually in the midtwenties—remains.

I then invite the student to read off their list and to have other students in the class snap their fingers if they hear a leadership trait that they also disliked.

It turns into the world's worst spoken-word poetry jam.

"Arrogant." *Snap*

"Entitled." *Snap*

"Condescending." *Snap*

But together we paint a clear and comprehensive picture of what ineffective or downright abusive leadership looks like.

I then make the case to the class that even though we know what bad leadership looks and feels like, and we, at least intuitively, know what great leadership looks and feels like, we face a leadership crisis in the world today.

According to a 2021 Gallup report, only 20 percent of people globally feel engaged at work.[4] In the US and Canada, that figure is about 33 percent, but that still means that two-thirds of folks are disengaged and, at best, not contributing much or, at worst, actively bringing down morale, effectiveness, and impact throughout the organization.

So if we know what bad leadership looks like and what good leadership feels like, why do we have such an abysmal state of leadership in the world?

I believe it's because for too long we have mistaken leadership as something bestowed upon someone because of title.

But leadership is something we do. It's not something we are.

LEADING THROUGH NETWORKS

The second twenty-first-century leadership skill is leveraging the power of networks.

"The world doesn't change one person at a time," authors and activists Margaret Wheatley and Deborah Frieze write. "It changes as networks of relationships form among people who discover they share a common cause and vision of what's possible."[5]

In a networked world, leadership is no longer about what you alone can control and influence but rather what and how you can contribute alongside other collaborators toward a common goal.

While it may seem daunting to try and get a whole network of people aligned and working in concert, research by University of Pennsylvania professor Damon Centola and colleagues paints a powerful and inspiring picture of what it means to be a changemaker leading effectively in a network. In the paper "Experimental Evidence for Tipping Points in Social Convention," they conducted experiments within social networks where they had "confederates"—people in on the study—change behavioral norms.[6] Their findings, as summarized in a *Fast Company* article, "The Magic Number of People Needed to Create Social Change," show that "only 25% of people need to adopt a new social norm to create an inflection point where everyone in the group follows."[7] This means that leading change through a network is much more accessible than many of us think, and that the influence any of us as individuals can have is likely much larger than we would imagine.

Small, Sustainable Steps

I helped Sebastien, a middle manager at a manufacturing company, put Centola's insight into action at his workplace. Passionate about sustainability, he tried for months to get colleagues to compost their food waste but still found himself as the lone composter. Backed by this tipping-point insight, he realized that trying to get the entire two-hundred-person office to compost at once was virtually impossible. I helped him focus his strategy:

first, to convince just fifty or so of his colleagues to begin composting. He set up composting bins in new and more strategic places around the office, which helped him to gain traction among this smaller group. By empowering them to help encourage their own colleagues and contacts to compost, Sebastien's composting effort took off. While he couldn't reach all two hundred coworkers effectively at once, he could reach fifty, and then he helped those first fifty inspire their own friends and colleagues. Within a month, his vision had been realized: Composting became the norm office-wide, thanks to the power of inspiring and activating networks.

Networked Leadership and the Social Justice Movement

This approach to leadership is also playing out in some of the most important social-change movements of our time, which are now being built around networks rather than individuals.

Take, for instance, Black Lives Matter.

While some may critique the BLM movement and wonder why this generation hasn't produced the next Martin Luther King Jr., Malcolm X, or other singular leader, this is actually a deliberate and strategic approach that shows what's possible through networked leadership.

As historian Barbara Ransby writes in a *New York Times* editorial, "The suggestion that the organizations that have emerged from the Black Lives Matter protests are somehow lacking because they have rejected the old style of leadership misses what makes this movement most powerful: its cultivation of skilled local organizers who take up many issues beyond police violence."[8]

Ransby adds that NAACP leader Ella Baker believed that this old model of a single, top-down charismatic leader "disempowered ordinary people, especially women and low-income and working-class people, because it told them that they need a savior."

What Black Lives Matter forgoes in terms of a singular leader—though, of course, some of its cofounders have taken on more prominent roles—it more than gains through distributed leadership. Its network-based model is more adaptable to local needs and conditions and creates a greater sense of ownership among a broad base of people. The values and aims of the organization unite its members while ensuring that there is no single point of failure.

Martin Luther King Jr.'s individual work was, tragically, cut short. Today's Black Lives Matter movement, with its many members, its many leaders, and its networked approach to leading change, would be far more difficult, if not downright impossible, to stop. Instead of a single change-maker, today's social movements increasingly look toward and are led by networks of many changemakers to effect positive change. What results are more complex organizations, yes, but also ones that are much more resilient, connected, and expansive.

Four Steps to Networked Leadership

How can one become an effective changemaker working within networks?

In the *Stanford Social Innovation Review* piece "The Most Impactful Leaders You Have Never Heard Of," Jane Wei-Skillern, David Ehrlichman, and David Sawyer outline four specific principles to follow.[9] You'll see that each of these principles tracks very closely to aspects of the changemaker mindset you've already developed in previous chapters, showing that changemakers are well positioned to be this type of twenty-first-century networked leader.

The first way to be a networked leader is to focus on trust, not control. This means building relationships, especially long-term relationships. It may also require taking a trust leap to partner with others whom you may not know well yet. Jean Guo put this into action when she decided to scale her organization, Konexio, with new local partners despite the future not yet being perfectly clear.

The second is to focus on humility, not brand. This means putting one's ego aside for the greater good, aiming not for fame but collaboration, creating a healthy culture of working together. This is a hallmark of Black Lives Matter.

The third is to be a node, not a hub. This means understanding the contributions of others and how your leadership can support and complement them, rather than trying to do everything yourself. Gwen Yi Wong, the former CEO of Tribeless, embodies this approach in how she stepped back in her organization to support others in stepping up.

The fourth way to be a networked leader is to focus on mission, not organization. This means buying into long-term, collaborative goals, and being part of painting that larger vision together. Muhammad Yunus has taken this approach to heart, inspiring countless others to launch microfinance initiatives in their own cities and countries.

Changemakers who can leverage the power of networks will be well positioned to amplify their change efforts through and with others, and to remain strong for the long haul.

LEADING WITH PURPOSE

The third twenty-first-century leadership trait is leading with purpose.

How important is purpose? The virtual coaching company BetterUp conducted a study on meaning and purpose at work, in which it surveyed 2,285 American professionals, representing twenty-six different industries, along with different demographics and pay levels.[10] The findings are powerful.

The survey asked participants how much of their entire future lifetime earnings they'd be willing to give up in order to have a job that was always meaningful. What do you think the data show? A gobsmacking 23 percent! On average, people would be willing to give up more than one-fifth of the money they would otherwise expect to make. (To put this in perspective, the average American spends 21 percent of their income on housing.) The survey results make clear just how much people today are yearning for meaning, for a sense of purpose. And you, as a twenty-first-century changemaker leader, can be well positioned to lead these people, through learning to lead with purpose.

The Three V's

I break down leading with purpose into a model of three V's: vision, values, and victories.

Remember the research from chapter 4 on the traits people look for in a colleague versus a leader (see page 98)? Being forward-looking was by far the biggest differentiator. This tells us that your ability to paint a picture of the future is what separates effective leaders from dependable colleagues.

Leading with vision is a superpower when it comes to instilling a sense of purpose in your team. To illustrate this, here's a story that may be apocryphal but is a great one nonetheless: A journalist was walking the halls of NASA when she struck up a conversation with a janitor. "What do you do for NASA?" she asked him. "I help launch rockets into space," he responded.

This story shows complete buy-in, from top to bottom, around the mission of NASA. The janitor (who does important and often thankless and underpaid work—let's be clear about that) is so bought into NASA's mission that he's able to connect his job to the agency's larger vision. As a changemaker, can you continually paint that picture of the future for folks on your team and help them connect each of their individual parts to the overall vision you are creating together? That's the first step in leading with purpose.

Leading with values means giving your team a way of working that connects them to something greater. When I was looking at joining a business school, I was initially a bit skeptical about whether a change-maker like me would fit in, and whether or not I would be happy in what I had stereotyped a business-school culture to be, which I imagined focused primarily on finance and profits at the expense of everything else. But as soon as I saw Haas's Defining Leadership Principles—its values—I realized that its culture would actually be a significant driver of purpose for me. When in my very first interview for the executive director position I was asked which defining principle was my favorite and why (and I got to expand upon my belief in beyond-yourself leadership), I felt an incredible sense of connection to the place and to the mission of the school.

But it's not enough to simply have values written down somewhere. As leaders we must ensure that we make them come alive to connect with that sense of purpose. In my early conversations with Rich Lyons, who was Haas's dean at the time, we discussed an ethical challenge—the possibility of a partnership that would bring in some much-needed revenue to the school but came with some significant moral concerns. How should we go about making this challenging decision amid declining state support for public education?

We leaned into our values.

"Our values aren't there to help us make the easy decisions," I argued. "They are here to help us make the most difficult ones. This is why we invest in our values; this is why we must lead with them. And this is one of those hard decisions where we must lean into them."

To this day, one of the most impressive and inspiring leadership decisions I've ever witnessed is when Dean Lyons decided not to pursue that much-needed revenue, because he saw that Haas's values were in conflict with the outcome. Despite the financial downside from such a decision, he made the determination resolutely, confident that our values should guide us.

Celebrating small wins and creating a sense of progress is what is meant by <u>leading with victories</u>. We changemakers often have such deep passion for the changes we pursue that we can stay strong for the long haul individually, pushing past the inevitable ups and downs, especially with big change initiatives. But not every teammate will share that same sense of indefatigable passion as early excitement fades. As a twenty-first-century leader, you have an opportunity to keep that sense of purpose and team morale high by paying attention to the small victories. While you might be fixated on the long-term change you are pursuing, it can feel abstract or even impossible some days for your teammates. Don't be afraid to celebrate even the smallest actions that bring you closer to reaching your long-term goal, so that your team can viscerally feel a sense of progress. It will make a big difference to your teammates and their long-term commitment to joining you in pursuing meaningful change.

LEADING WITH YOUR EARS

For so long, many of us have equated the person with the loudest voice in the room with being the most natural leader. But in modern times, where we fluidly move our interactions across in-person and digital realms, and as we communicate across channels ranging from Zoom to Slack to SMS, it's no longer the loudest person who is the obvious leader. In fact, being loud and talking over others is now more of a leadership liability than a strength. Instead, the best listeners are often the best leaders, and asking powerful questions to activate our listening is the fourth quintessential twenty-first-century leadership skill.

Researchers Scott D. Johnson and Curt Bechler set out to look at the connection between effective listening and effective leadership.[11] And in their twelve-week study of "leaderless" work groups, where none of the participants had ever met, they found a powerfully strong correlation between a participant's effective listening skills and their leadership ability.

These data back up what I've observed in the changemakers I've worked with as well. One of the common themes among these efficacious changemakers is their ability to ask insightful questions of others. While you may start out as a subject expert—say, in coding or contract writing—as you move up in an organization, you begin leading others who are experts in their own respective fields. Imagine being promoted to COO. You have two choices for how you will lead: Either try to become an expert at everything from HR policies to IT infrastructure, or learn how to ask powerful, clarifying, and catalytic questions. While not all of us can become experts in all of these different fields, we can all learn to be curious, and we can all learn to ask questions that bring out the best in others and surface new insights across teams and areas.

Consider acting like a journalist or an anthropologist. Rather than coming in with your own perspectives, lead with curiosity and ask questions of those around you, to explore with wonder. As journalist Kate Murphy says, "Everybody is interesting if you ask the right questions. If someone seems dull or uninteresting, it's on you."[12]

Lean into your curiosity, and instead of asking leading questions to force a conversation to where you might want it to head, embrace the unexpected that can arise through a catalytic question like "What might happen if…?" or "What is just one more possibility I might not have considered yet?" These questions invite divergent thinking. And you, as a leader and changemaker, can begin seeing connections across the many different conversations you have. The more you let your curiosity guide you, the more new insights you'll be able to pull together into your own ability to lead effectively.

THE NEW LEADERSHIP PLAYBOOK

While living in Stockholm, I had the privilege of running an incubator for some of the top entrepreneurs and innovators in Scandinavia with the organization Reach for Change. Theoretically, my role was to select and invest in amazing entrepreneurs and then help them with scaling their impact and revenue.

But what I actually ended up doing was much simpler and much more powerful: I supported these changemakers' growth as leaders. This helped me realize that it doesn't matter if you have the best ideas or the best strategy; you need leadership to make real change happen. Sure, I provided lots of ideas on how to measure impact and rolled up my sleeves to help rethink revenue models. But mostly I helped people reevaluate and reimagine their own approaches to leadership to become the leaders that their teams—and the world around them—needed.

These next chapters on changemaker leadership detail what it means to be an effective and inspiring leader of change today. You'll learn why the old models, from generations past, no longer work for changemakers in our fast-paced, interconnected world. I'll show how you can practice a concept called microleadership, shifting your view of leadership from titles and formal authority to an accessible choice to act on individual leadership moments. You'll learn to become the leader you've wished you had and help those around you be at their very best through practicing inclusive leadership and finding your own style of leadership that is true to who you are. And you'll start identifying opportunities to lead from where you are, including how to catalyze change through culture shifts.

The leadership playbook is being rewritten right now, and you can help write it with your actions. Those bad leadership examples we've all experienced can now be put where they belong: in the past. Embracing these fresh approaches to leadership will help you reinvent your own leadership and more effectively lead change around you.

BE THE CHANGE

Key Insights

- Stop waiting for permission to be a leader. Be like Suzanne McKechnie Klahr of BUILD.org and give yourself permission to lead.
- Increasingly, change is being made not by a single person but by a network. Embrace network-based leadership to create more resilient, sustainable change movements.
- Our values aren't there for the easy decisions; they are there for the really hard ones. Lean into your values when times get tough.
- If you feel uncomfortable in a new leadership position and feel pressured to have all the answers, focus on asking really great questions.

Changemaker Challenge

- Reflect on some of the worst examples of leadership you've experienced: moments where leaders frustrated you or let you down. Come up with a list of negative traits and use them as inspiration to reinvent your own leadership, and choose to create a style in opposition to these.

Chapter 7

Microleadership

The story of leadership is often told through the lens of a single leader and a singular act, like Lech Wałesa climbing over a fence to join strikers at a shipyard in Poland, Eleanor Roosevelt leading the creation of the Universal Declaration of Human Rights, or Steve Jobs pulling the first-ever iPhone out of his pocket during a keynote.

These people are impressive leaders and inspiring changemakers, to be sure. But they also set a leadership bar so high that it can feel unobtainable to most of us.

In putting these leaders on a pedestal, we often conflate *acts* of leadership with *positions* of leadership.

This narrative, however, has obfuscated what it truly means to be a leader. While leaders might be scarce, leadership is abundant. It is not something bestowed upon a person by virtue of a title or position but the sum of a series of opportunities in which a person consciously decides to act.

Leadership, then, is not a single act but a continuous mindset to serve others. It is therefore egalitarian; there is no requirement to wait until being anointed a leader in order to be a leader. Rather, leadership is something each of us can choose to practice every day through our own actions, whether we are an intern or a CEO, a parent or a child, a contractor or a client.

As Drew Dudley reminds us in his brilliant TED talk, "Everyday Leadership," the informal acts of leadership are often those that stick with us the most.[1] There is not a single constraint to performing these acts of leadership, except for our own self-limiting beliefs of what it means to be a leader.

The bravest act is to stand up and believe that you can be a leader. Instead of looking for someone else to give you permission to lead, you can constantly look for your own opportunities to serve someone else.

This chapter introduces a concept I call microleadership. It's a radically inclusive call to each and every one of us to start seeing ourselves as leaders right now and to begin seizing the leadership moments in front of us every single day. Microleadership shows that you don't have to be the CEO to perform acts of leadership; it's a framework for rethinking how simple and achievable it actually is to take on small leadership acts consciously and consistently.

This chapter is an invitation to you to start changing the way you think about leadership, from believing it's something that other people do, to something you do. Microleadership is inclusive and accessible. Microleadership is for all of us.

THE FOUR KEYS

There are four keys to embracing microleadership. They build upon one another, and while each is deceptively simple on its own, they make for a powerful combination. This framework will help you start becoming a leader in your group, team, organization, family, and beyond, even if you aren't the formal leader.

Believe It, Be It

You may not have a traditional leadership title or years of experience, but that doesn't mean anything about your ability to actually go practice leadership. The first key to microleadership is to fully believe that you can be, and likely already are, a leader. For many, this requires a cognitive shift to rethink the story of leadership we've heard over and over, that certain people are "natural-born" leaders while others are not. This concept is built upon biased beliefs around race, class, gender, and ability, and it limits the potential of so many of us who feel inspired to be a leader but simply want to do so in our own way.

I taught and mentored an administrative assistant who for years yearned to feel like she could effect change among the senior executives with whom she interacted. But the power dynamics of her organization and the traditional story of leadership reinforced for her this arbitrary bifurcation of leaders and nonleaders. She simply believed she was not a leader and could never become one. As a result, she let so many ideas she desperately wanted to share with her colleagues pass idly by without taking action on them.

We worked together on her own perception of what it means to practice leadership, and she came to realize that while she did not have the title or formal authority of the senior execs around her, she could absolutely practice leadership every single day. She embraced the first key to microleadership: to start seeing herself as a leader (even if those around her might not have yet). When she did, she finally felt more comfortable stepping up to take initiative, make suggestions, and use the tools of influence (which we will cover in more detail later in this chapter) to start becoming a leader from where she was. While she, of course, didn't have the same formal authority as those to whom she reported, she began to realize she was just as capable of making meaningful contributions in small, consistent, and substantive ways.

Give Yourself Permission

No one needs to give you the okay to embrace microleadership, so don't wait to receive it. Give it to yourself. This could be asking a reticent teammate for their opinion when they've been quiet the whole meeting or being willing to ask the questions no one else will.

Instead of waiting for approval for everything, microleaders seize the opportunities in front of them. We often overglorify leadership and conceptualize it as being about one powerful person in one room telling others what to do. But in reality, so much of what it takes to be a leader is a bottom-up approach. Leadership is really about rolling up our sleeves and getting involved. No one will ever tell you not to arrive early to help set up or to stay late to help clean up, but we can give ourselves permission to take on these small acts of leadership at any time.

A changemaker whom I helped fully embrace microleadership had recently joined a big multinational firm and was frustrated that there was no employee resource group (ERG) for LGBTQ+ employees. I encouraged them to seize the leadership moment. If they felt this way, surely many other teammates felt similarly. Instead of waiting for senior leadership to create an ERG, I suggested that this changemaker give themselves permission to step up and create one. They started with the first key to microleadership and began believing that they already were a leader. And then they followed key number two. They established an ERG with a small initial networking event, giving themselves the only permission they really needed to start leading: their own.

Serve Others

Whereas traditional leadership models often feel centered around being able to command and control, microleadership counters this. Microleadership is about seizing small leadership opportunities to help serve others, and to do so consistently.

Once you begin practicing the third key to microleadership, you'll realize that these small acts to make a difference are appearing all around you, likely dozens of times every day. Microleadership is a new lens on leadership, encouraging us to consistently seek out and regularly seize these small opportunities for service.

An app that fully embraces key number three is Be My Eyes. The concept was developed by Danish furniture craftsman Hans Jørgen Wiberg, who is visually impaired. The app connects blind and low-vision people with sighted volunteers, who provide on-demand visual assistance through live video calls. Volunteers lend their sight to help tackle challenges and solve problems together—anything from checking expiration dates, distinguishing colors, reading instructions, and navigating new surroundings. The experience on the volunteer side requires only one thing: the conscious choice to serve others.

Since 2015, over five million volunteers in over 150 countries and speaking 180 languages have engaged with over three hundred thousand blind and low-vision people through the app. Be My Eyes brings this third key to microleadership to life, transforming individuals with a bit of free time and a willingness to help out into microleaders who make connections, engage in community, and meaningfully serve others.

Take Action

Key number four: Take action and continue to take it—again and again and again. It adds up! Seize the leadership moments in front of you with courage and consistency. While CEO is an impressive title, the actual work of a CEO is mostly about taking regular action on many smaller leadership moments all day long. Small moments like these are opportunities, no matter who you are or what formal authority, or lack thereof, you might have. Microleadership levels the playing field and lets anyone have agency to practice leadership as long as they choose to take action.

Now that you know the four keys to microleadership, you'll begin seeing the world around you in a different way: It's filled with opportunities for you to step up and take action.

These opportunities for action can happen in the community: Eighteen-year-old Paige Hunter, who has experienced her own mental health challenges, started writing "notes of hope" and attaching them to Wearmouth Bridge in Sunderland, England, in 2018. Her notes, providing perspective as well as information and resources, are credited with saving the lives of several people.[2]

These opportunities can also happen in the workplace: for instance, choosing to take the time to thoughtfully share constructive feedback with a colleague; being willing to say no when everyone else is saying yes, or being willing to say yes when everyone else is saying no; and electing to respond with kindness when a colleague greets you with anger or fear.

A world filled with acts of microleadership is one where it's possible for everyone to be a leader even without being *the* leader. It's one where leaders are the exceptional many rather than the exceptional few. It's a world completely within our reach if we stop waiting for someone to tell us we are the leader and instead choose every day to recognize the leadership moments right before our eyes. Let's give ourselves permission to take action in small ways, again and again, and embrace the opportunity to put microleadership into action.

Seizing Leadership Moments

Microleadership breaks leadership down into a simple and profound unit: the leadership moment. These tiny moments present themselves to us dozens, if not hundreds, of times per day all around us. In them, we can observe small opportunities to step up, to serve others, to make small differences. Here are a few leadership moments seized by some of my students.

Sophia Baginski was serving as a teaching assistant in a class where students felt disconnected. To bring them all closer, she launched a series of Frisbee get-togethers. When COVID hit, she then prepared herself to seize the next opportunity in front of her: to transform those hangouts into virtual experiences. "Microleadership," she reflects, "has made me realize just how many chances I have to make change in my everyday life and has turned me into a more active leader."

Karina Gulati talks about how embracing microleadership made her become especially conscious of making sure everyone on her team receives credit for their work and, in moments where she might be the one getting praise, ensuring that she shares that recognition with her teammates.

Sid Holland, a member of the UC Berkeley rugby team, says microleadership caused him to stand up and take action both on the field and off, even when he was one of the younger players. He gave himself permission to suggest a new tactic and to encourage others—not relying on only the senior captains to do so.

For Jennifer Pfister, microleadership made her more aware of all of the opportunities for leadership that appear around her every day. She now regularly seizes leadership moments, such as opening up her network to make connections to help others realize their goals, and always trying to be the first person to help someone who seems lost.

Leadership can feel intimidating to many people, especially those who are younger or who have internalized the notion that they should wait their turn. Microleadership makes being a leader accessible to everyone, and it all starts with seizing those leadership moments all around us.

TIKTOK-ING FOR CHANGE

The leadership moment was right there in front of her. Would University of Oregon basketball player Sedona Prince seize it?

"I was like, I could do this," she recounts. "I have the power to do this, and my mom is always teaching me to just stick up for myself and do the best thing that I can."[3]

Prince took the opportunity to practice microleadership, and so much has changed as a result of her one simple yet powerful choice to take action.

Prince was twenty-one years old, a college sophomore as she arrived at the NCAA basketball tournament in 2021. Both the men's and women's tournaments were taking place simultaneously, and due to COVID, each was hosted completely within a single city, with the men in Indianapolis and the women in San Antonio. Yet while the games took place at the same time, the experience behind the scenes for the men's and women's basketball players could not have been more different.

As Prince entered the women's weight room, to be shared by all sixty-four teams throughout the tournament, she saw a huge discrepancy: The women's weight room was stocked only with some yoga mats and a rack of dumbbells—in stark contrast to the well-equipped and expansive men's weight room. When combined with other differences she had already observed at the tournament surrounding meals and COVID-testing availability, Prince recognized an opportunity that called for action, a chance for her to step up and lead. She followed the four keys to microleadership perfectly, and with one seemingly small act, she catalyzed ripples of change throughout the sports world and beyond.

> First, she believed that she had the power to do something. Other athletes presumably also noticed the unequal treatment, but Prince decided that she could do something about it.
>
> Second, she gave herself permission to step up. She didn't look to her coaching staff, the NCAA, or even her teammates to determine whether she should seize the moment. She chose, on her own, to be the change.
>
> Third, her microleadership was firmly rooted in serving others—in standing up for her fellow female athletes and the women who would one day follow in her footsteps. It wasn't about gaining fame or attention; it was rooted in the opportunity to make things better for others around her.
>
> Finally, she took action. She created and posted a thirty-eight-second TikTok video that showed firsthand the differences between the two weight rooms. Posting her video and reposting it to Twitter were small acts that she hoped would have an impact—a perfect example of microleadership.

While Prince's acts may have been small, the response was absolutely enormous. When she woke up the next morning, she had received over one hundred thousand retweets and invites to appear on national television shows, including ABC's *Good Morning America*. Her one short video had catalyzed a national conversation. As of this writing, it had reached over eighteen million views on Twitter and twelve million views on TikTok.

More important than any of the individual attention Prince received, though, was that her video got the attention of the NCAA and the sports world. Sports stars—both women and men, including NBA star Steph Curry—weighed in on the conversation Prince had started, and as a result of the attention, the NCAA made the weight rooms equal.

Microleadership, because it is accessible to all of us, can catalyze one moment of action into many more. Such was the case with Prince, who has now taken the platform she built through her first action to continue taking action in support of others. She now has almost three million followers on TikTok, where she lifts up fellow athletes and advocates for further changes at the NCAA.

"I'm glad that she stood up," her coach, Kelly Graves, said. "She's, quite frankly, made change and that's super, super powerful."[4]

Indeed, microleadership is superpowerful.

LEADING FROM WHERE YOU ARE

Just as microleadership is egalitarian and accessible to all, so, too, is the opportunity to influence others. In fact, we changemakers often need to rely more on our ability to persuade others than our ability to tell others exactly what to do. Changemaking usually requires bringing together lots of different people, from different backgrounds, collaborating across sectors and silos, and working across, through, and around hierarchies.

One's ability to influence others irrespective of title or authority is often referred to as "lateral leadership."

In his classic book *Leadership Without Easy Answers*, Harvard University professor Ronald Heifetz helps us differentiate between leadership and authority.[5] Heifetz defines *authority* as "conferred power to perform a service." And while this chapter focuses on leading without authority, let's be clear that there are some cases where leadership with authority are not just welcomed, but necessary. Imagine the case of an emergency evacuation of a stadium filled with thirty thousand concertgoers. An egalitarian approach to evacuation, where each person would get a say on the best way to exit the premises, is not only hard to imagine; it would be downright dangerous. In times of emergency or distress, authority is crucially helpful. We need the direction it provides.

But we aren't living in emergency situations most of the time, so let's focus instead on how we can lead laterally when it comes to making change.

The First Follower

Perhaps my favorite YouTube video of all time (yes, beating out even the sports bloopers and outtakes from *The Office* you'll find filling my watching history) is a blurry, low-res video called "Leadership Lessons from Dancing Guy."[6] With brilliant insights delivered by musician and entrepreneur Derek Sivers, the video captures the power of what he calls "the first follower" in action.

The video begins with a lone man dancing enthusiastically at an outdoor music festival while other festivalgoers either look on or completely ignore him. He dances by himself for about twenty seconds until another person, a stranger, sees the guy dancing and decides to join him with his own silly gyrations.

Together the two dance for a while, waving their hands in the air, kicking their legs, until the man who recently joined in—the first follower—calls out to others with his hands, encouraging others to join.

Soon after, another dancer joins. Then another. Then a handful of folks. Until a steady stream of people get up from their picnic blankets and join the dance party.

Over the course of just three minutes, a movement is born, going from a single dancer (what Sivers calls a "lone nut") to a scene filled with nearly everyone dancing together, and from dancing as the minority activity to the majority one.

I love this video because it shows so viscerally the leadership roles we each can play in making change happen. Some of us will be the uninhibited dancing guy, the first person with a vision for change, who puts themselves out there. Some might be the first follower, the one who sees potential in someone else's vision and helps to catalyze it. Some might be the early adopters, those who see the change getting some traction and want to help shape it and build it (and, in doing so, make it safe for others who might be more risk-averse to join as well). And, finally, some might be the later adopters, who wait for the vision of change to be clearer.

As Sivers concludes in the video, the first dancer might get all of the credit for starting the movement. But actually, much of the credit should go to his first follower, the one who risked his own reputation to make it safe for others to join the movement. While the first follower might not traditionally see themselves as having a leadership role, this video shows us that their leadership is at least as important as, if not more than, anyone else's. It's a reminder that all of us lead, and all of us follow, depending on the day, the task, or the setting.

Your role in leading change might be different depending on the cause. Perhaps you are a first follower with new technologies and a late adopter when it comes to hitting the dance floor. But no matter one's formal role in initiating change, we all can play a leadership role in making change happen.

LATERAL LEADERSHIP

Whether at a festival or in the office, how can you lead laterally to make change happen? I believe lateral leaders need to embrace three leadership tools: seeing the best in others, building alliances, and asking others for advice. Let's look at each.

To see the best in others, I love the insight Liz Wiseman, author of the book *Multipliers: How the Best Leaders Make Everyone Smarter*, provides us. She says the critical question for "multiplier" leaders is not "Is this person smart?" but rather "In what ways is this person smart?"[7] "The job," she and fellow author Greg McKeown write in a related article, is "to bring the right people together in an environment that unleashes their best thinking—and then stay out of the way."[8] Lateral leaders are able to see the best in others, no matter their title or position, and engage them in effectively leading change.

This approach connects well to HR expert Lauren Keller Johnson's suggestion in a *Harvard Business Review* article that "coalition building plays a vital role in lateral leadership," because individuals working together will exert more influence than a single person.[9] She says when she spoke to Jay Conger of the London Business School, he explained that "by building coalitions, you gather influential people together to form 'a single body of authority.' " Johnson then advises us, "To assemble a powerful coalition, begin by asking yourself who's most likely to be affected by the change you're proposing."

We see alliance building in action among an influential group of climate activists from around the world. The young leaders Greta Thunberg (Sweden), Autumn Peltier (Wikwemikong First Nation, Canada), Vanessa Nakate (Uganda), and Xiuhtezcatl Martinez (Mexico) exemplify this coalition-based approach to change. They've come together because they and their communities are affected by climate change, and they've found ways to unite as leaders, despite geographic and cultural differences, and to bring their communities along to be part of the change. This lateral leadership has resulted in even larger, more powerful, and more diverse coalitions.

Inspiration sometimes comes to us from unlikely places, which I discovered regarding asking others for input. As you can imagine, there are many brilliant professors at UC Berkeley, including ten Nobel Prize winners. While I will never be on any of the Nobel shortlists, I do one thing that I don't believe any other Berkeley faculty members have ever done in their lectures: quote Mr. Worldwide himself, the singer and rapper Pitbull. Yes, this prestigious university, from which faculty are credited with discovering a number of chemical elements, including californium and berkelium, also has me playing a fifteen-second clip of a Pitbull music video in my classroom.[10] But his insight, which we apply toward learning to lead laterally, is a powerful one.

"Ask for money and get advice," he sings. "Ask for advice, get money twice."

Pitbull's advice for lateral leadership here is borne out by entrepreneurs seeking investments from venture capitalists. It's a well-known approach that instead of asking for money right up front, savvy entrepreneurs will ask VCs for advice on their startup, their pitch deck, or anything else they can think of. Folks are more likely to feel compelled to support an initiative if they feel like they've had some role in helping to shape and build it. As a lateral leader, can you find opportunities to ask others for their input and advice instead of, or at least in addition to, asking specifically for help?

UNDERSTANDING INFLUENCE

It may seem absurd, but one of the best (in my opinion) studies on the power of influence took place in hotel bathrooms. Researchers designed experiments to see how they could influence hotel guests' behavior when it came to environmental conservation. They posted different signs in hotel rooms encouraging guests to participate in a conservation program. In one version, they used language about what other people were doing, such as THE MAJORITY OF GUESTS REUSE THEIR TOWELS. In another version, they used more traditional wording, focusing on protecting the environment. They found that appealing to group norms was the most effective way to influence behavior.[11]

On top of that, proximity mattered, too! When they posted a sign that read THE MAJORITY OF GUESTS IN THIS ROOM REUSE THEIR TOWELS, it resulted in even stronger environmentally conscious behavior.

This fun example underlies a powerful concept: We humans are incredibly susceptible to small tweaks that can greatly influence our own behavior. Leading change isn't simply about having the right strategy—in this case, reusing towels. *How* we influence can ultimately make the difference in whether or not our change initiatives are adopted.

The Power of Reciprocity

Reciprocity is a powerful driver to influence behavior. If we do something for someone, that person then often wants to return the favor. This intuitive concept was brilliantly proven out by researchers in a paper called "Sweetening the Till: The Use of Candy to Increase Restaurant Tipping."[12] (Side note: Between spending time in hotels and restaurants to observe behavior, I think influence researchers have figured out how to have the most fun possible with hypothesis testing!) In this study, researchers looked at what happened to tips on restaurant bills when servers gave each guest a fancy piece of chocolate along with the check, compared with tips from a control group, who received no chocolate.

When diners received a single piece of candy, tips increased, on average, by 3 percent. Not a huge result, but statistically significant.

Fascinatingly, when instead of one piece, a server offered each guest two pieces of candy, the tips grew exponentially, to 14 percent!

What about when a waiter starts off by offering one candy per guest, begins to walk away, and then pauses, turns back and says, "You nice people can each have an extra piece"? Tips skyrocket to a 21 percent increase over no mint at all.

While these insights are interesting, I can't help reading studies like these and walking away feeling a little sleazy. These particular examples, relating just to candies and towels, are mostly trivial, but the power of influence can be used in manipulative ways and too often is. As a result, I'm not a fan of the type of influence techniques that can feel transactional or scheming. That trick of giving an extra candy to the "nice people" at the table might work the first time, but rest assured if a waiter tried the exact same technique on the same group for a second or third time, not only would it no longer work, it might even backfire. So how can we influence others in a more grounded and sustainable way?

INFLUENCE SUPERPOWERS

Whether you're aware of it or not, influence is all around us, and we are regularly attempting to influence others. Even if we don't imagine we will ever see a person again, our reputations follow us. So it's therefore not just an ethical imperative but an efficacy imperative that we use our influence powers for good, not for manipulation.

When I teach about influence in my class, I introduce students to what I call "influence superpowers," which focus not on short-term gains but rather on long-term connection toward meaningful goals. Let's learn about these five influence superpowers and how you can apply them to your own influential leadership.

Relationships

As opposed to transactional one-off influence opportunities—like a single hotel stay or a restaurant meal like the one you just learned about—the first superpower focuses on building relationships way before you ever need to call in a favor. As we learned from Margaret Wheatley and Deborah Frieze in chapter 6, change takes shape as we build networks of relationships. The more you can invest in relationships up front, the more effective your ability to make a successful ask of someone will be, because you will have developed trust and rapport and you'll have insights on how to best motivate them to join you.

And sometimes people will join your change initiative not because they particularly care about the specific change you are leading but just because they care about you. A friend of mine decided to run a marathon to raise funds for a rare disease that was afflicting a loved one of his. While, of course, I cared about helping fund research for the disease, it wouldn't have been in my top one hundred causes about which I am most passionate. But when he asked me to support him, I chose to do so enthusiastically—not because of his cause, per se, but rather because of my relationship with him. He probably could have asked me to support any of ten thousand good causes, and I would have been all in. And that's because we had developed a meaningful relationship, where if something matters to him, it matters to me as well. He leaned into our relationship in making the ask, and I felt great about supporting him.

Vision

The second superpower is vision. We define vision as painting a picture of the future that others feel called to follow. Can you paint such a vibrant and exciting future that someone can't help but be excited to join? Remember to make it clear and compelling and use the power of aspiration, of helping others see what's possible and believe that they can help make it a reality with you. Use vision to bring everyone along—from the NASA janitor to the executive team whose buy-in you require—to imagine this new future with you. Jean Guo, whom we met in chapter 2, is very effective at leveraging vision to influence key stakeholders. Konexio's vision is "to create a more inclusive society, in which no one is marginalized due to lack of access to digital skills,"[13] and I've watched firsthand as, with this vision, she's encouraged talented colleagues to leave existing jobs to join Konexio, and brought on board partners and investors who feel equally stirred. This inspiring vision lights up so many, and Guo leans into it to excite others to join her in making it a reality.

Empathy

When attempting to influence, empathy is required to actively seek to understand what's in it for the other person and why they should care. As changemakers, we often fall in love with our own ideas, but empathy forces us to see things from another's perspective and understand that perhaps they like the idea but feel scared to join, or they want to help but perhaps not at the level we might be asking. Employing empathy—influence superpower number three—helps us shape our asks and our influence to be human-centered, not one-size-fits-all. Labor leader Dolores Huerta, whom we met in chapter 5, has leveraged empathy throughout her changemaking career to influence all kinds of different people. So much of her success to build powerful and diverse coalitions has come from her ability to tailor her message to emotionally resonate with each distinct audience, whether that's policymakers, farmworkers, or non-profit leaders. She is able to imagine the perspective of others, and by deploying empathy she can understand how to best influence those around her, resulting in groundswells of support.

Passion and Positivity

People can't help but feel inspired when a leader shows up with authentic enthusiasm for what's possible. The fourth superpower—passion and positivity—is impossible to fake. While I absolutely love teaching, if I were forced to teach accounting at Haas (don't worry, Dean Harrison, I would never even think to try), it would be clear from the first moment that my heart wasn't in it. I wouldn't be able to influence others toward becoming great accountants the same way I attempt to do when it comes to helping students become changemakers. Our workplace-composting hero, Sebastien, whom we met in chapter 6, made passion and positivity his influence superpower in encouraging a new behavior throughout his office. He galvanized others to join him in his composting efforts in part through his sheer excitement, and that same enthusiasm started a chain reaction. His first supporters were called to join him because of his passion, and then they themselves transmitted that same zest in rallying their own networks to join in.

Making It Safe

As we learned in chapter 2, we all have different appetites for risk, and many of the people you will meet along your changemaker journey are more scared than you are to take action. How can you proactively make it safe for others to join you? This final influence superpower is one I've had to refine in attempting to lead positive change in a big bureaucracy like UC Berkeley. By first employing empathy, I may realize that a colleague appreciates the vision of a proposed change effort but is scared about what might happen if it doesn't succeed. This reminds me to connect back to Jim Collins's mirror-and-window insight (see page 66). I tell them that I know they are taking a risk to join me on this change initiative. And I promise that if the initiative fails, I will take all the blame and make sure that they don't receive any negativity for having trusted me. And meanwhile, if it succeeds, I will make sure they get credit. Here, the power of humility ensures we make it safe for others to join us.

Choosing which influence superpower to use isn't zero-sum. Each of them is helpful in certain circumstances, and they can even be used in combination. The most influential changemakers will develop a fluency with all five and call upon the best ones depending on the situation. You likely have one or two that feel the most comfortable to you, and one or two that feel like the biggest stretch. So as you think about your own ability to influence, consider which one is already your superpower and which ones, through a bit of practice, might make you even more influential.

Leadership can feel intimidating, especially if we are waiting for someone to give us the title of leader or permission to lead. But if we can adopt microleadership and begin seeing leadership not through rank or position but instead through moments to be seized, we can each be a leader in our own way. So give yourself permission to start harnessing the power of microleadership.

INFLUENCE IN ACTION

Jon Chu, the director of *Crazy Rich Asians*, the first major studio movie in twenty-five years with an entirely Asian cast, kept trying to find the right songs for the film's pivotal final scenes.

He tried songs from big names like Rihanna and Sia, but nothing was quite right. He felt he simply had to use Coldplay's "Yellow" as the final song, to hit just the right emotional notes.

There was just one problem: Coldplay's record label had already said no. Though we don't know for sure the reasons why, perhaps there was some concern that the song's title, which is also a commonly used slur against Asians, would put the band in uncomfortable territory.

It's precisely for this reason Chu felt this just had to be the song he used for this breakthrough film. "We're going to own that term," Chu told the *Hollywood Reporter*. "If we're going to be called yellow, we're going to make it beautiful."[14]

Chu had a vision for how and why that one song would end his movie, but he was faced with some stark power dynamics. He was a virtually unknown filmmaker, and he needed to convince Coldplay, one of the most successful bands in the world, to lend one of its biggest hits to a project whose popular reception was completely uncertain.

Chu clearly had no authority; the one thing he could do, though, was try to influence. And Chu put every influence superpower into action in an attempt to get Coldplay to come over to his side.

He decided to write a letter addressed directly to the members of Coldplay: Chris Martin, Guy Berryman, Jonny Buckland, and Will Champion. He set out to build a relationship, even if one didn't exist at the time.

He began his letter by making a personal connection with them, building bridges and finding commonalities; he talked about being called the derogatory term himself in school and the complicated feelings he'd had with the word until seeing Coldplay's music video: "For the first time in my life, it described the color in the most beautiful, magical ways I had ever heard: the color of the stars, her skin, the love. It was an incredible image of attraction and aspiration that it made me rethink my own self-image."

Now that he had set the stage with an initial connection, he pivoted into painting a picture for Coldplay, laying out his vision for the scene that would take place in the movie while the song "Yellow" crescendoed on top. Calling it an "empowering, emotional march," he described in delightful detail how "Yellow" would fit perfectly into and complement the narrative.

From there, he pivoted back to empathy, putting himself in the band's shoes: "I know as an artist it's always difficult to decide when it's ok to attach your art to someone else's—and I am sure in most instances you are inclined to say no." He leaned into the tension he was sure Coldplay would feel here, owning the potential discomfort.

He then attempted to make it safe for Coldplay, outlining some of the initial accolades the film team had received and how the movie was based on a best-selling book, recognizing that it might feel risky for a world-famous band to trust a filmmaker without a long résumé behind him. He couldn't make it totally safe, but he could at least point to some external recognition the project had received in its early days.

In closing his letter, Chu leaned heavily into his strongest superpower here: passion and positivity. Talking about the impact that the band's song could have on a generation of Asian Americans, he wrote, "I want all of them to have an anthem that makes them feel as beautiful as your words and melody made me feel when I needed it most."

Less than twenty-four hours after Chu sent the letter, Coldplay approved his request.

He'd be able to bring the song he wanted more than any other into his film and, in so doing, end his film on an emotional high note, all while bringing his dream of reclaiming the term *yellow* to life.

Chu didn't have power, and he didn't have authority. But he did have influence. And to quote the lyrics from "Yellow," he turned that influence "into something beautiful."

BE THE CHANGE

Key Insights

- Microleadership breaks leadership down into its simplest and most profound unit: leadership moments. You can seize these moments whenever they arise; you don't need permission to practice microleadership.
- Sedona Prince and Jon Chu led change not through formal titles but rather through influence without authority. Prince fully embraced microleadership to seize a leadership moment, and Chu applied multiple influence superpowers to persuade one of the world's biggest bands to join his change effort.

- Influencing can sometimes feel sleazy, but by practicing influence superpowers like investing in relationships, employing empathy, and making it safe for others, you can influence effectively in honest and transparent ways.

Changemaker Challenge
- Pay attention to all of the leadership moments that pop up around you in the next week. Commit to performing at least one act of microleadership in the first day, two in the second day, and all the way to seven by the seventh day.
- Choose one or two of the influence superpowers you most want to develop, and then select one of these challenges below to put those superpowers into practice:
  o Select a favorite nonprofit organization and convince someone you know to post about the organization on social media.
  o Choose a favorite animal and use your influence superpower to get a friend to send you a picture of them posing like that animal, without telling them why.
  o Convince a stranger to sing you happy birthday after you tell them that it's not actually your birthday.

Chapter 8

Becoming the Leader You Wish You Had

Whether it's student changemakers at UC Berkeley, water-access change-makers I've coached in Phnom Penh, or technology changemakers I've advised in the Midwest, one common thread in their prowess of leading positive change is "applied empathy." Not just seeing things from another's perspective, but actively doing something with that newfound perspective.

I have the wonderful privilege of getting to know so many change-makers at the very beginning of their journeys, when they are filled with raw energy and excitement for change but unsure of where to channel it. One simple maxim I offer is: "Be the _____ you wish you'd had." Be the boss you wish you'd had. Be the mentor you wish you'd had. Be the parent you wish you'd had. Be the teacher you wish you'd had. Or be the friend you wish you'd had. It's a simple but inclusive way to put empathy into practice: We know what it is like to lack something, and so we can consciously decide to provide it to others.

This is especially applicable as we think about establishing and defining our own leadership styles. Is there something you wish other leaders had done for you? If so, what a perfect opportunity to make sure those you lead don't miss out like you did. As a student attending a hypercompetitive high school, I often felt a lack of "psychological safety" (we'll explore this concept later in this chapter). So on the first day I stepped to the front of the Berkeley Haas lecture hall, I decided then and there that one of the tenets of my leadership as an educational changemaker would be to ensure that all of my students feel psychologically safe—something I so wish I had felt when I was sitting in their place years ago.

In this chapter, we will help you become the leader that you wish you had. We'll explore essential leadership practices that bring out the best in others and in your teams: inclusive leadership and psychological safety. We'll discuss why diversity is an essential asset to any team and share some perspectives on how to apply lenses of diversity, equity, and inclusion to your change efforts. And because there is no single "right" way to lead, we will discuss different approaches to leadership and help you find the style that is true to who you are as a leader and changemaker.

This chapter is a thoroughly inclusive invitation to become the leader you wish you had. The people you lead deserve it.

PICTURING INCLUSIVE LEADERSHIP

There's a single image indelibly seared into my mind that I immediately picture when I think of the term *inclusive leadership*. It's a photo of New Zealand's prime minister, Jacinda Ardern, and representatives of the Muslim community in Christchurch in March 2019. The community was reeling from a mass shooting in a local mosque, where over fifty members had been killed by a xenophobic murderer less than twenty-four hours previously.

The photo shows Ardern wearing a black headscarf, hands clasped in front of her, with a look on her face that somehow simultaneously conveys compassion, resolve, concern, and love. Her posture, the look in her eyes, and her decision as a non-Muslim to show respect by wearing a headscarf all combined to tell us everything we need to know about her leadership style.

When US president Donald Trump called her and asked what the United States could do for New Zealand at this sorrowful moment, Ardern could have asked for anything she wanted.

Her response was unambiguous: to offer "sympathy and love for all Muslim communities."[1]

Her focus as her nation's leader was making sure that the most vulnerable under her watch felt safe. Her attention and care was on them, not on herself—choosing first to take care of others.

That's inclusive leadership, and it's remarkable to see this example coming from a head of state at the scale of national and international politics. And while Ardern led from the highest position of power and authority, changemakers of all kinds can bring that same inclusive leadership approach to those around them, whether in smaller groups, teams, or organizations.

UNDERSTANDING INCLUSIVE LEADERSHIP

Management consulting firm Korn Ferry defines *inclusion* as "leveraging the wealth of knowledge, insights, and perspectives in an open, trusting, and diverse workplace."[2] I think this is a pretty good definition, and to give a leadership lens to it, I'd like to add two amendments: Inclusive leadership extends beyond the workplace and is equally important and impactful in teams, partnerships, and formal groups; really, any time that people gather together in some way, leading inclusively matters. Second, inclusive leadership empowers people to be their full selves.

But before we learn how to practice inclusive leadership, let's first look at why it matters.

In 2017, global consulting firm Deloitte looked at thousands of employees across industries to attempt to measure the impact of inclusive leadership.[3] The results are staggering.

One of its major findings is the power of a single inclusive leader. Deloitte found that one inclusive leader on a team can account for an up to 70 percent increase in the number of employees who feel highly included. One need not be the CEO to lead inclusively, and these data show that even a lower-level manager can have outsized impact.

The positive ramifications are wide-ranging when inclusive leadership is present. Deloitte found that teams are 20 percent more likely to say they make high-quality decisions and 29 percent more likely to report collaboration. Inclusive leadership unlocks better and more integrated decision-making at the team level. But when entire organizations have an inclusive culture, Deloitte found that they were twice as likely to meet or exceed financial targets and six times more likely to be innovative and agile.

The data are clear: Inclusive leadership matters for the individual to be at their best. And, increasingly, inclusive leadership is necessary for teams and organizations to thrive as well.

Inclusive Leadership: What Not to Do

Juliet Bourke, adjunct professor at the University of New South Wales in Australia, and organizational psychologist Andrea Titus have done terrific work on identifying six keys to becoming an inclusive leader.[4] Let's start by reviewing what their research says are the traits that the *least* inclusive leaders have, so that we can be aware of these noninclusive traps.

By comparing the most inclusive leaders with the least inclusive leaders in their research set, Bourke and Titus were able to isolate three behaviors common to the least inclusive leaders:

<u>Overpowering others.</u> This is a trait all too common in the "old" style of leadership we discussed in chapter 6. For so long, leaders have (mistakenly) held the belief that good leaders force their ideas on others. In actuality, when a leader overpowers others by trying to have all of the answers, it limits the ability and motivation of those around them to contribute and participate themselves. I worked with a senior vice president who by most accounts was a successful leader, but feedback showed his team didn't feel comfortable participating in meetings he led. Deloitte's data makes clear that this means the team was missing out on important insights. He and I realized together that he mistakenly thought leadership meant always having the answer, so he felt pressure to always tell the team what to do. But he learned to step back and ask more questions so that others might actively participate. I encouraged him to ask questions, even when he felt sure of the right approach; if and when someone

mentioned the idea he'd had all along, he would praise that person for their terrific contribution so that more and more people would feel comfortable sharing their suggestions.

Displaying favoritism. Whether it's along lines of race, class, age, or gender, or perhaps shared personal interests and backgrounds, it's all too common to play favorites. This could manifest in younger leaders showing a regular bias toward the contributions of fellow younger colleagues, at the expense of more experienced ones. Or it could manifest itself as regular Monday morning discussions that center on weekend activities like golfing or skiing, which some, but not all, colleagues participate in, leaving those who don't spend time on the links or the slopes feeling excluded. We've likely all had the experience of seeing someone playing favorites by regularly praising or placing more attention on someone else, and we know how exclusionary that can feel. We must regularly reexamine our biases—especially those we might not be conscious of— to ensure that we aren't leaving others feeling left out, even if we aren't doing so purposefully.

Discounting alternative views. As we'll learn in this chapter, teams that are more diverse and have a wider range of experiences and viewpoints perform better and are more innovative. But simply having a diverse team is not enough. As leaders, we must regularly show that we are open to diverging perspectives, especially when they go against what we might initially think or believe.

One leader with whom I worked was incredibly creative and resourceful, and exceptionally good at selling his ideas. He also had a penchant for speaking first. He would jump right into a brainstorm and effectively convince everyone in the room that his idea was the best before anyone else could weigh in. Occasionally, some people would push back, but he often got his way without others weighing in. He then wondered to me why he appeared, at least to himself, to be the only creative person on the team. I helped him see that because he presented his ideas so quickly and so forcefully, others didn't feel comfortable sharing their own ideas. Together, we worked on having him fight his impulse to always share his idea first and instead to make space for others to share theirs. Sometimes, those people would come up with the same idea he'd had; other times, they would offer divergent views. But by making space for others to weigh in, he learned to be a more inclusive leader who showed he welcomed others' perspectives and contributions, leading to wider-ranging and more effective brainstorms.

SIX TRAITS OF INCLUSIVE LEADERSHIP

Now that we've identified the traits of noninclusive leaders, let's turn our attention to the six key traits Bourke and Titus identified and explore how each of these connects to aspects of the changemaker mindset we've already learned.[5]

Visible commitment to inclusivity. We need to make inclusion a personal priority and articulate it to the team. Here's where beyond-yourself lessons come into play: As a leader, can you articulate a vision for the inclusive team you want to lead? And can you practice servant leadership in ensuring that your commitments are realized?

Humility. In the words of Bourke and Titus, this means to "admit mistakes and create the space for others to contribute." It's important to recognize that we as leaders need not have every answer ourselves and that we believe—and our actions consciously show—that we value the contributions of others to make all of us better. As we learned from Amy Ou and her colleagues, who studied humble CEOs (see page 65), this matters to the way organizations are run, decisions are made, and teammates feel included.

Curiosity about others. We must be willing to listen first and activate empathy to put ourselves in the shoes of our teammates. Here we may find Steve Zaccaro's "emotional flexibility" especially powerful as a tool to unlock our ability to connect with others—especially those different from us. Our ability to ask great questions as we lean into our curiosity and wonder will also help us be more inclusive leaders.

<u>Cultural intelligence.</u> It's necessary to be attentive to others' cultures and adapt as required. I experienced this myself during my first day of work in Stockholm, as I met with one of the most inclusive leaders I've ever known, Pär Viktorsson. As the only non-Swede in the office (and with Swedish language abilities on par with an average Swedish preschooler), I was navigating a brand-new culture. Pär welcomed my divergent path and did everything possible to make sure I felt included, from ensuring that documents were translated into English to offering me American holidays like the Fourth of July off from work. Though I never took him up on the holiday offer, the gesture meant the world to me. And as I reflected on how powerful this inclusive cultural intelligence was for me, I thought about how much more meaningful it must be when people from marginalized communities get to experience it. Working in Sweden was also a humbling experience for me as I sought to build cultural intelligence. I transitioned from being quite comfortable with a single culture to recognizing that to lead change I needed to adapt to a new culture as well. Pär led with such high cultural intelligence that I felt included from the first day. And that feeling of inclusion inspired the way I saw myself, even in a vastly different culture and context.

<u>Effective collaboration.</u> This means going beyond lip service, actively ensuring that everyone feels comfortable to share their perspectives and that the team welcomes diverse thinking, especially ideas that question the status quo. We saw in chapter 3 how a bias toward collaboration is a key changemaker trait; it shows up again here as a way to not just lead change but to inclusively invite others to be part of the change with us.

<u>Awareness of bias.</u> We all have blind spots, and while we may want to build a world that is more meritocratic, we must recognize the larger flaws in the system that prevent it from being so. Our biases take so many different forms: racial, gender, class, ability, sexuality, and more. There are also biases that may seem innocuous but still get in the way of being an inclusive leader. I've realized that one of my blind spots includes working primarily with entrepreneurs. As an entrepreneur myself, I feel a kinship

with others who are crazy enough to try and launch their own organization. As a result, when we did our initial hiring for StartSomeGood, we heavily biased our recruitment toward fellow entrepreneurs. Yes, entrepreneurs can be wonderful. But we also have lots of flaws—including, often, a lack of focus on operations and logistics. I realized that we had built a team of entrepreneurs that felt comfortable to me, but it wasn't an inclusive team when it came to skills or personality (or ability to create spreadsheets).

There's a natural tendency to want to avoid recognizing our own biases, because, let's face it—it can be uncomfortable! But perhaps my favorite finding from Bourke and Titus is this: When an awareness of bias is combined with high levels of humility in a leader, this increases employees' feeling of inclusion by 25 percent on average. The lesson here is so powerful. We all have biases. But when we also have the humility to recognize and actively work on them, applying a growth mindset instead of feeling shame and ignoring them, that combination enables us to be even more inclusive, because it helps us take action to address our potential biases.

IS IT SAFE?

An ambitious, high-growth company like Google, staffed by some of the brightest minds from around the world, might not be what first comes to mind when we think about psychological safety. Yet it's that very dichotomy that makes Google such a terrific case study to anchor our discussions of creating environments and teams where people feel psychologically safe.

If there's one thing Google knows, it's data. So it's no surprise that when the company set out to discover what makes certain teams at Google most effective, it turned inward to examine its DNA and began a rigorous, data-informed study of its teams, encompassing more than one hundred thousand employees.

If you were to take a guess, especially at a company like Google, you might reasonably surmise that the most effective teams have strong technical expertise. Or they might have both highly qualified and well-trained engineers and businesspeople. That was certainly my first thought as I began reading Google's results from its project code-named Aristotle (a tribute to Aristotle's koan: "The whole is greater than the sum of its parts").

Google's researchers analyzed team effectiveness across four dimensions:[6]

1. Executive evaluation of the team
2. Team leader evaluation of the team
3. Team member evaluation of the team
4. Sales performances compared to quarterly quotas

The results were striking. What Google found is that "what really mattered was less about who is on the team, and more about how the team worked together." Researchers found that team traits like dependability and purpose were important. But there was one singular trait that stood out above every other variable: psychological safety.[7]

Even in a company like Google, which prides itself on innovation and questioning the status quo, it wasn't about individual traits but rather about team culture. And the most significant (statistically and culturally) aspect of team behavior is this single powerful concept. Let's explore what it is, why it matters, and how you can create it in your teams.

Psychological Safety

Harvard professor Amy Edmondson deserves credit for identifying and bringing the concept into modern management science. Edmondson is an expert on teams and the process of teaming up to accomplish goals, and her research mirrors that of Google's.

Edmondson defines *psychological safety* as "a shared belief held by members of a team that the team is safe for interpersonal risk taking," "a sense of confidence that the team will not embarrass, reject, or punish someone for speaking up," and "a team climate characterized by interpersonal trust and mutual respect in which people are comfortable being themselves."[8] Google adds to this definition, asserting that when psychological safety is present, members of a team "feel confident that no one on the team will embarrass or punish anyone else for admitting a mistake, asking a question, or offering a new idea."[9]

Put simply, it's a feeling of security that comes from knowing that all members of the team can be themselves, and can put themselves out there, without risking their reputation or well-being.

For any of us who have felt suffocated from teams that lack psychological safety, it's like a breath of fresh air to be our full, creative changemaking selves.

The Safety to Innovate

While Google's study stands out for its scale and scope in proving the importance of psychological safety, it's a concept getting more and more research attention elsewhere as well. Markus Baer, a professor at Washington University in St. Louis's Olin Business School, has also studied the concept in great depth and in diverse fields, with a particular lens on its role in innovation. From reviewing many separate studies by Baer, Edmondson, and others around the world, we can see the positive impact of psychological safety in absolutely unambiguous terms. The data from these studies show that the presence of psychological safety:

- Improves the likelihood that a given attempted innovation will be successful, while also improving overall innovation at the team level[10]
- Increases the amount of learning team members gain from making mistakes[11]
- Boosts employee engagement and retention[12]
- Makes it more likely that teammates will embrace and harness the power of diverse ideas from their teammates[13]

How can you establish and reinforce the presence of psychological safety in your teams, whether or not you are the formal leader? Here are some suggestions based on Edmondson's research and some tactical approaches that have worked well for my teams.

The first suggestion is to frame each challenge as a "learning problem" rather than an "execution problem." When challenges are presented this way, we can acknowledge uncertainty (which will no doubt be there in any change effort you pursue!) and lean into our interdependency. When a challenge is simply about execution, its focus on converging—without time to diverge—might be efficient, but it will often exclude other voices, perspectives, approaches, ideas, and connections that could be leveraged in pursuit of learning about a problem.

The second suggestion is to acknowledge our own fallibility. By modeling the very behavior you hope to engender among others, it helps those around you feel safe to do the same. It takes courage, and some humility, to lead in this way, but the power of leading by example helps show others that it's safe to take risks and be imperfect.

The third suggestion is to model curiosity. Instead of watching us as leaders provide the "correct" answer, seeing us instead lean into curiosity and powerful questions sets the stage for others to feel comfortable putting forward their own ideas. It reinforces that we are pursuing learning, not just execution, and by showing ourselves to be curious, it inspires this same approach in others.

A Tactical Approach

Here are some strategies you as a changemaker can use to ensure that everyone on your team feels psychologically safe. These tools are based on what I've experienced in my own work.

First, <u>give everyone a chance to put ideas forward before making a decision.</u> It can be tempting to settle on the first idea that seemingly sounds good to most people and doesn't get any initial pushback. But this is like settling for "compromising" instead of "collaborating" in the TKI model (see page 78). It's the path of least resistance, but if you as a leader are not waiting for others to speak up, you might be missing out on their ideas because they don't feel safe to suggest them.

You can create this environment in multiple ways: during a meeting, as you go around the room inviting everyone for their input; sending out a survey before or after you meet; or leveraging other tech-enabled platforms to let everyone add their voice to the conversation. It may take longer to ensure that everyone has a chance to share their perspective but consider making it a practice to actively ask everyone for their ideas and perspectives, instead of relying on the loudest voices to emerge. You want to make sure all members of your team feel included and comfortable sharing their voice.

Next, embrace Zaccaro's "cognitive flexibility" (see page 111), the ability to actively consider two different and potentially conflicting scenarios simultaneously. There are often pressures and cognitive biases that push us to go with our first instinct. While this may end up being the answer we go with, a leader who can consider multiple perspectives—especially those that directly diverge from their own—makes it safe for others to disagree or weigh in with minority opinions.

Next, celebrate failing forward. One of the values important to my team at Reach for Change in Sweden was that we would "proudly and consciously fail forward." We would open every single weekly team meeting by going around the group with answers to two questions: What was your win of the week (the thing you did that propelled us closer to our goals)? And how did you fail forward last week?

The phrasing here is deliberate. We didn't just celebrate any failure (for instance, not responding to a crucial email) but rather we doubled down on the learning that failure can bring us. Doing so accomplished two specific goals: It reminded teammates every single week that we wanted them to try out new things (even if that meant failing at them), so that we could continue learning from our failures and each other; and it modeled the exact type of psychological safety we wanted to cultivate in everyone on the team, from interns to executives. By normalizing failure, it made it safe to admit mistakes, no matter what role someone had, because we all failed, and we all encouraged failure-enabled learning in each other.

Finally, <u>be watchful for absolute unison on the team, especially for an idea you yourself proposed.</u> It may be the case that you came up with a brilliant idea (in that case, congratulations!), but it might also be the case that others don't feel comfortable diverging from your strong opinions or confidence, like with the senior vice president we met earlier in this chapter, whose team was hesitant to participate in his meetings. In this case, consider asking someone—even if they agree with you—to take the opposite position and point out potential flaws in the idea. At worst, you'll gain some new perspectives that will strengthen the existing idea. And you will signal to others that you want the strongest answer, not just the easiest answer, which will encourage them to take risks and put bold new ideas forward.

A DEI LENS ON CHANGEMAKING

The most fundamental belief running throughout this book is that anyone and everyone can be a changemaker. And I hope that this book is, indeed, a radically inclusive playbook for changemakers of all kinds to lead positive change that is true to them—including, and especially, you.

However, we must also recognize that the process of developing an identity as a changemaker and learning the skills to turn ideas into reality is not the same for each of us. Each of us puts our own changemaker identity on top of existing identities that are core to who we are, and these identities intersect with our ability to lead positive change in myriad ways—some in incredibly helpful ways and others in ways that present systemic barriers beyond us as individuals.

While I have done my best to write this book as inclusively as possible, I know I have my own blind spots and recognize that there may be parts of this book that, for whatever reason, don't quite work for your unique situation. Changemakers recognize that talent is equally distributed but opportunities are not. And that, in and of itself, is a meaningful call for change.

Changemakers can, and must, build a more meritocratic system. But we are not there yet. Changemakers can, and must, ensure that everyone has access to opportunities. But we are not there yet. Changemakers can, and must, create a world that works for each of us. But we are not there yet.

So there is important work to be done in diversity, equity, inclusion, and more. And as changemakers, we choose to actively lean into this reality not as an insurmountable challenge but as the opportunity of a lifetime to inspire other changemakers to realize their potential as well.

Diversifying Your (Team) Portfolio

One place to start is by consciously building and contributing to diverse teams.

We shouldn't need data in order to find motivation to invest in cultivating a diverse team. I'm wary of the request we often hear for the need to make the "business case" for diversity, when the real motivation should simply be to do the right thing in dismantling historical patterns of bias and oppression. But it may also be helpful to remember that for our changemaker endeavors, the data are clear: More diverse teams lead to greater innovation and better performance.[14]

The University of Maryland's Cristian Dezsö and Columbia University's David Ross teamed up to look at the intersection of gender diversity and performance of the top firms in the S&P Composite 1500 list. Their results showed that, on average, "female representation in top management leads to an increase of $42 million in firm value."[15] Further, the "innovation intensity" of these firms (defined as the ratio of research-and-development costs to total assets) goes up alongside gender diversity.

We observe similar relationships between innovation and racial diversity. Orlando Richard, a professor at University of Massachusetts Amherst's Isenberg School of Management, and colleagues studied the executives of 177 US banks and their operations, and found that racial diversity was positively correlated to innovation.[16]

A diversity of viewpoints also greatly matters. In a supercreative study, researchers Denise Lewin Loyd, Cynthia S. Wang, Katherine W. Phillips, and Robert B. Lount Jr. had 163 participants read a murder-mystery story and make a claim about who they thought committed the crime.[17] They also asked these participants whether they identified as a Democrat or a Republican. The participants were then asked to write an essay to make their case to convince another group member that their murder suspect committed the crime. In each case, participants were told that the person they would meet with disagreed with their opinion, but they would need to come to an agreement with that person nonetheless. Half of the participants were told that they'd be making their case to a member of the same party as them; half that they'd make the case to someone from the opposite party. The results were striking: Democrats prepared much more for meeting with a Republican than for someone from their own party; the same pattern held true for Republicans. According to the authors, "When disagreement comes from a socially different person, we are prompted to work harder. Diversity jolts us into cognitive action in ways that homogeneity simply does not."[18]

FINDING YOUR LEADERSHIP STYLE

As we close out this chapter on becoming the leader you wish you had, I want to proactively address something so many of my students struggle with when I ask them, for their first paper of the semester, how they would describe their leadership style. So many students have been conditioned to believe that there is a single leadership style, the pinnacle to which we must all aspire. And while there absolutely are mindset and leadership traits that I believe the best leaders and changemakers have—concepts we've discussed already, including empathy, resilience, courage, and kindness—there is no single, prototypical way to lead.

For so long, we have put a singular type of leader on a pedestal:

the extrovert, the schmoozer, the visionary, the hyperconfident. But this does a disservice to both individuals who don't fit this incredibly narrow mold and to the world that suggests that people must conform to one archetype in order to be effective. It leads individuals to doubt their own ability to self-identify as a leader (a pattern I've unfortunately seen be especially pronounced among women and people of color in my courses) and, therefore, to limit their own capacity and potential as a leader.

So let's be clear: There is no single way to practice leadership and no singular way to be a changemaker.

Six Leadership Styles

In my early days leading StartSomeGood, a mentor gave me a copy of psychologist Daniel Goleman's classic piece from 2000, "Leadership That Gets Results."[19] Goleman articulates six leadership styles used by managers, each with its own strengths and weaknesses. I quickly skimmed the paper, and then while I was out for a run, a light bulb went off: I had been trying for so long to make my own leadership style fit what I thought others wanted of me, trying to force a square block into a round hole. For instance, despite always being very focused on relationship building in other roles, I mistakenly started believing that by virtue of my new leadership title, I now had to focus exclusively on bottom-line results, even though this narrow focus always felt discordant to me. Instead of taking the time to coach and support a teammate to grow into a stretch role, I started believing that I needed to tell them exactly what to do in order to maximize efficiency.

But I learned it's not about having a singular leadership style; it's about being able to pull on the right leadership style at the right time, while applying a changemaker mindset to each. I cut my run short (as if I needed any extra motivation to do so) in order to go read the piece properly. I studied the article then, and I continue to practice all six leadership styles at different times, depending on what a situation calls for. Some come more easily to me than others, but what I so love about Goleman's framing is that he shows that each of us can develop all six of these leadership styles, no matter our natural personality or previous leadership experiences.

1. Coercive, or the "Do what I say" approach. This approach demands immediate compliance and is best in a disaster, a turnaround situation, or when working with difficult teammates. It is crucial in some circumstances—for instance, in a burning building, where direction is needed—but it can often hurt both flexibility and the motivation of others.

2. Authoritative, or the "Come with me" approach. This approach mobilizes people toward a vision and is best when a team is lacking direction. Here, a leader states the larger goal but leaves individuals the flexibility and freedom to figure out how to best achieve it. This is challenging if you are less experienced or less traditionally qualified than others on the team.

3. Affiliative, or the "People come first" approach. This approach creates harmony and builds emotional bonds. Affiliative leadership is terrific for increasing team morale and ensuring that everyone gets along well. But its downsides include allowing underperformers to continue without reprimand. And because these leaders are less likely to offer advice, sometimes employees are frustrated when they need more direct input.

4. Democratic, or the "What do you think?" approach. This approach forges consensus through participation. It's great for building flexibility, driving up responsibility, and bringing in fresh ideas. But the downsides can include meandering meetings and confused employees who clamor for stronger direction.

5. Pacesetting, or the "Do as I do, now" approach. This approach sets high standards for performance, exemplified by the leader's own actions. For highly motivated teams, pacesetting works really well, but some teammates may feel overwhelmed by such drive and resent a pacesetting leader's tendency to take over a situation.

6. <u>Coaching,</u> or the "Try this" approach. This approach develops
    people for the future and works especially well to help team-
    mates improve their long-term performance or develop long-
    term skills. Coaching works well for motivated teammates but
    struggles for teammates who aren't keen on changing their ways
    in the first place.

I bet, like most of my students, as you read about these leadership
styles, one or two of them jumped out at you as approaches you feel
comfortable with and regularly put into practice. And I'm sure there was
at least one style, and perhaps multiple styles, that made you feel uncomfortable, or that you couldn't ever imagine using to lead.

I find Goleman's approach hugely liberating for us as changemakers,
because it shows us that we need not try to fit our personality into one
single leadership style. Instead, these are approaches we can try on like
various hats, depending on the situation and the needs we and our team
are facing. We can put on our "authoritative" leader persona to get something done for a day without defining ourselves with that label. We can
be a pacesetter when our team needs leadership by example, but then we
can switch to a different style when that tool has done its job.

Just like changemaking is not one-size-fits-all, neither is our leadership style. We can all lead in a way that is true to ourselves. And if we
decide to be the leader we wish we had, we can ensure that we bring out
the very best in those around us while we do so.

BE THE CHANGE

Key Insights
- Psychological safety is the most important success factor Google found among
  its teams. It's characterized by a feeling of mutual trust and respect, where
  risk-taking is embraced and where it's clear that the team will not embarrass
  or reject someone for speaking up.

- The most powerful way to be an inclusive leader is to combine a recognition of our biases with the humility to know we need to work on them.
- Bringing a diversity, equity, and inclusion lens to our changemaker work is not only the right thing to do; it also increases the chances of innovation and solutions that will work for more people.

Changemaker Challenge

- Reflect on the six leadership styles presented at the end of this chapter. Think about which of these you most commonly use and which is most challenging for you. Try to apply each of them, at least once, in the next week. What happens when you try out these different styles?

PART 3

CHANGEMAKER ACTION

Chapter 9

Sparking Change: From Idea to Action

At its best, entrepreneurship is about so much more than go-to-market strategies and business plans. It's a deeply personal endeavor, a way to transform one's values, perspectives, and experiences into a real-world manifestation.

That's a lesson I learned myself as I retraced my family's roots along the backstreets of Shanghai, China.

As Jews living in Berlin and Vienna during the rise of the Third Reich under Adolf Hitler, my relatives faced increasingly grave danger. Though they had loved living in these cultural capitals, they began to realize that Europe was no longer safe for them and they had to leave. Fearing for their lives, they wanted to come to the United States, but they could not get a visa. So they applied what I think of as an entrepreneurial mindset to find other solutions and eventually found a place that would take them: Shanghai, China.

Shanghai was an open port and didn't require documentation. My family set sail on a twenty-four-day voyage, departing from Trieste, Italy, on the ocean liner SS *Conte Verde*, headed for this unexpected country. In all, about twenty thousand refugees ended up in what was called the Restricted Sector for Stateless Refugees, and most stayed until the end of the war in 1945. My relatives ended up living in a Jewish ghetto (sometimes called Little Vienna), separated from much of the city.

Nearly eighty years later, work took me to Shanghai, and I set out to investigate this part of my family's history.

I was armed with a book my dad had given me, containing the addresses of all known Jews in Shanghai during the 1940s, with Chinese addresses translated into German. I took these addresses, translated them into English and then, with the help of Google Maps and Google Translate, into the modern-day Chinese street names.

I managed to find the exact address, on which stood the very same building, where my grandmother's side of the family lived. And while I couldn't find the precise address for my grandfather's side, I traversed the dilapidated back alleyways close to their home where I know he would have walked daily.

I also visited the Shanghai Jewish Refugees Museum, which is located right in the heart of the Hongkou District, where they lived.

Not only did this experience change forever how connected I felt to my family, but it also transformed the way I thought about entrepreneurship.

I had always heard about how my family had started a Viennese café in the middle of their Jewish ghetto in Shanghai as a way to bring a bit of their old-world life to this new world in which they were living.

I never fully appreciated this endeavor until I toured the museum and I saw photo after photo of their café highlighted as a crucial part of the Jewish refugee experience in Shanghai. I pressed a button on an interactive display in the museum and saw the Viennese café come to life. I asked the tour guide about the café, and he went on and on about how it was a center for connection and joy for residents, amid their many challenges, including their sorrow for an old life they all missed.

There's no question there was much despair among the residents of this restricted sector. But my family took action, bringing its values to life in a café that ended up becoming so much more than a place for coffee or a pastry. I saw what entrepreneurship looks like in its truest sense—a passionate undertaking—and a way in which your values, beliefs, and work can extend far beyond yourself.

As I walked the Hongkou streets alone, I imagined my very family walking these same streets decades earlier (likely feeling similarly alone and disoriented), and I felt an indescribable connection. Though the Viennese café no longer stood, its values and its impact did. So did its connection among other refugees, and even its connection to an American grandson almost a century later.

As musician Joan Baez says, "Action is the antidote to despair." Standing on the streets of Shanghai as the traffic and commotion swirled around me, I thought back to my relatives. I imagined for the first time what it really must have been like for them here then and recognized just how meaningful it was to me that my family chose in those moments to take action.

THE CHANGEMAKER IMPACT EQUATION

Building on the words of Joan Baez, I will begin this chapter with a challenge for you.

By this point, you have developed a changemaker mindset and you've expanded your changemaker leadership skills. Now I'll introduce what I call the changemaker impact equation:

$$(\text{MINDSET} + \text{LEADERSHIP}) \times (\text{ACTION}) = \text{IMPACT}$$

This simple equation shows that your impact as a changemaker is a function of the sum of your mindset and your leadership multiplied by the action you take.

In other words, the impact you have as a changemaker can be measured by the mindset and leadership you bring to your work multiplied by the action you take with them.

In class, once I've presented the equation, I call on a math or physics major and ask them to answer another important math question. They perk up, probably ready to quote some theorem I've never heard of. But then I ask them quizzically, "What does a number multiplied by zero equal?"

"Zero," they quickly reply.

"But what happens if you multiply a huge, huge number by zero?" I ask again, feigning incredulity.

"Still zero."

Even if you have a finely tuned changemaker mindset and sharp leadership skills for catalyzing positive change, if you never take any action, you will never have any impact as a changemaker.

The changemaker impact equation serves as the jumping-off point as we explore together how to take action to catalyze change for ourselves, our communities, and our world.

Even the most talented changemakers I know struggle with taking those first steps on a new idea or project. Therefore, this chapter focuses on those crucial first steps to help you spark an initial idea into reality. We'll see how changemakers in fields ranging from medicine to art to sports to business took their first steps and we'll explore what we can all learn from the broader field of entrepreneurship—even though most of us will never be entrepreneurs ourselves—about starting something that matters.

StartSomeGood has supported thousands of changemakers in taking the first step in their changemaker journey. This has afforded me the most incredible privilege of having a vantage point into the lessons we can all learn about what it takes for changemakers to go from nothing to something, taking those scary but crucial first steps. Combined with supporting my students with their inspiring changemaker projects, I've seen consistent patterns around what actually helps changemakers get started—based on what really works, not oversimplified memes or empty inspirational rhetoric. I've distilled these insights down into six lessons, which I will share with you in this chapter.

You'll develop the art of agency—the ability to simultaneously feel frustration or despair while also believing you can go do something about it. You'll learn how to first fire bullets, then cannonballs—to first take lots and lots of small actions to give you confidence when it comes time to make a big, bold move later. You'll see how to reduce resistance to action by reframing problems and leveraging existing resources. You'll learn how to validate your ideas and then use the "lean startup" methodology to start small and iterate quickly. Finally, you'll learn how to know when it's time to take a leap—and why it's never a good idea to go discount skydiving! First, let's start with helping you develop your sense of agency. By the end of the chapter, I hope that the concept of taking action will feel much less scary, and that it will feel accessible to you.

THE ART OF AGENCY

I've learned that no matter who we are or what we are most passionate about, we almost always have greater agency to take action and create change than we might initially think. Let's look at how a couple of artists sparked changemaker initiatives at a local level, and then let's see how an entire nation banded together to start taking action collectively.

We begin by visiting Malpe Beach near Udupi in Karnataka, India. In 2018, this beautiful beach along the Arabian Sea was littered with countless plastic bottles that were ruining a picturesque shoreline and, more importantly, were wreaking havoc on the environment. Local artist and sculptor Janardhan Havanje sought a solution.

Using iron rods, he created a huge, open-netted fish-shaped sculpture named *Yoshi the Fish*. Alongside the sculpture were the words YOSHI LOVES PLASTIC. PLEASE FEED HIM.

The result? A fish-shaped piece of art filled with plastic bottles to be recycled, a beach free of debris, and a concept that would be copied on beaches around the world, perhaps most famously in Bali.

Havanje had reason to be frustrated. After all, he, as an individual, could never pick up all of the trash on the beach, but he found agency in his action and sparked positive change for his community.

For another example, let's travel to the US–Mexico border in El Paso, Texas, and Ciudad Juárez, Mexico, to see action taking place in a challenging locale. Virginia San Fratello and Ronald Rael, both professors and artists in the United States, had been scheming for around ten years about an art installation they might create at the border. In 2019, in the midst of deportations and family separations, they installed bright-pink seesaws through the fence so that children on both sides of the wall could play together. Not only did this installation create a moment of human connection, but it also presented a powerful philosophical viewpoint: that actions on one side of the wall—just like a seesaw—affect those on the other side of the wall. Rael explained to the *Guardian* that he wanted the seesaws to provide "a literal fulcrum" between the countries and to bring "joy, excitement and togetherness at the border wall."[1]

To be clear, this art installation itself doesn't change policies or laws. That would require "systems change," a changemaker approach we will discuss in chapter 11. But this installation, which received wide media coverage, took action in the face of despair and helped many see the wall, and its related policies, in a brand-new way.

The same feeling of agency to create change that these artists found can also be applied collectively in a group—even an extremely large one. Let's look at how collective action took shape at the nation-state level. In 2019, the citizens of Ethiopia banded together to tackle the existential threats of deforestation and climate change by planting trees. And not just a few trees. In a single day, over 23 million Ethiopians came together to plant 353 million trees![2] Students were granted time off from school, and civil servants time off from work, to contribute to the planting initiative. Climate change can feel like an intractable problem for any one individual (the world record for trees planted in a single day by a single person is about fifteen thousand in 2001). But with each of us choosing to take action, a collective sense of agency to begin addressing even the biggest challenges becomes possible.

Giving ourselves permission to start taking action can be hard, especially for first-time changemakers. Sometimes inaction feels like the safer or easier path. But as facilitator and coach Brandi Nicole Johnson reminds us: "Inaction is an action."[3] So let's choose action.

CANNONBALL!

Of all the things I'd imagined investing a good amount of time in while running StartSomeGood in the early days of its existence, spending hour after hour on the phone with banks and pleading with payment processors was certainly not one of them. We had envisioned that StartSomeGood would support changemakers all around the world. We therefore decided to go all in to being a global platform from day one—an inspiring endeavor, to be sure, but one that tested my patience as much as my ability to navigate customer-service phone lines at all hours of the day. We didn't fully appreciate the challenge of being able to support transactions on our site like having a supporter in Mexico contribute toward a venture in Thailand—an experience that forced me to learn more about currency exchange markets than I ever wanted to know.

Our intentions were good, and our vision for global change was noble. But with limited resources, we simply took on way too much complexity early on, diverting my time and attention away from building our website and community to instead getting on a first-name basis with at least a dozen call-center employees around the world, whom I had to constantly turn to for help. We did too much too soon, instantly attempting to be global, instead of starting off with some incremental first steps toward internationalization. This rush to the big change we want to create is one I often see in changemakers I mentor, as well.

During my office hours, an undergraduate student, Samar, presented a change challenge to me: He's an outstanding swimmer and is passionate about his part-time job as a swim teacher. He's even come up with a bunch of creative swimming techniques that are extremely effective. But Samar's manager at the swim club refused to give him permission to teach these techniques, or anything that deviated from the required curriculum.

Samar wanted to create change; he had a clear vision for all of the new stroke techniques he would teach. He was confident in his ability to help these young swimmers realize their full potential if he were just given the chance to do so. However, with the power imbalances between Samar and his manager, and the negative response from his manager to any of his innovations, his only path forward seemed to be to keep teaching the same less effective technique. He wanted so badly to question the status quo but felt there was no path around his stubborn manager.

He asked me what to do, and I recalled the insights from Morten Hansen and Jim Collins: First fire bullets, then fire cannonballs.[4]

Through their review of big organizations, the authors help us see that often what looks like one single big bet on a strategy is actually the sum of lots of small tests, which then provide the confidence to go big.

Apple's iPhone was a big bet, but Apple didn't start with the iPhone. It tried the iPod first, in 2001. Then, in 2003, the iTunes music store. These were bullets—relatively smaller tests to see whether Apple could hit the target. As the company got a better and better sense of where the target was and how to reach it, it gained confidence in 2007 to go big and fire the massive cannonball: the iPhone. When Steve Jobs pulled the iPhone out of his pocket during his keynote, it seemed to many observers to be a singular bold action. But because he was informed by Apple's previous "bullets," Jobs was able to unveil the iPhone with the confidence that it would succeed.

So often with change initiatives we think we have one single shot and it's a make-or-break moment. Samar was envisioning one contentious meeting with his boss where he would lay out his entire refreshed curriculum and give his manager an ultimatum to let him try all of these techniques or else he might leave. That would be far too much pressure on everyone involved and would be unlikely to provide his best shot at hitting the target. Instead, I encouraged him to think about how he could try some smaller tests to gain confidence and feedback before going big.

When I asked Samar how he might apply this concept to his teaching, he got it immediately: He said he could try teaching one single new technique to one child and see how it worked. He could offer to volunteer for one hour with the more advanced children alongside another coach. He could model the more effective technique himself without asking any children to copy him.

At the start of our office hours, Samar couldn't find any path forward toward leading change besides launching his cannonball, but he left office hours with lots and lots of ideas for small bullets to fire as a way to start overcoming the knowing-doing gap. He ended up convincing his manager to let him try a single new technique with a single swimmer. Once that swimmer's times improved, Samar then got more leeway from his manager to bring his new ideas into his teaching. While he didn't overhaul the entire curriculum (at least within a few months), Samar got to bring lots of his techniques into the pool, and everyone was better off for it.

THE BUILDING BLOCKS OF CHANGE

Sometimes a change initiative will call for creating a brand-new company, organization, or endeavor. If so, this is great, but this can feel overwhelming or intimidating to many changemakers, who might not feel called to start something new. Sometimes change happens from within; this is called intrapreneurship, the cornerstones of which are seeing problems in a new way while leveraging existing resources effectively. Changemaker Luis Sota embodies both of these, and his story shows how thinking differently and then bringing together the resources of his company and key stakeholders within his community helped him take his first steps of leading change.

In 2008, CEMEX, a leading building materials company, operated on four continents, with 260 distribution centers and over two thousand facilities around the world. Though its headquarters are in Monterrey, Mexico, the company's traditionally premium-priced products were struggling to gain traction in its home market, especially among low-income families aspiring to safer housing in semi-urban and urban areas.

The company considered traditional corporate social responsibility (CSR) models to make its products available to these families, such as donating a portion of revenues to provide free building materials. It also considered selling smaller, less expensive bags of concrete in lower-income neighborhoods.[5]

Its intentions may have been good, but its results were nonexistent.

Sota integrated his ability to weave together insights, empathy, and community and was able to view CEMEX's challenge in a completely new way. He then leaned into this new way of thinking and the resources he could leverage, including CEMEX's existing brand and infrastructure to start taking action. He envisioned a program far different from what CEMEX had imagined previously, which would both improve the lives of local families while also improving the bottom line for the company.

Sota set out to support people like Esperanza, a mom of two, who lived with her husband in their house of just eighty-six square feet, protected only by a leaky tin roof, and with just curtains separating the kitchen from the sleeping area.[6]

Sota's changemaker impact began with a simple but powerful realization: Families like Esperanza's weren't interested in the cement itself but rather in what that cement would make possible. They weren't motivated simply by access to cheaper materials; they, like everyone else, cared about building a safe and healthy space for their families.

Practicing empathy and designing solutions around actual community needs, Sota went back to CEMEX. Rather than start a new organization, he began taking action from within the company, finding ways to focus its resources toward this new opportunity for change. He transformed its product offerings from simply bags of cement to a full-featured suite of products. He convinced CEMEX leadership to offer these families not just cement but a wide variety of targeted innovations, including materials, microfinance, technical assistance, and logistical support. Families would also receive fixed pricing, so that if a housing build took a long time, families wouldn't find themselves unable to afford materials halfway through construction (and to allow for just-in-time deliveries throughout a project instead of risking theft along the way). CEMEX also offered advice from architects to help families avoid poor construction design at the outset. And Sota pioneered the option of fixed weekly payments—something CEMEX had never considered before.

All told, these innovations became Patrimonio Hoy, a new part of CEMEX, which works with local families to help them take control of their homes and lives. Through a combination of access to microcredit and building advice from the beginning of the build until the end, Patrimonio Hoy helped Esperanza and her family build a new housing unit. Sota's change initiative had, for the first time in her entire life, made a safe and healthy home accessible to her. She marked this new chapter by burning all of the old photographs of her old, unsafe home.

Patrimonio Hoy started with just a single family within a single community. From that initial action, spurred on by Sota's creative reframing of the opportunity, Patrimonio Hoy has now supported over five hundred thousand families, and its timely repayment rate is an incredible 99 percent. Sota's spark of action set in motion lasting positive change for consumers, and a profitable line of business for CEMEX. Sota reminds us that although sometimes change calls for something totally new, sometimes it calls for seeing things a bit differently.

What Is Intrapreneurship?

While intrapreneurship is sometimes defined as "corporate innovation," I prefer to think of the concept in a broader context. University College London (UCL) professor Tomas Chamorro-Premuzic describes it as "acting like an . . . entrepreneur, but within the ecosystem of a larger, more traditional organization."[7]

Intrapreneurs are the ones who can take a previously all-analog business and help it adapt to a digital-first world. Intrapreneurs are the ones who can deftly navigate internal politics and roadblocks to launch a new product or service. Intrapreneurs are the ones who can address what economist and management expert Clayton Christensen named "the innovator's dilemma," which explains why great companies often fail to adjust to new technologies.[8] In his book of the same name, Christensen shows us that the same practices that lead businesses to initially be successful can also eventually lead to their demise because of management and leadership approaches that fail to support continual innovation. Intrapreneurs are uniquely suited to lead the necessary changes to ensure that organizations continue to innovate even, and especially, when they have already found some success.

As the concept of microleadership shows us, one need not be an entrepreneur, or even an intrapreneur, to lead change. We can create change in even the smallest and simplest of ways. Changemaking is far more inclusive than entrepreneurship or intrapreneurship; what really matters is one's ability to combine a changemaker mindset and changemaker leadership skills together with action. But I've found that many of my students find a lot of inspiration in learning about the path of intrapreneurs, because it gives them a lens to start spotting opportunities for change from the very first day of their job—especially if they are at a big or more traditional organization.

IS YOUR IDEA A GOOD ONE?

One of my favorite books to read to my son is Kobi Yamada's brilliant story *What Do You Do with an Idea?* It's a picture book that tells the beautiful story of an idea and the child who brings it into the world. The title of his book is also one of the most common questions I receive from changemakers who are searching for validation of their idea. As you'll learn in the next section, the lean startup methodology—which is applicable far, far beyond traditional startups—is a perfect way to start seeing whether your idea is worth pursuing further. But so often changemakers fail to get started with taking action simply because they don't have confidence that their idea for change is a valid idea in the first place. I want to preempt that common question here with two terrific and accessible ways changemakers identify ideas worth developing: from data-driven insights and from lived experience.

Nadine Burke Harris trained as a medical doctor and began her career practicing medicine in San Francisco in 2005. About three years into her practice, she read a medical research paper that would introduce her to the idea that would transform her career: "The Relationship of Adverse Childhood Experiences to Adult Health: Turning Gold into Lead" by Vincent J. Felitti.[9] The study, based on research done in San Diego, showed a linkage between the presence of adverse childhood experiences (ACEs), such as divorce or an alcoholic parent, on all kinds of negative future health outcomes, from cancer to heart disease. This idea, backed by rigorous, data-informed medical research, became the cornerstone of Burke Harris's changemaker efforts. She gave a TED talk on the topic to raise awareness of the idea, and she created partnerships to create new clinical models for doctors to screen for and support children with ACEs.[10] She would go on to become the state of California's first-ever surgeon general, where she integrates awareness of and interventions for toxic stress throughout the state government, from public transportation to public education to, of course, public health. Burke Harris's changemaker work all came from an idea. And for her, this idea was data-informed and research-based.

Sam McCracken, a member of the Fort Peck Sioux and Assiniboine Tribes, began his career at Nike in 1997, working at the company's warehouse in Wilsonville, Oregon. Three years into his role, he developed an idea that was informed by all of his experiences to that point: both his community experiences and his professional ones. He pitched the idea for an Indigenous-inspired line within Nike, which would leverage the brand and its resources to encourage increased athletic participation among Indigenous communities. How did McCracken know this was an idea worth pursuing? "I heard there was a need in my community and I listened," he says.[11] How did he know this idea would be a fit with Nike? His idea for the N7 Fund, which is directly supported through sales of the N7 line of shoes and clothing, was anchored by Nike maxims like "It is our nature to innovate" and "Do the right thing." "I use the Nike brand for inspiration," he says. "We have a series of eleven maxims and I use them all." To date, the fund has raised nearly $8 million and has supported over five hundred thousand children.

The inspiration for your idea may be like Burke Harris's and informed by research, or your idea may be based on your own lived experience—personally, professionally, or beyond—like McCracken's. Both are valid, and both are powerful. Now that you have more confidence that your idea is one that is worth pursuing, let's see how the lean startup methodology can make putting it out into the world a bit less intimidating.

LEAN STARTUP FOR CHANGEMAKERS

Based on Steve Blank's customer development methodology and popularized by Eric Ries's 2011 book *The Lean Startup*, the essence of lean startup methodology is helping figure out if a proposed idea is worth pursuing as quickly as possible.[12]

Though *startup* is in the name, I believe this approach is helpful for any kind of change initiative, extending far beyond traditional startups. I've helped changemakers leverage this concept to take action on all kinds of different change initiatives, especially those far removed from startups or even corporate environments. So whether your change is in the arts, the sciences, or your community, the lean startup can help you learn how to confidently conceptualize and then take action on your ideas.

What's the opposite of the lean startup? It involves creating products with long build cycles, high up-front costs, late (if any) feedback, and lots of wasted time, energy, and money.

Enter the lean startup.

The lean startup is built around a cycle called the build-measure-learn loop. The cycle begins with an idea. It could be an idea for a startup business, a feature, or even a technique; think of Samar's more efficient swimming stroke.

We take that idea and build a "minimum viable product": the smallest, simplest test that will allow us to get feedback from users as to whether this idea has potential.

Minimum viable products come in many different forms:

- Dropbox cofounder Drew Houston had a vision for a file-syncing app, but he knew that building it would be incredibly costly. So he filmed a video mock-up showing what his app would do and he posted it to Reddit for feedback. People seemed to love the idea, and this initial feedback buoyed his confidence that the app was worth creating.

- Pebble was one of the first-ever smartwatches—way ahead of Apple Watch. Would people want a smartwatch? Its founders weren't sure, so they launched a minimum viable product; they put the concept out on the crowdfunding site Kickstarter, inviting people to back the product and receive a watch months later for doing so. Not only did Pebble pre-fund all of the manufacturing costs, but it also became the most successful campaign to that point in Kickstarter's history, showing that there was, indeed, demand for its watch.

Once we build a minimum viable product, we measure its response by collecting data. These data inform whether our initial hypotheses about the idea we came up with are true or not.

There are strong connections here to the scientific method. The lean startup helps us transform ideas into tests, from which we can then learn.

Not every minimum viable product will be successful like Dropbox's and Pebble's, and that's a great thing! Time is our most valuable nonrenewable resource, and a minimum viable product that doesn't work out is a gift, because it tells you that an idea isn't on the right path—at least yet—before you waste lots of time pursuing it.

In the lean startup methodology, there isn't anything like failure, only "validated learning." If you try to launch an after-school tutoring program for middle schoolers but no one shows up, this isn't a failure. This is an insight for you: that your idea didn't quite land. You've validated that a tutoring program for middle schoolers isn't the approach to take.

Based on the data you have collected, you can then use these insights—this validated learning—to go back to the beginning of the cycle again and come up with a new idea. Maybe you will try an after-school tutoring program for high schoolers instead. Or maybe you will try a weekend-tutoring program for middle schoolers.

The build-measure-learn loop repeats, going around and around and around, as you come up with an idea, build a minimum viable product, measure it by collecting data, learn from the data, and continue iterating again and again and again.

It's extremely unlikely that you will come up with a perfect idea for change, which requires no tweaking at all, by yourself right off the bat. Much more likely is that you have the beginnings of a really good idea, and through practicing the tenets of the lean startup, you can gain more and more confidence that you are, in fact, on to something and that your idea has potential.

The lean startup helps us test, not guess.

MAKING THE LEAP

There's a lot of fear wrapped up in change, especially in leading it. I tell this next story to my students to remind them that putting one's ideas out into the world is inevitably scary. It's totally normal to feel afraid; we all do. Often this feeling is simply a sign that the time has come for your idea to leap out of your head and off into the world.

In an effort to confront fear head-on, friends and I decided to use a Groupon discount for a suspiciously cheap price on our first skydiving experience. Of all of the things to never, ever use a half-off coupon for, I'd say skydiving should be at the very top of your list.

Fortunately, I lived to tell the tale (though I purposefully didn't tell my mom about this adventure until I was safely back on the ground), but there were so many warning signs we should have heeded before getting in the plane. I thought we would be taking off from a small airport. Nope. More of a grassy field with some dirt tracks. I thought we would get a full-on training of how to jump and what to do in every possible scenario. Nope. We got a ten-minute workshop, where the biggest takeaway was to try and not land on the ground standing up. I thought we'd have professional experts strapped to us in a tandem jump, who would ensure that every safety precaution was followed. Nope. I was strapped to a guy named Chuck, and I only learned once we were in the air that he didn't actually work at the center, he just volunteered to help out when a professional skydiver called in sick. I thought we'd have military-grade airplanes. Nope. We had planes that looked straight out of World War II, with a pilot who was also wearing a parachute (not exactly trust-inducing).

We were going skydiving on the day that I'd decided to quit my full-time job to focus exclusively on StartSomeGood. While I was doing work I loved at my nine-to-five, trying to run a high-growth social enterprise starting at 5 p.m. meant that I wasn't sleeping until 3 a.m., wasn't taking care of myself, and wasn't being the teammate either company needed of me.

Strapped to Chuck, with my feet dangling out of the plane as we reached our exit altitude nearly two miles up in the air, I knew it was time to go.

Just as looking out of the door of that old plane from ten thousand feet, the wind violently flapping my cheeks, was scary, so is being at the crossroads between having an idea and deciding to put it out into the world. Eventually, though, the time comes to check your parachute and jump.

Brené Brown teaches that on the other side of vulnerability is courage. And sometimes the most vulnerable thing imaginable is to put ourselves and our ideas out there.

While skydiving comes with physical danger, putting an idea for change out can feel equally dangerous, if just on the emotional side.

I made two big, scary leaps that day: one out of a plane, one into a change I cared deeply about pursuing.

It may never be perfectly logical to jump. After all, what person in their right mind would say it's a good idea to jump out of a plane? (Certainly not my mom.) And there are always reasons that would make us feel it's better to be safer, to take the easy path, and to never put our idea out into the world.

But I know that, as a changemaker reading this book, you have an idea inside you that can change the world.

I invite you to find that courage, to feel the fear, to embrace the vulnerability, and to still take action: Go take that leap.

BE THE CHANGE

Key Insights
- Action is how you put your changemaker mindset and changemaker leadership skills into practice to create impact.
- Before you start a new initiative, challenge yourself to see the existing obstacles in a fresh light and to examine whether existing resources can be used in a new way.
- Whether your idea comes from data-informed research or your own lived experience, you can use the lean startup model of build-measure-learn to test ideas early and often.
- Don't go for a discount skydive!

Changemaker Challenge

- Remember that the lean startup is not just for startups! It's helpful for change initiatives of all types. Think of a change you'd like to see become a reality, and come up with a minimum viable product that will allow you to take a small first step.
- Give yourself permission to practice the art of agency. Then go launch that minimum viable product and see what happens.

Chapter 10

Leading Change When Change Is Hard

"I was like, oh my goodness, I have to calm my nerves," Carolyn Davis said as she reflected on the moments before she delivered a three-minute speech in front of twenty-five thousand people at a packed University of Arkansas arena. She'd heard the boos that greeted the speaker before her. She said, "I'm thinking I'm next. And I think my heart just sunk even further."[1]

On the surface, Davis might have seemed like an unlikely person to be about to step up to address Walmart's executive leadership team and tens of thousands of shareholders. She's an associate at a Walmart store in the Outer Banks of North Carolina. Her town of Bayboro has a total population of 1,210, equivalent to less than 5 percent of the number of people in the crowd that day in June of 2017. She had never sought out the spotlight, especially with the risks that she knew might come from speaking out about an issue at her job. But as she recounted later on the podcast *WorkLife*, "The will to help people outweighed the notion that I might be fired."

Davis is a mother of two grown children and one grandchild, something that informed her decision to step up and become a changemaker. One of her colleagues was pregnant and was stuck in the unsettling position that so many new moms face: how to pay her bills while taking time off from work to recover from birth and be with her new child.

Davis realized that company executives received their full salary and ten weeks of paid family leave when they had a child, while associates like her received only half pay for six to eight weeks maximum. What could Davis do to change this? She started by talking to others.

She began with conversations. And when those conversations indicated that many other associates had struggled with the same issue, she took the next step: trying to engage a wider community on social media. From there, she did surveys to discover what store associates really needed, and then launched a petition to call on Walmart executives to change the company's policies. She'd expected a few hundred signatures. But Davis had tapped into a collective need. To her absolute shock, she gathered over one hundred thousand employee signatures. "To have a group behind you, giving you support, it makes a huge difference," she said. "There is power in numbers."

Davis had consistently wondered whether it was worth her time and effort to try and make change—especially when the odds were so stacked against her, due to power dynamics and fixed corporate policies. But her drive for giving a voice to others, and the feeling of knowing so many people were standing with her (even if they chose to remain anonymous, sending encouragement via email instead of signing their name), gave her purpose and encouraged her to keep going.

Armed with a box containing all the signatures, Davis and other colleagues hand-delivered it to the office of Walmart's CEO. Soon after, this reluctant public speaker was about to step up to the microphone, twenty-five thousand pairs of eyes fixed upon her.

"My name is Carolyn Davis, from store 1300. And I am a Walmart associate from the Outer Banks of North Carolina, where I proudly serve our customers," she began.[2] She then made her call for change clear: "Investing in associates means that new parents in Walmart are allowed time to bond with our children. Walmart's female executives receive ten weeks of paid family leave. Let's do the same for hourly associates, women and men." She used the remaining three minutes of her time to continue making the case for equality for all workers and to stand up for associates like her colleague who wanted time to be with her baby without worrying every day about whether she could still pay her bills.

By building a groundswell of support, and by giving voice to so many others, Davis had tapped into something powerful. Unlike the speaker before her, she was greeted with claps, and shouts of "Yes!" Davis didn't set out to be a vocal leader, but by taking many successive small steps, she was able to grab the microphone with the power of thousands behind her.

A few months after Davis's address, Walmart announced an expanded policy for paid family leave. Now all employees, including hourly employees, would receive ten weeks of full pay.

Davis said she was still in disbelief that it happened. "So many who wanted to stay anonymous because they are scared of retaliation... were in my inbox congratulating me, thanking me... for being brave for speaking out."

Davis had the odds against her when she started her change efforts. But, as we will learn in this chapter, she applied some crucial approaches for leading change when change is hard, from engaging different groups of stakeholders in unique ways to leveraging culture as a catalyst for change, to overcoming the status quo bias.

This chapter will give you the tools to keep pressing forward with your change efforts, teaching you approaches and tactics, so that even when you feel the inevitable fear and self-doubt, you will know that, just like Carolyn Davis, when the time comes for you to step up and lead change, you will be ready.

OH, THE PEOPLE YOU'LL MEET

NOBL (pronounced "no-bell") Collective is a group of organizational psychologists and change management experts who help individuals and teams lead change. They have identified "the three types of people you'll meet while implementing change," which is a helpful place for us to start as we begin thinking about how to lead change when change is difficult.[3] These are labeled as champions, cynics, and fence-sitters. Let's look at each, and the best ways I've learned to work with all three types.

Champions

Champions are inspired by the possibility of the change we are articulating.

NOBL suggests that we "get champions involved," by delegating projects and decision-making to them, supporting their ideas (when possible), and showing appreciation for their enthusiasm.

Clem Auyeung was perhaps the first champion of StartSomeGood. He sent me an email out of the blue, which I had to reread multiple times to make sure I was seeing it correctly. In it, Clem articulated how inspired he was by our vision, and he asked if there was any way we might consider bringing him on as an intern. At that point, we didn't have an organizational chart or business cards, let alone an internship program, but I could see that we had ignited something within Clem. His email was so compelling that we brought him on board on the spot.

I didn't yet know how talented Clem was or even what we would have him do for us. But I recognized a champion of our mission when I read that email and knew I wanted him to be involved. He would go on to work with us for a couple of years in various capacities and with increasing responsibility, and he left an indelible mark on our organization and our team. He was a champion from the very beginning, and we are so fortunate that he brought his enthusiasm to our vision. Champions help build a movement.

Cynics

Cynics are those who actively oppose change.

NOBL recognizes that "cynics' negativity can be annoying," but engaging with them and trying to convince them can often be a huge time suck when it comes to leading change. Here's the magic: "cynics are just disappointed idealists." Perhaps they have gotten their hopes up about change only to be let down.

Unlike a fence-sitter, a cynic is at least actively engaged with the change effort so spend your time delivering "something that matters" to your cynics, because actions will speak much louder than words. And if you are successful, your greatest cynics, once won over, will often become your greatest advocates.

This is something I experienced firsthand in the early days of Start-SomeGood, when our site was plagued by the inevitable bugs that come with launching a new, and early, technology. I received all kinds of emails from disappointed users, expressing emotions I couldn't have imagined generating from an early-stage startup. But rather than fighting them or telling them why their distrust of us or our platform was wrong, I tried to hear their complaints and then do something about them.

When a skeptic expressed disappointment at a missing feature, I didn't tell them why we had deprioritized it. Instead, I thanked them for their feedback and then as soon as that feature shipped, I would send them a note to ask them to help us test it out. Some of the cynics who authored some of the angriest of emails ended up becoming among our strongest and most ardent supporters once we proved to them that change was, indeed, possible. Optimism in action often won over even our harshest cynics.

Fence-Sitters

Fence-sitters are those who aren't sure what to think when it comes to change.

NOBL suggests leaving the fence-sitters to others. "Get some small wins on the board," NOBL advises, "and then let the champions and converted cynics take care of the fence-sitters." Just as we learned in the video of the dancing guy, once there is momentum, even the most persistent of fence-sitters will often come around.

I saw this firsthand with the fundraising campaigns we hosted on StartSomeGood, where changemakers would create a funding goal (totals ranged from a couple of hundred dollars all the way to hundreds of thousands of dollars) and a time frame to reach that goal (between one and sixty days). Only if the organization reached its funding goal by the deadline would it receive the funds; otherwise, no money would ever change hands. Digging into the data during the first two years of operations, we discovered something that absolutely blew us away: At that point, among hundreds of fundraising campaigns, every single fundraiser that reached 42 percent of its total funding goal would end up reaching or exceeding its goal. In other words, if a campaign could reach 42 percent of its target, it was virtually guaranteed to reach at least 100 percent.

At first we couldn't explain this phenomenon, but the framework of fence-sitters helps us understand why. The early supporters of a campaign are likely the champions. The fence-sitters, meanwhile, might think an organization is doing interesting work but may be skeptical of its ability to actually deliver on its proposed change. However, once the early champions have become engaged and there is a groundswell of momentum, these fence-sitters will more readily jump off the fence. In instances where an organization can't reach a modicum of success—42 percent of its goal—with early champions, the fence-sitters are less likely to engage. But if the organization and its champions can get early wins and build momentum, the fence-sitters are likely to jump in and help the change efforts grow to even greater heights.

Bringing It All Together

Carolyn Davis shows us what becomes possible when approaching each of these three groups with distinct strategies to catalyze change. Her first step was to build a community of champions. These people were willing to be among the first to sign their name to the petition and to work with her to help raise awareness at their own local stores, far from Davis's home store in North Carolina.

A large number of associates were fence-sitters. A lot of them liked what she was saying but were scared to speak up. Once Davis had engaged enough early champions, though, it became much safer for the fence-sitters to join in and help the campaign go from a small group to a huge groundswell, until a hundred thousand people from across the United States had joined in.

Finally, while Davis faced a number of cynics who questioned whether change would ever be possible at this scale, she welcomed their input behind the scenes and then won them over with her compelling speech and the surge of support behind her, convincing them that this time it might, actually, be different.

CATALYZING CHANGE THROUGH CULTURE

We learned in chapter 1 that there are three ways to radically accelerate your ability to effectively lead positive change:

- Become a changemaker yourself.
- Surround yourself with other changemakers. We'll talk more about this in the coming chapters as you build your changemaker community.
- Help others become changemakers. In fact, I believe the highest impact a changemaker can have—just like Laura Weidman Powers and Tony Carr (see page 26) have done—is to help others see their own potential to lead positive change.

If you believe, as I do, that everyone can be a changemaker in their own way, then each of us can help those around us become changemakers.

Culture, therefore, is one of the most powerful levers to catalyze positive change. Just as I believe that you can lead positive change from wherever you are, so, too, can you lead and shape culture from wherever you are.

Norm Entrepreneurship

This is one of my favorite changemaker concepts. The idea of norm entrepreneurship is most often applied in the world of political science and international relations. We might describe how a nation-state is acting as a norm entrepreneur, for instance, in advocating for climate change policy. Christine Ingebritsen, a professor at the University of Washington, explores this in her paper "Norm Entrepreneurs: Scandinavia's Role in World Politics."[4] In it, she explains how a "group of militarily weak, economically dependent, small states" can have an outsized influence on international affairs. In contrast to traditional political science studies on "material power," she charts how these countries exert "social power," influence on sustainable development, environmental goals, and collective security, through setting and reinforcing collective norms.

In the 1998 paper "International Norm Dynamics and Political Change," political scientists Martha Finnemore and Kathryn Sikkink were the first to discuss the goal of norm entrepreneurship, which defines or creates specific behavioral standards such that others within the community follow them.[5] Legal scholar Cass Sunstein adapted this concept from the nation-state level to the individual level.[6]

Just as an entrepreneur creates and scales a new venture or company, a norm entrepreneur creates and scales a new culture.

What I love so much about this concept is that it's inherently democratic: anyone can be a traditional entrepreneur, anyone can be a norm entrepreneur. No matter if you are an intern or an entry-level employee, you can help to shape culture. The norms that you create can be both formal and informal. On the formal side, you might push for a culture that ensures equal pay for all employees. On the informal side, you might try to create a norm that improves the start of all virtual Zoom meetings by inviting each participant to do a quick check-in on how they are doing.

Just like with launching a new business, there is no guarantee that a new cultural norm will successfully take hold and scale. But there's nothing holding you back from giving it a shot, from taking a cultural norm you would like to see be part of your workplace or your community and attempting to embed it in the existing culture. Sebastien, whom we met in chapter 6, created an office-wide norm around composting. And like him, as a norm entrepreneur you can lead change through culture from wherever you are.

A PRESCRIPTION FOR CHANGE

UCSF Health, in San Francisco, is at the forefront of research, scholarship, and medical innovation. Its medical center is where my family placed our most vulnerable trust when my dad underwent cancer surgery in the summer of 2018, ultimately saving his life.

By all measures, UCSF is an exceptional place for healthcare.

But Julie Kliger, then the program director of the Integrated Nurse Leadership Program, noticed a startling trend: medication dosing errors. Imagine expecting a loved one to receive a specific medication and specific dosage yet learning that they'd received either the completely wrong medication or an inappropriate amount of the correct one. These mix-ups can be deadly. Kliger realized that these medication errors made up the largest proportion of medical errors in the hospital.[7] Understanding the gravity of the situation, Kliger approached this challenge with curiosity and humility, asking, "How might we reduce this error rate?" She made it clear that she was not on a mission to critique the nurses.

Rather than jumping right in to try and solve the problem, she began her changemaker efforts by observing nurses' efforts at multiple Bay Area hospitals. She found something striking: Nurses kept getting interrupted by doctors, over and over and over again. Doctors or even fellow nurses might see a nurse standing with their back to them, not realize they were dispensing medication, and interrupt them with a question or request.

Joanne Mette, chief nursing officer at Kaiser Permanente's Fremont and Hayward hospitals at the time of the study, put the scale of these interruptions into perspective; per Mette, it wasn't uncommon for a nurse to be interrupted five to ten times while trying to dose out a single medication![8] With that type of distraction, is it any wonder there were so many medication errors?

How did Kliger process these data? Reprimand doctors? Teach nurses to ignore all requests? Both of these changes would have been difficult to catalyze and scale. Instead, she developed a simpler and far more effective approach.

She created a new norm at UCSF. When a nurse was preparing medication, they would wear a bright neon-yellow vest that had the words

DO NOT INTERRUPT printed on the back. This became a visual cue to everyone in the hospital that a nurse was focused on an important task and needed to retain their full attention.

Of course, there was some pushback: Some nurses didn't want to wear the vests. Some doctors didn't like the new norm of delayed communication.

But the data from this intervention spoke volumes: an 88 percent drop in medication errors over thirty-six months across nine Bay Area hospitals.

Starting change doesn't always mean creating a new product or organization. Julie Kliger's changemaker efforts resulted in scalable, sustainable, and measurable change. She was a changemaker from within a hospital, yet her impact rippled throughout the entire medical profession, all through norm entrepreneurship.

YOUR THEORY OF CHANGE

As changemakers, we are often fighting our way through uncertainty and ambiguity. In fact, this unpredictability is one of the defining features of leading any change initiative. Anything we can do, therefore, to achieve more clarity and certainty will help us be more strategic with our resources and help us blaze the trails ahead of us with greater confidence.

There's a powerful tool I teach my students called the "theory of change" model, which helps changemakers visualize and overcome precisely this challenge.[9] Though we can never eliminate uncertainty completely, this tool has helped countless changemakers proceed with their efforts in spite of the inevitable unpredictability they face.

I always like to lead with the why behind tools and concepts, and here, the why is abundantly clear: The theory of change model can serve as the foundation for what a change effort does and why it does it. And it can provide you with clarity for mapping out how your actions connect to the larger change that you want to create. A theory of change should fundamentally answer three questions:

1. What is the impact or change that you're hoping to make?
2. What is the mechanism, the actions through which you can pursue and make that impact or that change?
3. How will you know when you've achieved that change?

Though it is most often used in nonprofit settings, I believe this tool is applicable to visualizing and strategizing changes of all kinds, irrespective of sector or scale.

The essence of a theory of change model is creating a logically sound set of linkages, in which you map out how the work that you do leads to an outcome that you want to achieve. (That's why versions of it are also sometimes referred to as a "logic model.") There are a few different versions and iterations of the theory of change model, but we'll explore the most popularly used one.

Working the Model

Creating a theory of change model shifts your change leadership efforts from a strategy challenge to an execution challenge. It helps you connect where you are now with where you want to be, and it helps you understand what it will take to get there. A thoughtful theory of change model clarifies what action to take and when to take it, and provides confidence that what you do on a daily basis is in line with your vision for change and your strategy to achieve it.

The first step is identifying your long-term goals. Where do you want the world to be in the future—say, twenty years from now—because of this change you are leading? Let's use a global reduction in single-use plastics as the goal we want to eventually achieve.

Next, we do backward mapping and connect the preconditions necessary to achieve that goal. In other words: What would have to be true in the world for that outcome to become a reality? In our example, we might say there needs to be decreased demand among consumers for plastic and also decreased plastic production among the companies. For there to be less plastic in the world, both of these conditions would need to be met.

From there, we identify some of the basic assumptions underlying our view of the change we are pursuing. What would have to be true to have decreased plastic demand and decreased plastic production? We might need to assume that there are adequate material substitutes for plastic, that if and when we reduce plastic production, there are other materials that can take its place. We might also need to reach a point where people in general believe it's a worthy goal to try to reduce plastic use. If neither of these assumptions are true, it's hard to imagine we would ever reduce the amount of plastic in the world.

Next, we think about our initiative's interventions, laying out the change work that we will do in pursuit of that desired change. What are the tangible activities that you'll actually do on a daily, weekly, or monthly basis? To reduce plastic use, maybe we'll launch a social media campaign targeted at consumers, encouraging them to reduce their plastic consumption. Maybe we'll go around to local coffee shops and try to encourage them to no longer offer plastic straws. Or maybe we'll go and lobby Congress for plastic-related policy changes.

Then the final step is to develop indicators to assess the performance of our change initiative. What will we measure that will tell us that, yes, we are on the right track? Perhaps it's a percentage reduction in plastic use among a target group of consumers. Or maybe it's measuring the number of coffee shops that eliminate straws due to our efforts. These are all examples of indicators that would tell you that the activities we're taking in the near term are having the desired impact, which will likely eventually lead to that long-term outcome, due to the causal connections we have logically outlined.

inputs → activities → outputs → outcomes (short & long)

If you are more of a visual learner, you might prefer a logic model that applies the same concepts in a more visually appealing way:

- Working backward from the future to the present, we begin with the outcomes we want to achieve, both short-term (two to three years) and long-term (twenty years).
- We identify the measurable outputs of our initiative—for instance, how many individuals change their behavior as a result of our work.
- Next, we detail the activities we will undertake. This could include outreach, training, launching new programs, advocacy work, or other interventions or techniques that will result in producing those identified outputs.
- Finally, we list our inputs—what we are putting into this model—which can include all of the resources available to carry out this work, from human capital to financial capital to community.

Sometimes when we are leading change, we have a strong vision for the change we want to see and we can paint that picture for others to follow, but knowing how to get there remains fraught with uncertainty. By taking the time up front to create a theory of change model, you are able to break a big, ambitious change initiative down into logical steps to achieve it, so that you can spend your time focused on action, not paralyzed with fear and confusion.

OVERCOMING OPPOSITION

Even with all of these tools and approaches for leading change when change is hard, sometimes it's still just really hard! What do you do when you face fierce opposition to your change efforts? How do you persuade even your strongest detractors to come over to your side?

Here we will take a few lessons from sources as diverse as a Nobel

Prize winner, laundry detergent consumers, and stubborn professors to help you convince even the seemingly unconvincible that your change effort is, in fact, worth pursuing.

The Endowment Effect

Economists William Samuelson and Richard Zeckhauser first put an empirical underpinning beneath something that many of us have intuitively felt throughout our lives: a status quo bias. In the 1988 paper "Status Quo Bias in Decision Making," the researchers applied psychology, economics, and decision theory to show that many people prefer the status quo, even when the alternative is verifiably better.[10] They found, for instance, that whereas newer employees were more likely to choose a new healthcare plan, employees who had already been on a plan were more likely to stick with their old, but less favorable, one. The researchers found that existing employees were focused more on minimizing potential losses rather than considering any possible gains.

This also connects to the legendary work of Daniel Kahneman (2002 Nobel Prize winner) and Amos Tversky, whose prospect theory resulted in the expression "losses loom larger than gains."[11] In detailing "loss aversion bias," the pair show that people often focus more on what they have to lose than what they have to gain.

These biases can make leading change especially challenging, because changemakers, inevitably, are questioning the status quo and shaking up the accepted norm.

But just because some people have started to accept undesirable phenomena as the status quo, such as a warming climate, racial inequities, or outdated technologies, that doesn't mean we can't persuade people to change their minds. Understanding this quintessentially human desire to maintain the status quo is an important starting point for us changemakers to bring others on board.

Let's reflect on Jon Chu's letter to Coldplay (see page 165). He understood that the status quo in the music industry is to skew toward protection and limited use. By showing empathy to the way he thought Coldplay would be most likely to react to his change effort through the lens of status quo bias, he was able to address that head-on. "I know as an artist it's always difficult to decide when it's ok to attach your art to someone else's—and I am sure in most instances you are inclined to say no," he wrote. "However, I do believe this project is special." He then details the reasons why, concluding with, "It will give a whole generation of Asian-Americans, and others, the same sense of pride I got when I heard your song." Chu proactively articulated the status quo bias he knew he might be met with and successfully made his case for how and why to overcome it.

Anti-persuasion Radar

Let's now recognize that people do not like to be told what to do.

Wharton professor Jonah Berger recounts a paradoxical set of behaviors around, of all things, eating poisonous chemicals. A YouTube fad in early 2018 saw teenagers daring others to eat laundry detergent capsules, which were very clearly marketed for cleaning clothes and absolutely not for eating.[12]

The company who makes the product stepped up and filmed a catchy video with an NFL star, in which he wags his finger and authoritatively declares, "No!" when asked questions about whether people should eat detergent pods. "No! No! No! No!" he declares throughout the fun clip.

Executives thought that the message was clear and that consumption of the detergent capsules would finally stop. After all, they had communicated through a relatable and beloved sports figure, explaining in no uncertain terms not to eat the chemicals.

But what happened?

After the video was released, internet searches for the pods surged, and visits to poison control centers went up as well.

Berger attributes this to people's natural "anti-persuasion radar": a feeling that they were being told what to do and having their freedom to decide impinged upon.

One of Berger's suggestions for overcoming this instinct is to ask questions instead of telling people what to do.[13] By posing questions, you give people the feeling that they have an ability to decide for themselves—even if you are the one proposing the two options.

How might you apply this to your own change initiative? Try to drive buy-in by shifting the listener's role from thinking about all the reasons you are wrong to giving them the freedom to decide their own approach based on questions in which you help lead them. Offer two solutions instead of one. That way instead of deciding on change versus no change, which will activate status quo bias, you can see which of your changes they prefer. This invites potential change cynics to step up and give answers instead of being told what to do. And, remember, the endowment effect means we tend to love our own answers, because... well, they're ours.

Asking for Less

You might also need to ask for less in service of a greater change. When Dean Rich Lyons was leading an initiative to clearly articulate and put greater emphasis on the role of culture at Berkeley Haas, he faced a lot of pushback, especially from faculty members who saw culture as hard to measure, or even unimportant. Lyons knew that he wouldn't be able to get every faculty member on board in support of his culture initiative, so instead of asking for 100 percent of faculty to actively support his change efforts, he shifted his ask. He told faculty who didn't like his change that they could believe whatever they wanted and that he wouldn't force them to, for instance, teach about culture in their own classroom. But he made one clear reduced ask: No matter what you do, promise that you won't disparage the Haas culture in front of students. That was it; that was his only ask to stubborn faculty members. He got 100 percent commitment to his ask by offering a way to engage that didn't require much of any one individual yet ensured that a bunch of potential detractors didn't get in the way.[14]

One final recommendation as you prepare for leading change when change is hard: Remember to practice self-care so that you stay strong for the long haul. Any meaningful change won't happen overnight. Leading change is often a marathon, not a sprint, so practice "urgent patience," which leading change management thinker John Kotter defines as "acting each day with a sense of urgency but having a realistic view of time."[15] Remember that some changes, by their very nature, will take a while, and that's okay. You aren't doing anything wrong if you get some pushback. In fact, some resistance is likely a sign that you are on the right path.

BE THE CHANGE

Key Insights
- Get champions of your change initiatives involved early through delegation. Engage cynics by hearing them out and perhaps even making a smaller ask of them.
- Through norm entrepreneurship, you can lead culture change from wherever you are, both through formal and informal means.
- As a changemaker, you will be fighting the status quo bias. Be prepared to put in extra effort to overcome the many obstacles you may face.

Changemaker Challenge
- Identify a group you are part of and think about how its culture could better reflect some of the changemaker concepts you've been learning. Become a norm entrepreneur by attempting to create a new norm among your group, either formally or informally. Pay attention to how others respond and whether the new culture sticks.

Chapter 11

The Changemaker Canvas

"Um, Scott, your arm is bleeding. Are you okay?"

Those were the first words I ever uttered to Scott Shigeoka, now a good friend, and an incredible changemaker across many different arenas, whom we met in chapter 3.

Scott quickly retracted their outstretched hand from our handshake and excused themself. I sat, befuddled, staring at my iced coffee and wondering what in the world had just happened. Scott returned a few minutes later from the bathroom, arm all bandaged up, their trademark smile back, stretching from ear to ear.

Scott told me that, in a race to meet me on time, they fell off their bike somewhere on the streets of Washington, DC, but kept on going, unwilling to let a fall like that stop them.

If there was ever a metaphor for the way that Scott lives life—and leads change—this was it.

Shigeoka is a storyteller, an artist, a designer, and a (metaphorical) bridge builder.

In just the eight years I've known them, Scott has led change in more traditional roles, such as doing social impact design work at the firm IDEO and writing for outlets like the *Washington Post*.

But Shigeoka has also brought their full identity, a self-identified queer Hawaii-born creative yonsei (fourth-generation Japanese American), to imagine and reimagine projects that don't fit into any traditional change categories.

Scott created an art and music festival in rural Iceland, despite never having set foot in Iceland before, as well as a radically immersive art experience to help participants imagine their own death so that they might be able to live more fully in the present.

As the United States and many other countries around the world have become more polarized, Scott's focus now is on supporting national efforts to foster understanding and bridge divides across all imaginable cleavages.

Last year, Scott spoke to my class to share some lessons he learned on the road, and one in particular struck me. Scott said, "It's totally okay if your career path doesn't look like the conventional one." And, indeed, Scott's career path wouldn't fit into most MBA career-counseling brochures.

What has made Scott such a successful changemaker across so many different disciplines and so many unique concepts for positive change is their ability to draw from a changemaker toolkit. While the details of running a music festival are vastly different from a bridge-building road trip to overcome political and social divides, the underlying ways of thinking about leading positive change are remarkably similar.

Just as a medical doctor has their own set of tools and an artist has their own as well, so, too, does a changemaker have their own set of tools.

In this chapter, I will introduce you to a new model for leading change, called the Changemaker Canvas. I'll show you how you can take even the most complex, overwhelming, and even intimidating change initiative you might be imagining right now and make it understandable, actionable, and achievable, through this model and the toolkit it provides you.

A COMMON BOND

"Three! Two! One!" we yelled at the top of our lungs as we leapt from land and plunged into the Sea of Marmara in Turkey. I was privileged to be there as part of a fellowship for young social entrepreneurs from around the world. While I learned a lot about the intricacies of growing a social enterprise, I took away something far more powerful from our ten days together: connection.

As we all splashed around in the sea, the Mediterranean sun setting on the horizon, I felt an incredible bond with the nineteen people swimming around me. We could not have possibly come from more different backgrounds or places on Earth, yet there was something powerful that united each of us in our hopes and in our struggles.

While every changemaker is absolutely unique, with each of us bringing our own special blend of identities, experiences, and interests that inform the changes we lead, there is so much more that unites changemakers than divides us. As we swam, I realized that my new friend Muhammad Kisirisa, who works tirelessly to support and uplift his community in Bwaise, the largest slum in Kampala, Uganda, has a lot in common when it comes to changemaking with someone like Agustín Rodríguez Aké, who helps children in hospitals in Mexico nurture their own positive healing. Yes, their visions of change, their communities they support, and their geographies are vastly different. But they both spark positive change with a similar set of tools.

As the sun dipped down below the horizon, we headed out of the water and back to land. I realized that as different as all of us might be in terms of our backgrounds, experiences, and visions of change, we were now inextricably connected; I had just found my changemaker community.

Who do you consider to be part of your changemaker community? How might you connect with and nurture your relationships with them? Changemaking is a team sport, and we all benefit from surrounding ourselves with people who aspire to lead change just as we do.

THE CHANGEMAKER CANVAS

Whether it's Muhammad, Agustín, or others, I've realized that changemakers have a common set of tools for leading change, and that for all changemakers, leading change can be downright challenging and scary. To build the former up and challenge the latter, I developed a tool called the Changemaker Canvas.

Inspired by tools like the business model canvas, which takes the old-fashioned concept of a business plan and transforms it into a one-page strategy, the Changemaker Canvas does the same. It helps changemakers take change initiatives and break them down into smaller, manageable blocks. You will identify concrete steps and actionable activities to help you make your idea an impactful reality. The Changemaker Canvas attempts to help you balance the big picture of the world you are changing with the small changes that will get you there.

This tool provides changemakers with clarity on what needs to be done, confidence that they can lead the change, and insights on the first steps toward action. Unlike a business plan, which requires pages and pages of writing before you're taking action, the canvas is a tool to first promote reflection and then promote essential action. Each section should be answered with a maximum response of one paragraph. Often just a single sentence (which emerges from thinking and strategizing) is ideal.

The canvas is broken down into six sections: Vision, Opportunity, The Four S's of Change, Action, Community, and Approach. In the coming pages, I'll break down each section for you with instructions and examples, so that you can be like so many of my students and develop your own changemaker toolkit to put into action.

At the end of the chapter, you'll find the URL to access an editable copy of the Changemaker Canvas. I'll walk you through each of the blocks of the canvas and explain how to get the most out of the tool.

I've also included, throughout this chapter, an example of how the canvas can be used. In this case, the example canvas is for a twenty-four-year-old entry-level changemaker at a logistics company with offices throughout the US, who is passionate about making positive change in how the company engages with and supports workers around mental health.

VISION	**The Why.** Why do you care about creating this particular positive change? - - -	**The Vision.** In one sentence, describe the desired positive change and how you are creating it. - - -	
OPPORTUNITY	**Core Problem.** One succinct sentence describing the precise issue that you are addressing. - - -	**Consequences.** Short- and long-term implications if the core problem is not addressed. - - -	**Root Causes.** The underlying issues (social, legal, historical, cultural, environmental, etc.) that underpin the core problem. - - -
(CHANGE)s	**Substantive Impact.** The intended impact of your project, and 1 to 3 crucial indicators you will measure. - - -	**Scalability.** How you will scale this beyond a minimum viable project. - - -	**Sustainability.** How you will ensure that this project continues for the long term. - - - • **Systems Change.** How you will address root causes (laws, policies, mindsets, rules, etc.) to create systemic change. - - -
ACTION	**Minimum Viable Project.** The simplest test you can start running right now to learn if this project is worth developing further.	**Plan for Resilience.** The obstacles you may face and how you might proactively overcome them. - - -	
COMMUNITY	**The Doers.** The key changemakers who will be leading this change and their core skills. - - -	**The Evangelists.** The most important influencers and advocates whose support/approval are crucial. - - -	**The Community.** Who you are serving with this change and how you know this will be a positive change for them. - - - • **The Coalition.** Others who care about this and how you will involve them. - - -
APPROACH	**Changemaker Mindset.** The key aspects of a changemaker mindset needed to create this positive change. - - -	**Changemaker Leadership.** The key aspects of changemaker leadership required to create this positive change. - - -	

The Alchemy of Change

Perhaps my most beloved novel of all time is *The Alchemist* by Paulo Coelho, which tells the story of the shepherd boy Santiago's quest for a long-buried treasure.[1] It's a parable filled with so many pearls of wisdom for travelers, seekers, and changemakers, but there's one scene that is etched into my consciousness.

The king of Salem tells Santiago, as he hands him a spoon full of oil, to explore his castle without spilling the oil from the spoon. Santiago returns with the oil intact, but the king points out that Santiago missed all of the beauty of the castle, like the Persian tapestries on the wall, and the parchments in the library. Santiago sets out again, this time taking in the beauty around him, but upon returning, Santiago realizes that the oil in the spoon has completely spilled out.

"Well, there is only one piece of advice I can give you," the king says. "The secret to happiness is to see all the marvels of the world, and never to forget the drops of oil on the spoon."

I first read this book just as I was beginning my changemaker journey with StartSomeGood, and the concept regularly comes back to me as I teach others to lead positive change.

The secret to leading change is to be able to simultaneously see the big picture of the change you hope to create in the world while never losing focus on the crucial details and small steps in front of you as you go about creating it.

The Changemaker Canvas attempts to help you do both, balancing the big picture of the world you are changing with the small drops of change that will get you there.

VISION

Before we as changemakers can turn our focus toward the smaller details—the oil on our spoons—we can benefit from first immersing ourselves in the big picture. We begin our Changemaker Canvas here by reflecting on why, specifically, we care about making this change and outlining, in broad strokes, what that change will look like when we achieve it. As baseball great Yogi Berra said, "You've got to be very careful if you don't know where you are going, because you might not get there." Taking time at the beginning to chart our course will give us the confidence later on in the canvas to connect the dots backward and make sure we arrive at our desired changemaker destination successfully.

The Why

Mental health has affected me, my loved ones, and my colleagues, and I believe we all benefit from and deserve support.

As Simon Sinek instructs in his viral TEDx talk: Great leaders start with why.[2] He tells us that people don't buy *what* you do, they buy *why* you do it. What he calls The Golden Circle, from why to how to what, helps explain why many people are happy to buy many different products from Apple, not just a single "what." We buy into Apple's "why," which, as Sinek describes it, is: "Everything we do, we believe in challenging the status quo. We believe in thinking differently. The way we challenge the status quo is by making our products beautifully designed, simple to use, and user-friendly. We just happen to make great computers. Want to buy one?"

Leading with the why is where all great change starts, so it's the necessary first piece of your own Changemaker Canvas.

Begin by reflecting on the why behind leading your own change initiative. "Why statements" need three things to work: They must be compelling, authentic, and personal. A why statement should get others excited about the change you are leading; after all, if you aren't excited about it, why would they be? Second, it must be true to who you are. You can't fake it, especially since you will need to lean on it when times are tough. Finally, your why statement should be unique to who you are. Bring your own self into this. Your changemaker work is an extension of who you, as a person, are. Lean into this.

In addition to starting off your Changemaker Canvas, leading with why is a powerful leadership technique to engage others and make them feel included. For every single assignment I give in class, I always begin by explaining to students the why behind the task—the reason I chose this assignment out of an infinite possibility of assignments, and how I see this undertaking fitting into the overall goals and aims of the course. We get so used to doing what we are told to do in education that we often lack the context to understand why it matters in the first place.

The Vision

Mental health becomes as valued at our company as physical health.

The second block in our canvas, vision, connects back to many themes in this book. In chapter 4, we learned how to paint a picture for others to follow. Is your vision a clear and compelling one that will inspire others to want to join you? Is it aspirational? Does it activate our curiosity, wonder, and excitement? Consider bringing in the long-term goals you identified in your theory of change model and raise them up here to articulate what your change will make possible.

One particularly powerful vision statement consists of just four words: "Make autism a superpower." This belongs to an app, DayCape, that helps children on the autism spectrum gain more agency in their lives through daily planning and support. Founded and created entirely by a team of changemakers on the spectrum themselves, the tool enables children to not just mitigate against what we often perceive as the limitations of an autism diagnosis, but also lean into what their neurodiversity makes possible.

While the concept is terrific, it's the vision that catches us and makes us want to learn more. It helps us first imagine the world DayCape is creating, then invites us to engage further.

The Change

Increased awareness of, and support for, mental health throughout the company and our team.

Finally, we need to ask: What is the change?

In one clear, powerful sentence, explain what the change is that you are creating. You can't possibly explain everything, so instead focus on the essence of your change and leave others eager to learn more. Curious for a few examples? Here are some that students have used:

- Using gamification to get more children to read.
- Educating and inspiring students in Mexico City to be changemakers.
- Reducing food waste on campus through awareness campaigns.

In each of these examples, the change is simple and clear, even if the means to achieve it aren't yet apparent. We don't yet need to know how these students will bring game mechanics to drive more reading among children. All we need to know for now is where the proposed change is headed. The rest of the canvas will help us fill in the details.

With these three blocks, you've started to help us to see the world around us in a new way. We now turn our attention to the "drops of oil" on the spoon: the details for how you will make this change happen.

OPPORTUNITY

A quotation often attributed to Albert Einstein says, "If I had an hour to solve a problem I'd spend fifty-five minutes thinking about the problem and five minutes thinking about solutions."

Even so, so much of what we learn about problem-solving is the other way around: to get to the solution as quickly as possible.

The Changemaker Canvas helps us slow down and spend more time deeply understanding the problem we hope to address so that we can move forward with confidence that we are, indeed, spending our time solving the correct problem.

I know this doesn't come naturally. My students often remark how uncomfortable it is to simply sit with a problem as they spend time framing it, reframing it, and seeing it from all sides, instead of jumping right in to attempt to solve it.

In addition to the discomfort of sitting with a problem, I often find that many changemakers struggle to identify the right level at which to approach a problem. Should they look at a multifaceted problem with a wide lens? Focus on a narrow subset of the problem they see? Concentrate on downstream effects? Try and address systemic issues?

To help changemakers like you understand a problem, our canvas breaks down problem identification—or, as I prefer to call it, identifying the "opportunity" for change we seek to lead—into three distinct parts: the core problem, the consequences of the problem, and the root causes of the problem. All three are separate yet crucially connected aspects of recognizing an opportunity for change.

Core Problem

Inadequate support for mental health throughout the company and in its policies and practices.

I define the core problem as "one succinct sentence describing the precise issue that you are addressing." As I work with changemakers, they often struggle with whether the change they are working on should be at a hyperlocal level, a community level, or a state, national, or even global level. They wonder whether it should be broad in its scope or more narrow.

This tool purposefully provides room for any and all of those options, but I encourage changemakers at the start of their change process to shoot for a core problem that is inspiring yet achievable. In the case of better support for mental health, this is certainly a problem that needs to be addressed at not just local and state levels, but also national and even international levels. But as a first step, that could feel really overwhelming. Identifying the core problem invites you to start where you are. In our example case, it makes the most sense for the changemaker to begin leading change directly within their own company.

Defining the problem here with a narrower lens (the company) but showing that it's built upon multiple factors (including formal policies as well as informal practices) gives us a clear starting point: to begin small but still aim big.

Consequences

Exclusion; loss of opportunities; stigma; reduced participation; vulnerability; higher turnover; reduced performance.

Consequences are the negative implications that the identified problem brings about if not addressed. Put another way: If we don't solve the core problem, then what would happen as a result?

Changemakers sometimes conflate the core problem with the consequences. But because there are often so many consequences to an unsolved problem, trying to address all of them all at once usually will spread us way too thin, such that we'll be unable to realize any change at all.

Identifying the consequences gives us a road map for how we will measure the success of our change initiative and how we will determine downstream areas for future work, should we be successful in first addressing our core problem. (If the consequences fail to become a reality, we will know we were successful in driving change in our root problem.)

It is helpful to think about consequences from both the individual level (what happens if each individual fails to get the support they need and deserve) as well as the organizational level (what happens if the company fails to fully support its employees). In our example, the seven identified consequences are diverse and would be challenging to solve all at once, because they would spread our resources too thin. But if we successfully address our core problem, we should be able to make a meaningful impact on all of these consequences.

Root Causes

Underlying health conditions; trauma; stress; inadequate support throughout education systems; race and class disparities in access to care.

It's essential to pinpoint the underlying issues that are causing the core problem that you have identified. Often these root causes are social, legal, historical, cultural, environmental, or technological, reflecting greater systemic issues.

In fact, it's this very systems lens that encourages us to identify these root causes up front. By identifying them, you can start thinking about what those systems to change might be and where your greatest points of leverage might lie.

It's rare that we will be ready to work on systems change from the very start, so most likely you will still begin by addressing the core problem you identified. But having recognized these systems that need changing will give you both the perspective needed to keep these ideas in the back of your mind as you go about your first steps as well as the insight for where systemic change will occur as your initial changes take hold.

THE FOUR S's OF CHANGE

In 2012, my then girlfriend Rebecca got a job offer in Stockholm, Sweden. I had visited the city once before meeting her; she had never been.

The idea of exploring a fascinating part of the world together and experiencing life in a new country was compelling.

Rebecca and I visited Stockholm in July, the long Scandinavian summer nights providing the backdrop as we fell even more in love with each other—and with this new city we decided we would call home. Six months later, we made the leap and moved there together.

We moved in the middle of winter.

This California kid had never been colder in his life, and I learned so much: For instance, scarves aren't just a fashion accessory; they are the difference between being able to make the whole walk to the metro versus having to stop in random stores along the way just to warm up.

Despite the freezing climate, the excitement of exploring a new culture and context for changemaking was fascinating to me.

I am forever grateful that Reach for Change was willing to place its trust in me—a newly arrived, non-Swedish-speaking migrant—to run its incubator for social entrepreneurs. I felt so privileged to have this opportunity, and I committed to doing all I possibly could to help more people throughout Scandinavia become changemakers. In doing so, I was careful to not force my Silicon Valley mindset on others but rather to adapt to, support, and be a full partner in collaborating with my teammates and the greater social innovation ecosystem that was just beginning to blossom.

Reach for Change was a pioneer in inspiring and cultivating social entrepreneurs throughout Sweden, as one of the first organizations to recognize the opportunity for leading positive change in this way. We would select early-stage social entrepreneurs working in fields ranging from mental health to education to social inclusion, sometimes with just the beginning of an idea, and give them salary funding for three years (so that they could quit whatever else they were doing and focus on their organization full-time), as well as three years of coaching, advising, and support.

In deciding which entrepreneurs to select, we faced a monumental challenge. We received over five hundred applications for five annual spots—an acceptance rate of just 1 percent. While I worked extremely hard to find ways to support the other 495+ terrific ideas through informal means, that meant we still had to figure out how to find the five most worthy social enterprise ideas out of a huge, diverse, and deserving pool.

Along with my colleagues from around the world, we developed four key indicators—the four S's of change—that we would look for in these social enterprises, which would form the basis of our investment decisions.

These blocks of the canvas will help you get clarity on how to create a change that sticks and goes beyond yourself—irrespective of whether your change is related to social impact or something completely different.

Substantive Impact

# of employees participating in new mental health services; % of employees who say they feel better supported in their mental health (measured before/after our interventions).

Here you will list one to three crucial indicators that you will use to measure the intended impact of your project.

In other words, how will you know if you are actually on the right path to achieving your change? You can bring in both qualitative and quantitative measures here, but focus on identifying just a couple of the most essential measures that will inform whether you are indeed making the substantive impact you hope to create through your change.

It's important to have a measure for both the level of adoption (how many people are participating) and the difference (if any) the interventions make. In our example, the impact measurement of employees feeling better supported is self-reported. While this may not be ideal for a peer-reviewed publication, it can be a great way to get some quick and actionable data on the early impact of a change initiative.

For those who have an idea of the change they want to make but aren't sure how to implement it, LA-based design firm verynice created an incredible resource called Models of Impact, in which hundreds of ways we can embed impact into any type of initiative have been identified.[3] For instance, one of its models is "employment for traditionally excluded populations," like Jean Guo's Konexio pursues, and another is advocacy, which Dolores Huerta has pursued in various forms throughout her career. Or you might pursue a conditional discount to reward behavior, as Hummus Bar in Kfar Vitkin, Israel, does. The restaurant has a set price on the menu for its hummus plate, but it offers a 50 percent discount to parties who are mixed Jewish and Arab, to encourage connecting and finding community over food.[4]

And verynice itself uses a creative model of impact for its own change work, called #givehalf. It does 50 percent of its work for large companies like Google, Red Bull, and Apple, and then does 50 percent of its work, pro bono or discounted, for nonprofits and social enterprises like the National Resources Defense Council, the Pancreatic Cancer Action Network, and South Los Angeles community group Pando Populus. It uses the big contracts from big corporations to subsidize its ability to do world-class design for impact-driven clients.

Scalability

We will create an employee resource group with at least one member in each office throughout the US.

In MBA programs, scale is often taught in a particular way: If you have one successful food truck, you are taught that you inevitably need to create a second. If both trucks are successful, then you should quickly get to five. Then fifty. Then a food truck empire.

However, I believe that more isn't always better, especially when it comes to leading change.

I teach changemakers "smart scale," not "scale at all costs."

How will you scale your initiative beyond a minimum viable project? Though your project need not end up scaling—and certainly not right away—thinking about this from the very beginning will help you design a change project that can scale. Whether or not you yourself will lead the scaling, and whether or not you might create a replicable model for others to follow, lay out how you will ensure scalability from the start.

In our example, a big challenge to scaling is that the company is nationwide, with different leaders of each office. To quickly and effectively scale, it will be crucial to have a presence everywhere and engage local leaders in the change efforts.

Casting the Widest Net

We met Rosie Linder, founder of Peppy Pals, in chapter 5, when we discussed empathy. She's among the most inspiring social entrepreneurs we supported during my time at Reach for Change, not least because she was a finalist twice before being selected. She later told me that in both cases, after getting so close to being picked but ultimately receiving a rejection, she gave herself one day to cry and be upset and then immediately got back to work leading change.

Linder's ability to make Peppy Pals a global entity started with a single, deliberate choice, which set her up for smart scaling from day one.

Most children's apps have language in them, either written words or spoken. But Linder thought differently. She recognized that there are only about nine million Swedish speakers in the world; if she launched the app in Swedish, this would significantly limit its initial appeal. Similarly, English only would alienate other users. Translating the app into different languages would be really challenging, time-consuming, and expensive and Linder didn't have this linguistic expertise on her team.

Linder made the bold decision to create an app that had no language whatsoever. All of the game play would be based on engaging with adorable animated animals, following visual cues, and learning to read microexpressions.

Through a single decision, Peppy Pals was completely global from day one. It launched simultaneously in the Swedish app store and the American app store, as well as in France, Germany, Brazil, and more than twenty other countries.

Sustainability

We will ensure that funding for the program is included in the company's long-range budget alongside all healthcare costs.

It's imperative that you ensure that your project continues for the long term. Especially in the corporate world, companies' file systems are filled with change memos, strategies, and action plans that never resulted in lasting change. In order to sidestep these pitfalls, think about sustainability on both the financial and human capital sides. If you are leading change within an organization, how can you make certain that this change initiative will survive the next year's budgeting process? If you are creating a new community group, how will you fund not just its founding but also its steady-state operations?

On the human capital side, this project might just be powered by you at the beginning—which is totally fine! We will learn more, soon, about how to engage others in your project. But how can you ensure that your change initiative would survive the "vacation test" (where you, as the leader, are out of reach for two weeks)? Are there others whom you might enroll at the very beginning, even in a light-touch way, to guarantee that the project could continue without you if you were to switch jobs, move companies, or need a break?

Systems Change

We will be transparent and share our learnings with other companies; we will advocate for policy change at the state and national levels.

The fourth of the four S's is systems change.

What do we mean here by a "system?" A system is a set of things working together as part of a mechanism or network. The writing of Donella Meadows, who was a leading systems thinker, reminds us that a system can be "a corporation, an economy, a living body, a city, an ecosystem."[5]

Systems are also fascinating.

Rarely has an insight rendered me speechless, but physician Paul Batalden's observations on systems did just that. "Every system is perfectly designed to get the results it gets,"[6] he says. This means that if a process or network is giving us results we don't want, it's not the system's fault; we must go change the system.

In this block, you will outline how you will address the root causes you identified in the previous section (laws, policies, mindsets, rules, etc.) to create systemic change. Most change initiatives won't create systems change right off the bat, and that's to be expected. But after taking the time to identify the root causes, can you begin thinking about what some of the approaches might be to ensure that you aren't just putting a bandage on a cut but stopping the cut from happening in the first place?

In our mental health example, the changemaker will want to think about how changes in policy can complement or even replace some of the mental health services their company will provide in the short term. The changemaker will also want to think expansively, beyond just their company, considering how the model can scale to other companies.

Changing the System

How do we change the system? We might do it through shifting mindsets, changing policies, creating new frameworks, or rebalancing power structures.

Donella Meadows advises us to look for leverage points where one shift can create huge changes in a system—for instance, by changing the "rules of the system" (incentives, punishments, or constraints) or even the goals of the system.

What does systems change look like in practice? Compared with other countries, Sweden has pretty outstanding human rights, especially for children. But not every child knows their rights—like recent immigrants and, doubly so, unaccompanied youth refugees who have recently arrived in Sweden, having typically fled from countries with different social support systems and rules of law.

Founded by social entrepreneur Elin Wernquist, the Swedish-based venture Barnrättsbyrån, or the Children's Rights Bureau, works with a team of lawyers to ensure that these young people know their rights and are respected by local authorities—an important service on its own. Where what the organization does becomes system changing, though, is through its work on individual cases. Its lawyers learn where the cracks in the system are, gaining insight into where children are slipping by and the cases where rights aren't being upheld. Then, based on their individual "deep impact" work, they lobby, advocate, and inform policy change throughout the Swedish government. Their individual case support helps them see when the Swedish welfare system is delivering an undesired result, and then they advocate tirelessly to change the system so that no future children experience the same thing.

Barnrättsbyrån isn't just teaching about rights or providing rights. It is revolutionizing the way children are cared for by the entire public support system. That's systems change.

ACTION

This section of the canvas reminds us that it's not change*thinking*; it's change*making*. Here, you will strategize your first steps toward making your change a reality and get prepared to overcome the inevitable setbacks that go hand in hand with leading change.

Minimum Viable Project

Starting in one office, we will create "mental health days," which will be offered alongside sick days. To reduce potential stigma, every employee will be encouraged to take at least one in the next three months.

A play on the minimum viable product concept we explored in chapter 9, this block asks you to outline your "minimum viable project," or MVP: what the simplest, quickest way of validating your change initiative might be. Just as you saw with the lean startup examples of companies like Dropbox, the first steps of change often aren't elegant.

Before you commit lots of time, energy, and exertion into leading this change, you first need to figure out if you are, indeed, on to something. We want to move as quickly as possible from idea concept to tangible project, which can validate your initial assumptions.

The changemaker in our example has a lot of assumptions to test, including what role stigma plays in stopping people from getting mental health support; the extent to which it's possible to make it safe for everyone to be part of this change; and how willing different offices will be to start taking action. Mental health is multifaceted and complex, and it benefits from taking a holistic approach. Starting in one office with one first step, our changemaker can begin identifying what works well and where the specific barriers to change are within the company.

Plan for Resilience

We expect we may face some pushback from senior leaders and will come prepared with data. For instance, Mental Health America reports just 5% of workers in the US feel their employer provides a safe environment for mental health; 80% are at risk of burnout.

The second block in the "Action" section is your plan for resilience. Here, you will spend some time thinking about the obstacles you are likely to face and how you might proactively overcome them. There's a saying in the software development world that says a project usually takes about twice as long and costs twice as much as initially projected. This can be devastating if you build an entire launch strategy with no room for error on dates or costs. But if you factor these things in from the very beginning, you will be able to weather the storm. Rather than reacting after the inevitable roadblocks come up, spend some time now imagining how the change initiative could go off course and how you would then course-correct.

I know a group of three entrepreneurs who in the early founding stage of their company spent time talking through every single worst-case scenario—from one of them embezzling funds to two of them dying, leaving just one cofounder behind. These are never easy conversations to have! But their perspective was that it would be easier to have them up front, when there was less emotion and more time to think, than in the moment, when there would be chaos all around and getting clarity would be that much more difficult.

Making change happen requires a lot of action from you and your team, but before you jump right in, taking time to plan for how you will overcome inevitable hurdles will help you stay strong for the long haul.

MVP in Action

A group of my students wanted to create a "safe walk" system at UC Berkeley for students studying late at night at one of the libraries on campus who don't want to walk home alone. Their vision was to create an app where students could input their final destination alongside the time they wanted to leave, and then, using LinkedIn and Facebook data to ensure trust, the app would match students to safely escort each other home. Creating this app would take a lot of engineering time and brainpower—and, to be honest, they still weren't sure if the idea was a good one.

So they tested it, with a minimum viable project, or MVP.

They hung out in the late-night libraries and sent flyers to other students in close proximity via Apple's AirDrop capability. Students could then read about the concept, and follow a link to a private Facebook group (which required a berkeley.edu email address to join). There they could see which other students were at the library and also see right away if they shared any friends in common (which, while not a perfect proxy, at least ensured a quick level of social proof).

While it sounded like an intriguing concept in theory, my students discovered that the trust barrier was just too high of a hurdle to overcome digitally. Informed by the quick learnings from their MVP, this group of changemakers ultimately found that students preferred the safety that came with the official UC Berkeley night-walk service, even though many students remarked it was slow, ineffective, and often "awkward."

But this was a great outcome! It was validated learning, which told these changemakers that it was time to pivot from their original safe-walk concept because of an existing alternative. And, thanks to a bit of entrepreneurial hustle, my students were able to figure this out over only a couple of late nights, without needing to invest thousands of dollars and hundreds of hours in app development.

COMMUNITY

Changemaking is a team sport, and in order to make your change concept a reality, it will require working through and with other people in myriad ways. It's not as simple as identifying collaborators with whom you might work. There is crucial nuance here when it comes to engaging others in your change, and there are four distinct groups of people, each of which requires its own unique approach to bring on board. Let's take a look at each one: the doers, the evangelists, the community, and the coalition.

The Doers

Johanna: vision and team management
Ibrahim: communications
Daphne: policy research and budgeting

The doers are the core people on your team, actively rolling up their sleeves to make the change initiative a reality. If you're trying to lead change, you don't want to have a team composed entirely of five CEOs or five accountants. You want to build a mix of people with diverse personalities, approaches, experiences, and skills. Some priorities for putting together a changemaker team:

- Don't simply accept anyone who expresses an interest. Take time up front to think about how you want your team to fit together across roles and responsibilities.
- Going solo? Consider your "zone of genius." Think about what your core skills are and where you can make your highest-level contribution. Reflect not just on what you are good at but also what gives you energy. As much as possible, design a team that allows you to do the work you're great at and that inspires your highest-possible personal contribution. If you don't have any

specific collaborators in mind yet, that's totally fine! Sometimes, the early stages of a change initiative mean starting up by yourself. Take the time now to envision what the other roles on the team would be. If you are great at setting a vision, you might need someone else who can be COO to take care of operations. If you are great at finance, you might need someone who has a passion for and skills in marketing and PR. Identify the most important jobs to be done to make this change happen, and evaluate what an ideal team and division of roles and responsibilities would be.

- Have a team on board? Rather than taking an emergent strategy toward roles and responsibilities, have an up-front and honest conversation with your team. Discuss what everyone's areas of highest contribution are, as well as what everyone's time commitments will look like. Find where there is overlap and where there are gaps. Failing to do this was a mistake I made in the early days of StartSomeGood. My cofounder, Tom, and I were both good at the vision part and not so good at the operations. Comparatively, though, Tom was better than I was at vision, and I was less bad at operations, which led to a rough division of labor—albeit collaborative—along these lines. Had we done this exercise earlier, we would have realized that getting a hands-on COO should have been our top priority!

- Discuss how you will work together. A helpful tool here is having everyone on the team create their own personal user manual.[7] If each member of the team understands how the other members work, it will make working together easier. Have each person on the team write a one-page outline of how they work and how to best work with them. It might include, for instance, "I have parenting duties, so I won't be able to check emails after 5 p.m., but I will always check in first thing when my kids wake me up at 5 a.m.!" or "I tend to be very black-and-white in my first reactions to new ideas, so if I fail to see the nuance in an opportunity, please give me time." These outlines might cover personality traits, pet peeves, preferences on work environment, communication and conflict styles, and much more. Taking the time to create these user manuals up front can significantly reduce future awkwardness and increase collaboration efficiency so that your team can operationalize the change as effectively as possible.

Completing the "Doers" section helps you get clarity on what your active day-to-day team of changemakers will look like, and in what ways each person (or proposed role) will contribute in achieving your change.

The Evangelists

Executive leadership team (especially CEO and head of HR); general managers of each office.

In addition to your doers, you also need to identify and engage a group of evangelists. These are individuals who won't be active in supporting your day-to-day operations but whose approval or tacit support of your project will be crucial. Here, we want to identify who your evangelists are and how we might get them to be advocates for your project, even if they don't contribute much in terms of time or energy.

If I'm leading a change initiative at Berkeley Haas, I may need the support and approval of the dean, the chief operating officer, or perhaps the chief financial officer. All three are busy people and manage myriad projects every day. I can't reasonably expect them to attend daily stand-up meetings. But what I do want to ensure before I start this project is that I have identified whose approval will be crucial to this project becoming a reality and how I might get them on board.

In addition to ensuring that your project is in line with company or organizational goals by working with your evangelists, you'll find that evangelists can often do a lot for you and your vision in a very small amount of their time. Perhaps there's an intro they can make for you, a barrier they can knock down for you, or another contribution that is light on time for them but heavy on impact for you. There's also the additional benefit of the "social proof" that comes along with evangelists, a term coined by Robert Cialdini in his book *Influence*.[8] It's a social phenomenon that occurs when someone is unsure of the correct way to behave, so they look to other people for clues to confirm the correct behavior. In times of uncertainty, we tend to look to authority figures. So if someone is trying to figure out whether or not to be part of your change initiative, they might look and see who else is supporting you. If you have an impressive list of evangelists on board—whether formally, in an advisory board, or informally, through a green-lighting of your project—that's crucial social proof information, which may encourage others to follow the evangelists' lead in backing you.

The Community

We will create a diverse and inclusive advisory board of employees throughout the company to provide us with ideas and feedback.

Bryan Stevenson, whom we met in chapter 2, reminds us that there is power in proximity. He teaches us that we must get closer to, not farther from, those we serve. "If you are willing to get closer to people who are suffering," he has said, "you will find the power to change the world."[9]

Ask yourself two key questions as you engage the community in your change. The first is: Whom are you serving? And the second is: How do you know that this will be a positive change for them?

There's a bad habit in elite bubbles, like universities, think tanks, and consulting firms, to try and solve problems in an outside-in manner. For instance, many university classes on social entrepreneurship encourage students to come up with solutions to, for example, how to build a better school in Rwanda, despite the fact that most students aren't educators and haven't been to Rwanda in their life.

Instead, an approach laid out by Joanna Cea and Jess Rimington flips this model, as they detail in the article "Designing with the Beneficiary."[10] They make a compelling case that "end-users have a vital role to play in innovation," by showing how nonexperts who are close to a problem come up with product ideas that have both greater novelty and a great penchant for successfully "selecting and improving the best options among multiple prototypes." While their lens applies mostly to nonprofit projects, the concept holds for any type of change. Instead of guessing what type of change people most need, ask them—or, better yet, involve them in leading the change with you.

Maybe you are one of the people directly affected by the change. If so, that's a terrific place to start, since you already know the intricacies of the problem. But you will still want others' input, too. This starts with getting proximate, and it continues with the humility we learned about in chapter 3 to come in with more questions than answers and to be ready to really listen to others as they tell you more about what they need and the change they hope to see.

The Coalition

Regularly align with the National Institute of Mental Health, Mind Share Partners, Bring Change to Mind, and other nonprofits in the field.

The fourth and final group to engage in leading change is the coalition.

Here, we put our lessons around networked leadership into practice, by identifying others who care about the same change we are pursuing and may already be working on similar changes.

This could be a changemaker using similar methods but in a different geography. Or it could be someone pursuing a similar change but with different methods.

How can you leverage what others are doing and not reinvent the wheel? How can you use a smart division of labor to do what you do best and be part of a larger solution, rather than trying to do everything yourself?

Tristan Harris hit SEND on a presentation back in 2013, sharing it with a small community of fellow designers at Google, and then jumped in bed.

When he awoke, his presentation had gone viral within the company, and as he sat on the Google bus commuting to work the next morning, he saw laptop screen after laptop screen displaying his words.

His viral presentation, "A Call to Minimize Distraction & Respect Users' Attention," reverberated throughout Google, and beyond.[11]

In it, he made a compelling case that never before in human history had so few people, a small, homogenous group of designers in Silicon Valley, "mostly men, white, living in SF, aged 25–35...working at 3 companies [Facebook, Google, and Apple]...had so much impact on how millions of people around the world spend their attention."

Harris would go on to speak at TED[12] about how tech companies control users' minds through building products that promote addictive and unhealthy behaviors, such as "doom-scrolling" through Facebook feeds, which overstimulates our dopamine neurons with every "Like," every notification ping, and every moment of social media outrage.

He cofounded the Center for Humane Technology (CHT) to bring about positive change in the tech world. But he and his cofounders aren't trying to go it alone—far from it. The nonprofit has consciously engaged with and developed a powerful and wide-ranging coalition of partners all working in concert toward similar goals.

CHT sees itself as a "node, not a hub," as we learned in chapter 6 when we studied network-based leadership. The organization has brought together all kinds of changemakers working on different areas of addictive technology. From professors at UC San Francisco, Columbia, MIT, and Cornell to mathematicians, venture capitalists, entrepreneurs, politicians, and even Justin Rosenstein, the guy who invented Facebook's LIKE button in the first place.

Together they move forward to achieve the same vision, of "radically reimagined technology infrastructure and business models that actually align with humanity's best interests,"[13] and while CHT plays a role in bringing everyone together, each member of the coalition leads change in their own way: a law professor, working on legal aspects; a medical doctor, working on health implications; and so on.

As changemakers, every single one of us can catalyze change. But to make change a lasting reality, it often requires identifying, supporting, and learning from and with others who also care about the change.

That's the power of a changemaker coalition.

APPROACH

Our sixth and final section of the Changemaker Canvas brings us back to the changemaker impact equation (see page 193). Remember that your impact as a changemaker is the sum of your changemaker mindset and your changemaker leadership skills multiplied by your action. The first five parts of this canvas help you identify your strategy and prepare your action. The final part of the canvas helps you anchor your change back to the mindset and leadership you will need to make this change a reality.

Changemaker Mindset

> **Resilience to overcome initial pushback; long-term thinking to deliver on our big vision; dispositional flexibility to remain optimistic while also realistic about the challenges ahead.**

Start first with your changemaker mindset. What aspects of a changemaker mindset that you have learned are the most crucial? Which will be most applicable to helping you lead this positive change? Is it to remember how to question the status quo and zig when others zag? To regularly bring flexibility and empathy into your work? Or perhaps to focus on long-term thinking even when there will be pressure for short-term results? This is your own personal reflection on the mindset traits and attributes that you will commit to practicing in order to make this change a reality.

Changemaker Leadership

Influence without authority, to convince senior leadership; microleadership, to recognize and seize moments to serve others; inclusive leadership.

With your mindset traits in place, then begin reflecting on the changemaker leadership skills you will need to work through and with others to realize this change. Will you need to influence without authority? Practice network-based leadership? Perhaps a combination of microleadership and leading with purpose are the keys. There are no right answers here. This is your chance to identify up front what leadership techniques and approaches you think might be especially helpful, so that you can then put them into practice.

Muhammad Kisirisa, Agustín Rodríguez Aké, and all of the other changemakers I swam with in the Sea of Marmara have continued to keep in touch and to cheer one another on. Though our lives continue to traverse divergent paths, whenever I receive a WhatsApp group message from one of them, I feel a bit of comfort and a sense of connection. I'm reminded that while all twenty of us, spread out across six different continents, are working on very different initiatives, we are all forever connected by our shared struggles and victories in pursuit of positive change for our communities.

I built the Changemaker Canvas for them, for us, and for you.

I hope that with this canvas as part of your toolkit, you will feel equipped and prepared to move from idea to action and to take your crucial first steps of catalyzing change with courage and confidence.

BE THE CHANGE

Key Insights

- No matter what type of change we are leading, it can feel really overwhelming, especially at the beginning.
- Start with your why. Why are you committing your most scarce resource—your time—into creating this change?
- Your change will be powered through and with others, but remember to engage others in the process in different ways, from evangelists, who might provide approval or "social proof," to members of your coalition, who you will engage as collaborators.

Changemaker Challenge

- Download an editable copy of the Changemaker Canvas at changemaker.us /canvas, and begin filling it out for a change initiative you'd like to see become a reality! Share it with at least one other person for some early feedback.

Chapter 12

Catalyzing Your Changemaker Journey

Sarika Saksena was only eighteen years old when she signed up to take Becoming a Changemaker in 2019, the first semester I taught the class. I put my heart and soul into creating and teaching the course, and so there is nothing more meaningful than seeing a student like her become a changemaker right before my eyes.

But it's not so much what she did in my class that earned her an A+ on her final assignment, a grade I give out extremely rarely. It's what she did outside the classroom with her newfound changemaker mindset and leadership ability that showed me the collective power of changemaking in action.

I love when students question the status quo with assignments, and so rather than requiring students to write a traditional academic essay to display what they've learned in class, I provide them with other options—one of which is to write a fairy tale about what it means to be a changemaker. This not only activates students' curiosity and creativity, but it requires them to have such a command of the material that they can write about it in simple terms and in narrative form. I was not surprised at all when Sarika chose this option. She wrote a beautiful story about a little boy named Butru who lived with his mother in a small village. Through his interactions with a magical goddess, Butru learns lessons of empathy, courage, and resilience to help him make change for people in his village. A goddess helps Butru become a changemaker, but before the story ends, Sarika includes conversational questions to engage the children reading the fairy tale in learning the same lessons that Butru does.

Sarika told me she read her story to her middle-school-aged brother and engaged him in the questions at the end. The next week, Sarika recounted, "My brother told me that he spent his free time at school the whole week in a very different way than usual. He reached out for the first time and spent it hanging out with two kids: one who 'always sits by himself' and another who 'never plays with anyone.'" Both students, her brother would discover, always felt excluded from the other students— one because of a medical condition, the other due to shame from something far beyond his control. Her brother had felt sad about this, but he told Sarika that he felt like he finally knew what to do. He'd learned the same lessons Butru did about empathy, courage, and resilience, and felt called to action. He had always wanted to do something but never knew what to do or how to do it—until that magical moment he became a changemaker.

I've learned that changemaking doesn't just call upon each of us individually. It invites all of us collectively; it's a cumulative endeavor. And just as others can inspire us in our changemaker journey, we can, in turn, inspire others. As we learned at the beginning of the book, change can be challenging because it occurs exponentially. That same principle can become our greatest strength as changemakers. Like Sarika, you may not realize it in the moment, but when you start seeing yourself as a changemaker and give yourself permission to make change, you can inspire others to join with you. In fact, you may never know about all of the people whose lives you impact through your changemaker actions. But no matter who you are, where you live, or what change you go on to lead, the ripples of your work will reach places you never thought possible.

As you come to the end of this journey, you are joining a hungry, passionate, purpose-driven community of fellow changemakers, all ready to lead positive change from wherever they are. You are now connected to the corporate innovators and the grassroots advocates, the writers, the artists, the intrapreneurs, and the entrepreneurs. You belong to the changemakers of the world.

STANDING ON SHOULDERS

My passion for supporting changemakers comes from the humility to recognize that I can't possibly know everything the world needs. But I am absolutely positive that one crucial thing it needs is more changemakers: more individuals like you committed to creating the future and leading positive change from wherever you are.

Throughout this book, you've been introduced to changemakers who embody the crucial changemaker concepts of mindset, leadership, and action.

In the introduction, you met Shivani Siroya, an innovator who makes her impact at the intersection of finance, technology, and inclusion. She taught us how changemaker mindset concepts like curiosity, flexibility, and resilience represent how changemakers show up daily in their work and their life. And we discovered that these traits are learnable and practicable by anyone.

In chapter 1, we met my student Hana, whose idealism had faded when her new ideas for a more equitable and inclusive workplace failed to take hold right away. By finding inspiration in another changemaker— one who had also overcome setbacks and challenges—and telling that changemaker's story to our class, Hana herself became an inspiration to another student. Hana learned that one of the most powerful ways to practice a changemaker mindset is to help others become changemakers. She embodied learned optimism and realized that her initial setbacks weren't permanent. And since overcoming those initial doubts, she's gone on to lead DEI efforts with renewed confidence.

In chapter 2, we met legal changemaker Bryan Stevenson, who has charted his own impactful course by regularly questioning the status quo. We saw how he embraced his own curiosity—beginning as someone without any role models to look up to in the legal profession—to reimagine what justice could look like in the United States. We saw how he zigged when others zagged to advocate for the most powerless individuals in our society. And we saw how he took smart risks, courageously taking on legal cases most other lawyers chose to avoid, in service of leading positive change in the courts and halls of justice.

In chapter 3, we met Gwen Yi Wong of Tribeless, who embodies the concepts of "confidence without attitude." We saw how she had both the confidence to start and lead a high-growth organization, and the humility to know when it was time for her to step back so that someone else could step up as CEO. We learned from her that changemakers look for "both, and" solutions. She led with trust in her team, which allowed them to better collaborate, building a new product more rapidly than she'd ever imagined. She shows us that balancing both confidence and humility enables change to grow beyond any one individual.

In chapter 4, we met Emily Cherniack, who founded the organization New Politics. By identifying and supporting individuals who are servant leaders first and politicians second, she is raising up a leadership concept that is simultaneously ancient and cutting-edge. She inspires us to become leaders who go beyond ourselves and to think ethically and for the long term.

In chapter 5, we met Darius Graham, a changemaker who has led positive change in settings ranging from universities to foundations to law firms to grassroots nonprofits. Throughout each of the new opportunities he has seized, he's remained clear on his why—to better connect resources and solutions with problems to be solved—while being flexible on his how. He's remained resilient in spite of the challenges that have come from stepping into so many new roles, and he's used empathy to integrate community members into institutions in new and creative ways.

In chapter 6, we met Sebastien, a middle manager at a manufacturing company. Passionate about sustainability, he reached dead end after dead end in pursuit of getting his colleagues to join his composting efforts. But by practicing key twenty-first-century leadership skills, like leading through networks, he was able to empower many others to join him in his change efforts. By activating and inspiring others to be his "first followers," his composting efforts stuck, and he was able to go on to leading even more ambitious sustainability initiatives, never waiting for anyone to give him permission to do so.

In chapter 7, we saw how Oregon basketball player Sedona Prince embodies the concept of microleadership, as she seized a leadership moment and took action to call for equality. We also met film director Jon Chu, who was able to influence without authority to get one of the biggest bands in the world to give him the rights to use its song in the emotional, uplifting closing scene of the movie *Crazy Rich Asians*.

In chapter 8, we saw how New Zealand's prime minister, Jacinda Ardern, personified the very best of inclusive leadership following a shooting at a mosque in her country. She created a feeling of "psychological safety," a concept that we learned, from Google's organizational research, is the number one predictor of a high-impact team. And we saw how Ardern's cultural sensitivity reflects one of the keys of being an inclusive leader (its impact multiplies when we bring in humility as well).

In chapter 9, we saw how Luis Sota brought the changemaker impact equation to life, putting his mindset and leadership skills into action to develop new opportunities for low-income homeowners in Mexico. We also saw how sculptor Janardhan Havanje took the words "action is the antidote to despair" to heart and inspired people to clean up a beach in Karnataka, India.

In chapter 10, we met Walmart associate Carolyn Davis, who showed us how to lead change when change is hard. By engaging champions, cynics, and fence-sitters alike, she showed tenacity in advocating for—and ultimately achieving—equitable parental leave throughout the company. We also learned about Julie Kliger's successful efforts to reduce the number of medical errors at her hospital. Both Kliger and Davis used norm entrepreneurship to catalyze change through culture.

And finally, in chapter 11, we got to know Scott Shigeoka. Shigeoka has leveraged the full suite of instruments in the changemaker toolkit to lead diverse types of change, from experiential art and immersive music endeavors to a road trip with a singular goal of building bridges with people with different experiences. We learned that changemakers call upon a suite of tools brought together in the Changemaker Canvas, from articulating a vision to identifying the root causes of a problem to developing a minimum viable project, all depending on what the situation calls for, while remaining adaptable and able to find opportunities where others might only see challenges.

The changemakers we've met are exceptional in their impact, yet as you've learned throughout the research, stories, lessons, and studies in this book, changemaker mindset, leadership skills, and action orientation are accessible to each and every one of us.

In sharing their stories with you, my goal isn't that you feel pressure to follow in their footsteps. Armed with all that you've learned, you are now ready to do more than that: It's time for you to embrace your own identity as a changemaker and stand on the shoulders of these changemaker giants. This is your invitation to take the lessons you've learned throughout the book and apply them to your own life and the change that you are uniquely suited to lead. The world doesn't need a clone of Nadine Burke Harris or Sam McCracken. It needs a fresh new changemaker: you. We need you to bring all of your experiences, interests, passions, and skills—and, yes, changemaker mindset, leadership, and action—to driving forward change. We need you to lead change from wherever you are, in a way that is true to who you are, and to make the difference you are meant to make.

SUMMONING YOUR COURAGE

By now, you've developed your changemaker mindset. You've learned lots of new and effective changemaker leadership skills. You know what it takes to transform your idea into action, and you've filled up your changemaker toolkit with everything you need. You embrace the confidence from the Changemaker Index knowing that the Becoming a

Changemaker process works, and understanding that so many people just like you have transformed into changemakers as a result of these concepts and lessons.

There's just one thing left for you to do: summon the courage to go be a changemaker.

When I teach, I always close the semester with the words of novelist Anaïs Nin, a changemaker herself. She writes: "Life shrinks or expands according to one's courage."[1]

Now is the time for you to step into the courage that's been inside you this whole time, and expand your changemaker impact.

Can you find that courage calling out from inside you? The courage to stop thinking of changemaking as something that other people do, and tell yourself that it's now something you do. The courage to stop waiting until things are perfect before you begin to lead change and instead to commit to taking action right now, even if that means embracing some failures along the way.

It's okay, and perfectly normal, to feel a bit scared as you think about becoming a changemaker! As artist Damon Davis recounted about his work in raising up the stories of protestors in Ferguson, Missouri, "Courage is contagious."[2] The more you practice a bit of courage, the more your courage to make change will multiply.

You don't have to take a huge leap; you just have to find the courage to start. This is what thousands of changemakers before you have done, and now it's your turn to join them.

You now have everything you need to start leading positive change from wherever you are. You have become a changemaker.

The world has never been more ready for you.

And we can't wait to see what you do next.

Gratitude

To the extent I've accomplished anything in life or in writing, it's only because I have the immense privilege to spend my days surrounded, supported, and encouraged by the most incredible community of people. You all give me far, far more than I could ever deserve or possibly repay. From friends and family to colleagues, I carry each of you, and our shared triumphs and struggles, into this book. If I've mistakenly left you out here, please know that my gratitude extends off these pages and directly to you for all that you've done. (Also, let's blame it on my lack of sleep as a new dad. Deal?)

My first thank-you goes to my incredible students. You motivate, challenge, and inspire me every day. I often can't sleep the night after teaching you, because I am so lit up from the energy in our classroom and by the incredible passion and potential I see in every one of you. Thank you for giving me the most wonderful gift of being your teacher.

Thank you to my terrific Berkeley Haas community. To Jay Stowsky for believing in me, fighting for me, and giving me the greatest opportunity ever, of teaching at Haas. To Erika Walker for taking a chance on me and for all of your wise counsel. To Dean Ann Harrison for leading a school where a class on changemaking is not just allowed; it's supported and encouraged. To Laura Hassner, Brandi Pearce, Mariana Somma, and Rich Lyons, for your optimism, friendship, and indefatigable support of Berkeley Changemakers. And to all of my faculty and staff colleagues at UC Berkeley whom I'm honored to also count as friends: Thank you.

Thanks to Spotify's Deep Focus playlist for always being there for me—especially during late-night writing sessions. And to the MVBs (most valuable beverages) of this writing project: kombucha and iced coffee.

Thanks to all of the changemakers I've met along the way, both while writing this book and leading up to it. You've shaped me far more than you could ever know. A special thanks to each of the spectacular changemakers whom I profile in this book. Thank you for trusting me with telling your story, and for sharing your example with the world.

Thank you to my amazing agent, Jeff Shreve. Your email in April 2020 couldn't have come at a better time, and it started us on this wonderful journey together. Thanks for taking a chance on this first-time author and for answering every question I had along the way with wit and wisdom.

Thank you to my incredible editor and publisher, Nana K. Twumasi. From our very first conversation, you were the person I wanted to work with on this book, and you've exceeded every expectation I have. Thank you for always being in my corner, for bringing your brilliant editorial eye and sharp mind to this project, and for helping me fool readers into thinking I actually know how to properly use an em dash.

Thanks to all of my friends and family who supported me throughout the crazy process of writing a book! Your encouragement and support mean the world to me. To Justin Shifrin and Ryan Abelowitz for always taking time to check in about the book, even with everything you have going on. To Peter Roady for your indispensable advice early on in the project. To Ben Sands for being the first person to ever suggest I write this book, many years ago. To David Nahmias for being on the receiving end of the most lopsided deal in book-writing history: all of your immensely thoughtful input and feedback on this book in exchange for one plate of chicken shawarma and a beer.

Thank you to Alana Budak for believing in me and supporting this book in so many ways. Thank you to Emily Altman and Andrew Braunstein for such wide-ranging assistance with everything from helping me get time away for writing to answering my questions on statistical analysis. Thank you to Dave and Judith Altman for unwavering encouragement and support (and perfectly timed grandparenting!) throughout the writing process. Thanks to Mark Budak, Glenn Budak, Sherrie Bell, Phyllis Jerome, and Irwin and Gloria Altman for your kind belief in me and in this book always.

Thank you to my parents, Mo and Renee Budak, for teaching me the importance of values from a young age, for always encouraging me to be a changemaker, and for being the best (rogue and unpaid, but always appreciated) PR agents a son could imagine.

Thank you to Asher for always reminding me why I'm writing this book. Everything I do is for you, and you are everything to me.

And finally my biggest thanks to my wife, Rebecca Budak. None of this would ever have been possible without you and your wisdom, empathy, kindness, and love. You inspire me to be a better changemaker and, more importantly, a better husband, dad, and person every day. You are my only one.

Notes

Introduction

1. Abby Fifer Mandell, Megan Strawther, and James Zhu, *InVenture: Building Credit Scoring Tools for the Base of the Pyramid*, Greif Center for Entrepreneurial Studies, USC Marshall, December 1, 2015.
2. "Changemaker Skills," Ashoka, https://www.ashoka.org/en/collection/changemaker-skills.
3. Thomas L. Friedman, *Thank You for Being Late: An Optimist's Guide to Thriving in the Age of Accelerations* (New York: Farrar, Straus and Giroux, 2016).
4. Scott Brinker, "Martec's Law: Technology Changes Exponentially, Organizations Change Logarithmically," *Chief Martec*, June 13, 2013, https://chiefmartec.com/2013/06/martecs-law-technology-changes-exponentially-organizations-change-logarithmically.

Chapter 1

1. Carol S. Dweck, *Mindset: The New Psychology of Success* (New York: Ballantine, 2016).
2. Amanda Gorman, *The Hill We Climb: An Inaugural Poem for the Country* (New York: Viking, 2021).
3. Joe Pinsker, "People Who Use Firefox or Chrome Are Better Employees," *Atlantic*, March 16, 2015, https://www.theatlantic.com/business/archive/2015/03/people-who-use-firefox-or-chrome-are-better-employees/387781.
4. Stephen J. Dubner, "The Maddest Men of All," episode 198 transcript, February 26, 2015, *Freakonomics Radio*, https://freakonomics.com/podcast/the-maddest-men-of-all.
5. Snigdha Sinha, "Eco-Friendly Sanitary Pads Made of Banana Fibre—Saathi Pads's Solution to Menstrual Waste," YourStory, August 10, 2015, https://yourstory.com/2015/08/eco-friendly-saathi-pads/amp.
6. Rebecca Solnit, *Hope in the Dark: The Untold History of People Power* (Edinburgh: Canongate, 2005).
7. Shashank Bengali, "His Son Died in a Road Accident, so India's 'Pothole Dada' Fills His Family's Sorrow with Stone and Gravel," *Los Angeles Times*, August 15, 2018, https://www.latimes.com/world/asia/la-fg-india-pothole-man-20180815-story.html.
8. Martin E. P. Seligman, *Learned Optimism* (New York: Knopf, 1991).

9. Bill Snyder, "Laura Weidman Powers: Opening Doors for Minorities in Technology," Insights by Stanford Business, Stanford Graduate School of Business, June 21, 2013, https://www.gsb.stanford.edu/insights/laura-weidman-powers-opening-doors-minorities-technology.

10. "Our Culture," Berkeley Haas, https://haas.berkeley.edu/about/the-haas-difference/our-culture.

Chapter 2

1. "Bryan Stevenson," Gruber Foundation, Yale University, https://gruber.yale.edu/justice/bryan-stevenson.

2. Isaac Bailey, "Seeking Justice: Bryan Stevenson MPP/JD 1985 Is an Indefatigable Defender of the Powerless," Harvard Kennedy School, Summer 2018, https://www.hks.harvard.edu/research-insights/policy-topics/human-rights/seeking-justice-bryan-stevenson-mppjd-1985.

3. "Bryan Stevenson."

4. Equal Justice Initiative (EJI), Intro on Posts page, Facebook, https://www.facebook.com/equaljusticeinitiative.

5. Eva Rodriguez, "Bryan Stevenson Savors Victory in Supreme Court Ruling on Juvenile Life Sentences," *Washington Post*, June 25, 2012, https://www.washingtonpost.com/lifestyle/style/bryan-stevenson-savors-victory-in-supreme-court-ruling-on-juvenile-life-sentences/2012/06/25/gJQA8Wqm2V_story.html.

6. Lizzie Kane, "Bryan Stevenson: 4 Steps to 'Change the World,'" *Q City Metro*, January 29, 2020, https://qcitymetro.com/2020/01/29/bryan-stevenson-4-steps-to-change-the-world; "'Hope Is Your Superpower': Bryan Stevenson Speaks at Penn State Abington," Penn State, March 22, 2019, https://www.psu.edu/news/academics/story/hope-your-superpower-bryan-stevenson-speaks-penn-state-abington.

7. Svenolof Karlsson and Anders Lugn, "Laila Dials a Winner," Ericsson, https://www.ericsson.com/en/about-us/history/changing-the-world/the-nordics-take-charge/laila-dials-a-winner.

8. J. Nina Lieberman, "Playfulness and Divergent Thinking: An Investigation of Their Relationship at the Kindergarten Level," *Journal of Genetic Psychology* 107, no. 2 (1965): 219, https://doi.org/10.1080/00221325.1965.10533661.

9. Morten T. Hansen, "IDEO CEO Tim Brown: T-Shaped Stars: The Backbone of IDEO's Collaborative Culture," *Chief Executive*, January 21, 2010, https://chiefexecutive.net/ideo-ceo-tim-brown-t-shaped-stars-the-backbone-of-ideoaes-collaborative-culture.

10. Ian Leslie, *Curious: The Desire to Know and Why Your Future Depends on It* (New York: Basic Books, 2015); "Ian Leslie on Why Curiosity Is Like a Muscle," Quercus Books, May 7, 2014, YouTube video, https://www.youtube.com/watch?v=SOGqGOnlJCI.

11. Bruce D. Perry, Lea Hogan, and Sarah J. Marlin, "Curiosity, Pleasure and Play: A Neurodevelopmental Perspective," *HAAEYC Advocate*, August 2000.

12. Bethany Biron, "REI Is Defying Black Friday and Closing Its Stores for the 5th Year in a Row—and It Wants Shoppers to Join Its Plan to Fight Climate

Change," *Business Insider*, November 9, 2019, https://www.businessinsider.com/rei-closed-black-friday-for-the-fifth-year-2019-11.

13. Lizz Kannenberg, "Social Spotlight: REI's #OptOutside and How a Campaign Becomes a Movement," Sprout Social, January 22, 2020, https://sproutsocial.com/insights/social-spotlight-rei.

14. Emily Parkhurst, "That REI Black Friday Stunt? It Worked. REI Posts Largest-Ever Membership Growth," *Puget Sound Business Journal*, March 15, 2016, https://www.bizjournals.com/seattle/news/2016/03/15/that-rei-black-friday-stunt-it-worked-rei-posts.html.

15. Solomon E. Asch, "Effects of Group Pressure on the Modification and Distortion of Judgments," in *Groups, Leadership and Men*, ed. H. Guetzknow (Pittsburgh: Carnegie Press, 1951), 177–90.

16. Tyler Tervooren, "Finally, a Simple Way to Tell Smart Risks from Dumb Ones," Riskology, https://www.riskology.co/smart-risk-equation.

17. Anthony Ray Hinton and Lara Love Hardin, *The Sun Does Shine: How I Found Life and Freedom on Death Row* (New York: St. Martin's Press, 2018).

18. E. P. Hollander, "Conformity, Status, and Idiosyncrasy Credit," *Psychological Review* 65, no. 2 (1958): 117–27, https://doi.org/10.1037/h0042501.

19. A. A. Scholer et al., "When Risk Seeking Becomes a Motivational Necessity," *Journal of Personality and Social Psychology* 99, no. 2 (2010): 215–31, https://doi.org/10.1037/a0019715.

20. Miriam Cosic, "'We Are All Entrepreneurs': Muhammad Yunus on Changing the World, One Microloan at a Time," *The Guardian*, March 28, 2017, https://www.theguardian.com/sustainable-business/2017/mar/29/we-are-all-entrepreneurs-muhammad-yunus-on-changing-the-world-one-microloan-at-a-time.

Chapter 3

1. Gwen Yi, "To Lead Is to Let Go: Why I Fired Myself as CEO of Tribeless," *Medium*, December 5, 2018, https://gwenyi.medium.com/to-lead-is-to-let-go-why-i-fired-myself-as-ceo-of-tribeless-3f4c4eb46c.

2. Interview with Gwen Yi Wong, personal, June 22, 2021.

3. Amy Y. Ou, David A. Waldman, and Suzanne J. Peterson, "Do Humble CEOs Matter? An Examination of CEO Humility and Firm Outcomes," *Journal of Management* 44, no. 3 (September 21, 2015): 1147–73, https://doi.org/10.1177/0149206315604187.

4. Kibeom Lee and Michael C. Ashton, "Getting Mad and Getting Even: Agreeableness and Honesty-Humility as Predictors of Revenge Intentions," *Personality and Individual Differences* 52, no. 5 (April 2012): 596–600, https://doi.org/10.1016/j.paid.2011.12.004.

5. Samantha A. Deffler, Mark R. Leary, and Rick H. Hoyle, "Knowing What You Know: Intellectual Humility and Judgments of Recognition Memory," *Personality and Individual Differences* 96 (July 2016): 255–59, https://doi.org/10.1016/j.paid.2016.03.016.

6. Jim Collins, *Good to Great: Why Some Companies Make the Leap . . . and Others Don't* (New York: Harper Business, 2001).

7. *Public Trust in Government: 1958–2021,* Pew Research Center, May 17, 2021, https://www.pewresearch.org/politics/2021/05/17/public-trust-in-government-1958-2021.

8. "The State of Personal Trust," *Trust and Distrust in America,* Pew Research Center, July 22, 2019, https://www.pewresearch.org/politics/2019/07/22/the-state-of-personal-trust.

9. Esteban Ortiz-Ospina and Max Roser, "Trust," *Our World in Data,* July 22, 2016, https://ourworldindata.org/trust.

10. Rachel Botsman, "We've Stopped Trusting Institutions and Started Trusting Strangers," filmed June 29, 2016, at TEDSummit, Banff, Canada, video, 16:59, https://www.ted.com/talks/rachel_botsman_we_ve_stopped_trusting_institutions_and_started_trusting_strangers.

11. "University of Texas at Austin 2014 Commencement Address—Admiral William H. McRaven," Texas Exes, May 19, 2014, YouTube video, 19:26, https://www.youtube.com/watch?v=pxBQLFLei70.

12. Pauline Rose Clance and Suzanne Ament Imes, "The Imposter Phenomenon in High Achieving Women: Dynamics and Therapeutic Intervention," *Psychotherapy: Theory, Research & Practice* 15, no. 3 (1978): 241–47, https://doi.org/10.1037/h0086006.

13. Ruchika Tulshyan and Jodi-Ann Burey, "Stop Telling Women They Have Imposter Syndrome," *Harvard Business Review,* February 11, 2021, https://hbr.org/2021/02/stop-telling-women-they-have-imposter-syndrome.

14. Basima Tewfik, "Workplace Impostor Thoughts: Theoretical Conceptualization, Construct Measurement, and Relationships with Work-Related Outcomes," (PhD diss., University of Pennsylvania, 2019), https://repository.upenn.edu/edissertations/3603.

15. Brené Brown, "The Power of Vulnerability," filmed June 11, 2010, at TEDxHouston, Houston, TX, video, 20:03, https://www.ted.com/talks/brene_brown_the_power_of_vulnerability.

16. Morten Hansen, *Great at Work: The Hidden Habits of Top Performers* (New York: Simon & Schuster, 2018).

17. David Allen, "Opera's Disrupter in Residence, Heading to Bayreuth," *New York Times,* July 20, 2017, https://www.nytimes.com/2017/07/20/arts/music/operas-disrupter-in-residence-heading-to-bayreuth.html.

18. "Anna Deavere Smith, Yuval Sharon, and Kate D. Levin—Aspen Ideas Festival," The Aspen Institute, June 30, 2020, YouTube video, 23:04, https://www.youtube.com/watch?v=v3Sa1CRXbeE.

19. "Take the Thomas-Kilmann Conflict Mode Instrument," Kilmann Diagnostics, https://kilmanndiagnostics.com/overview-thomas-kilmann-conflict-mode-instrument-tki.

20. For more information and to see a visual representation of the graph, please visit "Thomas Kilmann Conflict Mode Instrument (TKI®)," Myers-Briggs, https://www.themyersbriggs.com/en-US/Products-and-Services/TKI.

21. Scott Shigeoka and Jason Marsh, "Eight Keys to Bridging Our Differences," *Greater Good Magazine*, Greater Good Science Center at UC Berkeley, July 22, 2020, https://greatergood.berkeley.edu/article/item/eight_keys_to_bridging_our_differences.

Chapter 4

1. Jim Heskett, "Why Isn't Servant Leadership More Prevalent?" Working Knowledge, Harvard Business School, May 1, 2018, https://hbswk.hbs.edu/item/7207.html.
2. Robert K. Greenleaf, *The Servant as Leader* (Indianapolis: Robert K. Greenleaf Center for Servant Leadership, 1970).
3. "Emily Cherniack," New Politics, https://www.newpolitics.org/emily-cherniack.
4. Adam M. Grant, *Give and Take: Why Helping Others Drives Our Success* (New York: Penguin, 2014).
5. Cone, "New Cone Communications Research Confirms Millennials as America's Most Ardent CSR Supporters," press release, September 23, 2015, https://www.conecomm.com/news-blog/new-cone-communications-research-confirms-millennials-as-americas-most-ardent-csr-supporters.
6. "2020 Edelman Trust Barometer," Edelman, January 19, 2020, https://www.edelman.com/trust/2020-trust-barometer.
7. Alison Beard, "Why Ben & Jerry's Speaks Out," *Harvard Business Review*, January 13, 2021, https://hbr.org/2021/01/why-ben-jerrys-speaks-out.
8. Phillippa Lally et al., "How Are Habits Formed: Modelling Habit Formation in the Real World," *European Journal of Social Psychology* 40, no. 6 (October 2010): 998–1009, https://doi.org/10.1002/ejsp.674.
9. *Measuring the Economic Impact of Short-Termism*, discussion paper, McKinsey Global Institute, February 2017, https://www.mckinsey.com/~/media/mckinsey/featured%20insights/long%20term%20capitalism/where%20companies%20with%20a%20long%20term%20view%20outperform%20their%20peers/measuring-the-economic-impact-of-short-termism.ashx.
10. Simon Sinek, *The Infinite Game* (New York: Portfolio, 2020).
11. James P. Carse, *Finite and Infinite Games: A Vision of Life as Play and Possibility* (New York: Free Press, 1986).
12. Brian Chesky, "Open Letter to the Airbnb Community About Building a 21st Century Company," Airbnb, February 14, 2018, press.atairbnb.com/brian-cheskys-open-letter-to-the-airbnb-community-about-building-a-21st-century-company.
13. Cameron Sperance, "Airbnb and Vrbo Significantly Outperformed the Hotel Industry but for How Long?" *Skift*, August 14, 2020, https://skift.com/2020/08/14/airbnb-and-vrbo-significantly-outperformed-the-hotel-industry-but-for-how-long.
14. James M. Kouzes and Barry Posner, "To Lead, Create a Shared Vision," *Harvard Business Review*, January 2009, https://hbr.org/2009/01/to-lead-create-a-shared-vision.
15. Matthew Kelly, *The Long View: Some Thoughts About One of Life's Most Important Lessons* (North Palm Beach, FL: Blue Sparrow, 2014).
16. Ashlee Vance, *Elon Musk: Tesla, SpaceX, and the Quest for a Fantastic Future* (New York: Ecco, 2015).

17. "Future of Driving," Volvo, https://www.volvocars.com/en-vn/why-volvo/human-innovation/future-of-driving.

18. Hannah Bae, "Bill Gates' 40th Anniversary Email: Goal Was 'a Computer on Every Desk,'" CNN Business, April 6, 2015, https://money.cnn.com/2015/04/05/technology/bill-gates-email-microsoft-40-anniversary/index.html.

Chapter 5

1. Mario T. García, ed., *A Dolores Huerta Reader* (Albuquerque: University of New Mexico Press, 2008).

2. Demetri Martin, *This Is a Book* (New York: Grand Central, 2012).

3. Thomas L. Friedman, "We Need Great Leadership Now, and Here's What It Looks Like," editorial, *New York Times*, April 21, 2020, https://www.nytimes.com/2020/04/21/opinion/covid-dov-seidman.html.

4. *The Flux Report: Building a Resilient Workforce in the Face of Flux*, January 2014, Right Management, https://www.rightmanagement.co.uk/wps/wcm/connect/350a18c6-6b19-470d-adba-88c9e0394d0b/Right+Management+Flux+Report+Spread.pdf?MOD=AJPERES.

5. Stephen J. Zaccaro, "Social Complexity and the Competencies Required for Effective Military Leadership," in *Out-of-the-Box Leadership: Transforming the Twenty-First-Century Army and Other Top-Performing Organizations*, James G. Hunt, George E. Dodge, and Leonard Wong, eds. (Bingley, UK: Emerald Publishing, 1999), 131–51.

6. Gunnar Bohné, "Emotions at Play: Gaining Emotional Knowledge Using a Video Game" (master's thesis, Uppsala University, 2014), http://uu.diva-portal.org/smash/get/diva2:747683/FULLTEXT01.pdf.

7. "Empathy Definition: What Is Empathy," *Greater Good Magazine*, Greater Good Science Center, UC Berkeley, https://greatergood.berkeley.edu/topic/empathy/definition.

8. Patti Sanchez, "The Secret to Leading Organizational Change Is Empathy," *Harvard Business Review*, December 20, 2018, https://hbr.org/2018/12/the-secret-to-leading-organizational-change-is-empathy.

9. Erik C. Nook et al., "Prosocial Conformity: Prosocial Norms Generalize Across Behavior and Empathy," *Personality and Social Psychology Bulletin* 42, no. 8 (2016): 1045–62, https://doi.org/10.1177/0146167216649932.

10. Anne Brice, "How Having the 'Wrong' Address Almost Cost One Graduate Everything," *Berkeley News*, May 13, 2021, https://news.berkeley.edu/2021/05/13/graduation-profile-aurora-lopez.

11. Elizabeth Levy Paluck, Hana Shepherd, and Peter M. Aronow, "Changing Climates of Conflict: A Social Network Experiment in 56 Schools," *Proceedings of the National Academy of Sciences* 113, no. 3 (January 19, 2016): 566–71, https://doi.org/10.1073/pnas.1514483113.

12. Byron Katie, "The Work Is a Practice," The Work of Byron Katie, https://thework.com/instruction-the-work-byron-katie.

13. Danielle D. King, Abdifatah A. Ali, Courtney L. McCluney, and Courtney Bryant, "Give Black Employees Time to Rest and Recover," *Harvard Business Review*, February 22, 2021, https://hbr.org/2021/02/give-black-employees-time-to-rest-and-recover.

14. Audre Lorde, *A Burst of Light and Other Essays* (Mineola, NY: Ixia Press, 2017).

15. Stephen R. Covey, *The 7 Habits of Highly Effective People: Powerful Lessons in Personal Change: 30th Anniversary Edition* (New York: Simon & Schuster, 2020).

16. "Habit 7: Sharpen the Saw®," FranklinCovey, https://www.franklincovey.com/habit-7.

17. Arnaldo Camuffo et al., "A Scientific Approach to Entrepreneurial Decision Making: Evidence from a Randomized Control Trial," *Management Science* 66, no. 2 (February 2020): 564–86, https://doi.org/10.1287/mnsc.2018.3249.

18. Though I hadn't watched it before creating the failure exercise, Jia Jiang's TED talk on purposefully being rejected for one hundred days straight provides more terrific insights: Jia Jiang, "What I Learned from 100 Days of Rejection," January 6, 2017, TED video, 15:31, https://www.youtube.com/watch?v=-vZXgApsPCQ.

Chapter 6

1. Herminia Ibarra, *Act Like a Leader, Think Like a Leader* (Boston: Harvard Business Review Press, 2015).

2. Herminia Ibarra (@HerminiaIbarra), "My new book #ActLikeaLeader," February 9, 2015, 3:45 a.m., https://twitter.com/HerminiaIbarra/status/564751835450597376.

3. "BUILD.org," Remake Learning, https://remakelearning.org/organization/build-org.

4. *State of the Global Workplace: 2021 Report*, "State of the Global Workplace," Gallup, https://www.gallup.com/workplace/349484/state-of-the-global-workplace.aspx.

5. Margaret Wheatley and Deborah Frieze, "Using Emergence to Take Social Innovations to Scale," 2006, https://www.margaretwheatley.com/articles/emergence.html.

6. Damon Centola et al., "Experimental Evidence for Tipping Points in Social Convention," *Science* 360, no. 6393 (June 8, 2018): 1116–19, https://doi.org/10.1126/science.aas8827.

7. Mark Wilson, "The Magic Number of People Needed to Create Social Change," *Fast Company*, June 22, 2018, https://www.fastcompany.com/90176846/the-magic-number-of-people-needed-to-create-social-change.

8. Barbara Ransby, "Black Lives Matter Is Democracy in Action," editorial, *New York Times*, October 21, 2017, https://www.nytimes.com/2017/10/21/opinion/sunday/black-lives-matter-leadership.html.

9. Jane Wei-Skillern, David Ehrlichman, and David Sawyer, "The Most Impactful Leaders You Have Never Heard Of," *Stanford Social Innovation Review*, September 16, 2015, https://ssir.org/articles/entry/the_most_impactful_leaders_youve_never_heard_of.

10. Shawn Achor, Andrew Reece, Gabriella Rosen Kellerman, and Alexi Robichaux, "9 Out of 10 People Are Willing to Earn Less Money to Do More-Meaningful Work," *Harvard Business Review*, November 6, 2018, https://hbr.org/2018/11/9-out-of-10-people-are-willing-to-earn-less-money-to-do-more-meaningful-work.

11. Scott D. Johnson and Curt Bechler, "Examining the Relationship Between Listening Effectiveness and Leadership Emergence: Perceptions, Behaviors, and Recall," *Small Group Research* 29, no. 4 (1998): 452–71, https://doi.org/10.1177/1046496498294003.

12. Kate Murphy, *You're Not Listening: What You're Missing and Why It Matters* (New York: Celadon Books, 2020).

Chapter 7

1. Drew Dudley, "Everyday Leadership," filmed September 30, 2010, at TEDxToronto, Toronto, Canada, video, 6:01, https://www.ted.com/talks/drew_dudley_everyday_leadership.

2. Sydney Page, "She Almost Jumped Off a Bridge. She Now Returns There to Post Notes That Have Saved the Lives of Others," *Washington Post*, June 3, 2021, https://www.washingtonpost.com/lifestyle/2021/06/03/suicide-bridge-note-kindness.

3. Gillian R. Brassil, "Sedona Prince Has a Message for You," *New York Times*, May 29, 2021, https://www.nytimes.com/2021/05/29/sports/ncaabasketball/sedona-prince-ncaa-basketball-video.html.

4. Nancy Armour, "Opinion: Sedona Prince Has Left Her Mark on NCAA Tournament, Women's Sports," editorial, *USA Today*, March 29, 2021, https://www.usatoday.com/story/sports/columnist/nancy-armour/2021/03/29/ncaa-tournament-sedona-prince-impact-women-goes-beyond-oregon/7042248002.

5. Ronald A. Heifetz, *Leadership Without Easy Answers* (Cambridge, MA: Belknap Press of Harvard University Press, 1994).

6. "First Follower: Leadership Lessons from Dancing Guy," Derek Sivers, February 11, 2010, YouTube video, 2:57, https://www.youtube.com/watch?v=fW8amMCVAJQ.

7. Liz Wiseman, *Multipliers: How the Best Leaders Make Everyone Smarter* (New York: Harper Business, 2017).

8. Liz Wiseman and Greg McKeown, "Managing Yourself: Bringing Out the Best in Your People," *Harvard Business Review*, May 2010, https://hbr.org/2010/05/managing-yourself-bringing-out-the-best-in-your-people.

9. Lauren Keller Johnson, "Exerting Influence Without Authority," *Harvard Business Review*, February 28, 2008, https://hbr.org/2008/02/exerting-influence-without-aut.

10. "Pitbull—Feel This Moment (Official Video) ft. Christina Aguilera," Pitbull, March 15, 2013, YouTube video, 3:49, https://www.youtube.com/watch?v=5jlI4uzZGjU.

11. Noah J. Goldstein, Robert B. Cialdini, and Vladas Griskevicius, "A Room with a Viewpoint: Using Social Norms to Motivate Environmental Conservation in Hotels," *Journal of Consumer Research* 35, no. 3 (October 1, 2008): 472–82, https://doi.org/10.1086/586910.

12. David B. Strohmetz et al., "Sweetening the Till: The Use of Candy to Increase Restaurant Tipping," *Journal of Applied Social Psychology* 32, no. 2 (July 31, 2002): 300–09, https://doi.org/10.1111/j.1559-1816.2002.tb00216.x.

13. Konexio (@Konexio_eu), "Our vision?," Twitter, January 28, 2021, 1:11 a.m., https://twitter.com/Konexio_eu/status/1354718835341930496.

14. Rebecca Sun, "'Crazy Rich Asians': Read the Letter That Convinced Coldplay to Allow 'Yellow' in the Movie," *Hollywood Reporter*, August 19, 2018, https://www .hollywoodreporter.com/news/general-news/read-crazy-rich-asians-director-s-letter -coldplay-yellow-1135826.

Chapter 8

1. Jason Le Miere, "New Zealand PM Says She Told Donald Trump to Show 'Sympathy and Love for All Muslim Communities,'" *Newsweek*, March 15, 2019, https:// www.newsweek.com/new-zealand-donald-trump-mosque-muslim-1365338.

2. Andrés Tapia, "The Inclusive Leader," Korn Ferry, https://www.kornferry.com /insights/this-week-in-leadership/the-inclusive-leader.

3. Juliet Bourke and Bernadette Dillon, "The Diversity and Inclusion Revolution: Eight Powerful Truths," *Deloitte Review*, January 2018, https://www2.deloitte .com/content/dam/insights/us/articles/4209_Diversity-and-inclusion-revolution /DI_Diversity-and-inclusion-revolution.pdf.

4. Juliet Bourke and Andrea Titus, "Why Inclusive Leaders Are Good for Organizations, and How to Become One," *Harvard Business Review*, March 29, 2019, https://hbr.org/2019/03/why-inclusive-leaders-are-good-for-organizations-and -how-to-become-one.

5. Juliet Bourke and Andrea Titus, "The Key to Inclusive Leadership," *Harvard Business Review*, March 6, 2020, https://hbr.org/2020/03/the-key-to-inclusive -leadership.

6. "Introduction," re:Work, Google, https://rework.withgoogle.com/print/guides /5721312655835136.

7. Charles Duhigg, "What Google Learned from Its Quest to Build the Perfect Team," *New York Times*, February 25, 2016, https://www.nytimes.com/2016/02/28/magazine /what-google-learned-from-its-quest-to-build-the-perfect-team.html.

8. Amy Edmondson, "Psychological Safety and Learning Behavior in Work Teams," *Administrative Science Quarterly* 44, no. 2 (1999): 350–83, https://doi.org/10.2307 /2666999.

9. "Identify Dynamics of Effective Teams," *Guide: Understand Team Effectiveness*, re:Work, Google, https://rework.withgoogle.com/guides/understanding-team-effectiveness/steps /identify-dynamics-of-effective-teams.

10. Markus Baer and Michael Frese, "Innovation Is Not Enough: Climates for Initiative and Psychological Safety, Process Innovations, and Firm Performance," *Journal of Organizational Behavior* 24, no. 1 (February 2003): 45–68, https://doi.org/10.1002 /job.179.

11. Edmondson, "Psychological Safety," 350–83.

12. Amy C. Edmondson, *The Fearless Organization: Creating Psychological Safety in the Workplace for Learning, Innovation, and Growth* (Hoboken, NJ: Wiley, 2019).

13. Maura Kessel, Jan Kratzer, and Carsten Schultz, "Psychological Safety, Knowledge Sharing, and Creative Performance in Healthcare Teams," *Creativity and Innovation Management* 21, no. 2 (June 2012): 147–57, https://doi.org/10.1111 /j.1467-8691.2012.00635.x.

14. Katherine W. Phillips, "How Diversity Makes Us Smarter," *Scientific American*, October 2014, https://www.scientificamerican.com/article/how-diversity-makes-us -smarter.

15. Cristian L. Dezsö and David Gaddis Ross, "Does Female Representation in Top Management Improve Firm Performance? A Panel Data Investigation," *Strategic Management Journal* 33, no. 9 (September 2012): 1072–89, https://doi.org/10.1002 /smj.1955.

16. Orlando Richard et al., "Employing an Innovation Strategy in Racially Diverse Workforces: Effects on Firm Performance," *Group & Organization Management* 28, no. 1 (2003): 107–26, https://doi.org/10.1177/1059601102250022.

17. Denise Lewin Loyd et al., "Social Category Diversity Promotes Premeeting Elabo-ration: The Role of Relationship Focus," *Organization Science* 24, no. 3 (May–June 2013): 757–72, https://doi.org/10.1287/orsc.1120.0761.

18. Phillips, "How Diversity Makes Us Smarter."

19. Daniel Goleman, "Leadership That Gets Results," *Harvard Business Review*, March–April 2000, https://hbr.org/2000/03/leadership-that-gets-results.

Chapter 9

1. Lanre Bakare, "Pink Seesaws Reach Across the Divide at US-Mexico Border," *Guardian*, July 30, 2019, https://www.theguardian.com/us-news/2019/jul/30/pink -seesaws-reach-across-divide-us-mexico-border.

2. "Ethiopia Plants over 350 Million Trees in a Day, Setting New World Record," *UNEP*, United Nations Environment Programme, August 2, 2019, https://www .unep.org/news-and-stories/story/ethiopia-plants-over-350-million-trees-day-setting -new-world-record. Note that Ethiopia's claim of 350 million trees has not been independently verified as of February 2022.

3. Brandi Nicole Johnson, "7 Things Leaders, Brands, Companies and Organizations Can Do to Support Black Employees," *Medium*, June 4, 2020, https://medium .com/@bnicolejohnson/7-things-leaders-brands-companies-and-organizations-can -do-to-support-black-employees-b182a44c4a72.

4. Jim Collins and Morten T. Hansen, *Great by Choice: Uncertainty, Chaos, and Luck— Why Some Thrive Despite Them All* (London: Random House Business, 2011).

5. *The Social Intrapreneur: A Field Guide for Corporate Changemakers*, Allianz, IDEO, Skoll Foundation, and SustainAbility, 2008, https://www.allianz.com/content /dam/onemarketing/azcom/Allianz_com/migration/media/current/en/press/news /studies/downloads/thesocialintrapreneur_2008.pdf.

6. "Patrimonio Hoy: A Home for Everyone," CEMEX, October 7, 2015, https://www .cemex.com/-/patrimonio-hoy-a-home-for-everyone.

7. Tomas Chamorro-Premuzic. "Why You Should Become an 'Intrapreneur,'" *Har-vard Business Review*, March 26, 2020, https://hbr.org/2020/03/why-you-should -become-an-intrapreneur.

8. Clayton M. Christensen, *The Innovator's Dilemma: The Revolutionary Book That Will Change the Way You Do Business* (New York: Harper Business, 2011).

9. Vincent J. Felitti, "The Relationship of Adverse Childhood Experiences to Adult Health: Turning Gold into Lead," *Zeitschrift fur Psychosomatische Medizin und Psychotherapie* 48, no. 4 (October 2002): 359–69, https://doi.org/10.13109/zptm.2002.48.4.359.

10. Nadine Burke Harris, "How Childhood Trauma Affects Health Across a Lifetime," TED video, September 2014, https://www.ted.com/talks/nadine_burke_harris_how_childhood_trauma_affects_health_across_a_lifetime.

11. *The Social Intrapreneur*, https://www.allianz.com/content/dam/onemarketing/azcom/Allianz_com/migration/media/current/en/press/news/studies/downloads/thesocial intrapreneur_2008.pdf.

12. Steve Blank, *The Four Steps to the Epiphany: Successful Strategies for Products That Win* (Hoboken, NJ: John Wiley & Sons, 2020); Eric Ries, *The Lean Startup: How Today's Entrepreneurs Use Continuous Innovation to Create Radically Successful Businesses* (New York: Crown Business, 2011).

Chapter 10

1. Adam Grant, "Who's the Boss?: Transcript," *WorkLife with Adam Grant*, TED Media, May 25, 2021, https://www.ted.com/podcasts/worklife/whos-the-boss-transcript.

2. "United for Respect Member Carolyn 'Cat' Davis Speaking at the 2017 Walmart Shareholders Meeting," United for Respect, October 7, 2019, YouTube video, 2:57, https://www.youtube.com/watch?v=ft3drtjhMFg.

3. "The Three Types of People You'll Meet When Implementing Change," Innov8rs, September 23, 2018, https://innov8rs.co/news/the-three-types-of-people-youll-meet-when-implementing-change.

4. Christine Ingebritsen, "Norm Entrepreneurs: Scandinavia's Role in World Politics," *Cooperation and Conflict* 37, no. 1 (2002): 11–23, https://doi.org/10.1177/00108367 02037001689.

5. Martha Finnemore and Kathryn Sikkink, "International Norm Dynamics and Political Change," *International Organization* 52, no. 4 (Autumn 1998): 887–917, https://doi.org/10.1162/002081898550789.

6. Cass R. Sunstein, "Social Norms and Social Roles," *Columbia Law Review* 96, no. 4 (May 1996): 903–68, https://chicagounbound.uchicago.edu/cgi/viewcontent.cgi ?article=12456&context=journal_articles.

7. Julie Kliger et al., "Empowering Frontline Nurses: A Structured Intervention Enables Nurses to Improve Medication Administration Accuracy," *The Joint Commission Journal on Quality and Patient Safety* 35, no. 12 (December 2009), https://doi .org/10.1016/s1553-7250(09)35085-0.

8. Victoria Colliver, "Prescription for Success: Don't Bother Nurses," *San Francisco Chronicle*, SFGATE, October 28, 2009, https://www.sfgate.com/health/article /Prescription-for-success-Don-t-bother-nurses-3282968.php.

9. For more information on the model and its development, see "What Is Theory of Change?," Center for Theory of Change, https://www.theoryofchange.org/what -is-theory-of-change.

10. William Samuelson and Richard Zeckhauser, "Status Quo Bias in Decision Making," *Journal of Risk and Uncertainty* 1, no. 1 (March 1988): 7–59, https://doi.org /10.1007/bf00055564.

11. Daniel Kahneman and Amos Tversky, "Prospect Theory: An Analysis of Decision Under Risk," *Econometrica* 47, no. 2 (March 1979): 263–91, https://doi.org.10 .2307/1914185.

12. Alison Beard and Jonah Berger, "Mastering the Art of Persuasion," episode 753, *HBR IdeaCast*, August 11, 2020, https://hbr.org/podcast/2020/08/mastering-the -art-of-persuasion.

13. Jonah Berger, *The Catalyst: How to Change Anyone's Mind* (New York: Simon & Schuster, 2020).

14. "Case Study: The Berkeley Haas School of Business: Codifying, Embedding, and Sustaining Culture," Berkeley Haas Case Series, cases.haas.berkeley.edu/case/berkeley -haas-culture.

15. John P. Kotter, *A Sense of Urgency* (Cambridge, MA: Harvard Business Press, 2008).

Chapter 11

1. Paulo Coelho, *The Alchemist* (New York: HarperOne, 1993).

2. Simon Sinek, "How Great Leaders Inspire Action," filmed September 16, 2009, at TEDxPugetSound, Newcastle, WA, video, 17:48, https://www.ted.com/talks/simon _sinek_how_great_leaders_inspire_action.

3. "Models of Impact," Verynice, http://www.modelsofimpact.co.

4. Jodi Rudoren, "Peace Deal Comes with Hummus at Israeli Restaurant," *The New York Times*, November 25, 2015, https://www.nytimes.com/2015/11/25/world /middleeast/peace-deal-comes-with-hummus.html.

5. Donella Meadows, "Leverage Points: Places to Intervene in a System," Donella Meadows Archives, Academy for Systems Change, https://donellameadows.org/archives /leverage-points-places-to-intervene-in-a-system.

6. Paul Batalden and Earl Conway, "Like Magic? ('Every System Is Perfectly Designed...')," *Institute for Healthcare Improvement*, August 21, 2015, http://www.ihi .org/communities/blogs/origin-of-every-system-is-perfectly-designed-quote.

7. There are lots of variations of this concept, but a great resource (with helpful templates included) comes from the company Atlassian, which uses these as part of new employee onboarding: "My User Manual," Atlassian, https://www.atlassian.com /team-playbook/plays/my-user-manual.

8. Robert B. Cialdini, *Influence: The Psychology of Persuasion* (New York: Collins, 2007).

9. Leandra Fernandez, "Empathy and Social Justice: The Power of Proximity in Improvement Science," Carnegie Foundation for the Advancement of Teaching, April 21, 2016, https://www.carnegiefoundation.org/blog/empathy-and-social-justice -the-power-of-proximity-in-improvement-science.

10. Joanna Cea and Jess Rimington, "Designing with the Beneficiary," *Innovations: Technology, Governance, Globalization* 11, no. 3–4 (Summer–Fall 2017): 98–111, https://doi.org/10.1162/inov_a_00259.

11. Tristan Harris, "A Call to Minimize Distraction & Respect Users' Attention," October 2019, https://idoc.pub/documents/a-call-to-minimize-distraction-respect -users-attention-by-tristan-harris-d47e1096j7n2.

12. Tristan Harris, "How a Handful of Tech Companies Control Billions of Minds Every Day," filmed April 28, 2017, at TED2017, Vancouver, BC, Canada, video, 16:52, https://www.ted.com/talks/tristan_harris_how_a_handful_of_tech_companies _control_billions_of_minds_every_day.

13. "What We Do," Center for Humane Technology, https://www.humanetech.com /what-we-do.

Chapter 12

1. Carol A. Dingle, *Memorable Quotations: French Writers of the Past* (Writers Club Press: Lincoln, Nebraska, 2000).

2. Damon Davis, "Courage Is Contagious," filmed April 24, 2017, TED2017, Vancouver, BC, Canada, video, 5:17, https://www.ted.com/talks/damon_davis_courage _is_contagious.

Index

Act Like a Leader, Think Like a Leader
(Ibarra), 135–36
agency to create change, 195–96, 209,
262, 278n2
Ethiopia's tree planting, 196, 278n2
Havanje's fish sculpture to eliminate
plastic waste, 195, 262
San Fratello and Rael, border seesaws,
196
Aguilera, Pablo, 115–16
Airbnb, 96–98
Alchemist, The (Coelho), 232
Apple, 91, 198, 233
Ardern, Jacinda, 170–71, 262
Asch, Solomon, 53–54
Ashoka organization, 5
Atlassian company, 280n7
Auyeung, Clem, 213

Baez, Joan, 193
Baginski, Sophia, 153
Baker, Ella, 140
Baltimore Museum of Art, 109
Batalden, Paul, 244
Bechler, Curt, 145
Be My Eyes, 151–52
Ben & Jerry's, 92–93
Benedetti, Ally, 9
Berger, Jonah, 224–25
Berra, Yogi, 233

Be The Change, 88
BetterUp, 142
Bezos, Jeff, 48
bias, 173, 175–76, 187
loss aversion bias, 223
status quo bias, 223, 224, 226
Bilhore, Dadarao, 24, 38
BlaBlaCar, 69
Black Friday, 51–52, 92
Black Lives Matter (BLM), 90, 92,
140–41
Blank, Steve, 204
Bohné, Gunnar, 113
Botsman, Rachel, 69
Bourke, Juliet, 172, 174, 176
Bridging Differences, 80
Brown, Brené, 76, 208
Brunell, Mia, 125
BUILD.org, 137
Burey, Jodi-Ann, 71
Burke Harris, Nadine, 203, 204, 263

"Call to Minimize Distraction & Respect
Users' Attention, A" (Harris), 254
Carr, Tony, 26–27, 216
Carse, James P., 95
Cea, Joanna, 253
CEMEX, 199–201
Center for Humane Technology (CHT),
254

Centola, Damon, 139
change, 10–13
  choosing a proactive path, 10
  companies in 1955, loss of, 42
  empathy and acceptance, 114–15, 117
  Martec's law, 12
  Moore's law, 11, 12
  secret to leading change, 232
  three levers of, 26–28, 216
  two maxims of, 10, 42
changemaker
  approach to barriers, setbacks, 5, 23,
    24–25
  defined, 5–6, 9
  a DEI lens for, 181–83
  personal qualities of Siroya and, 4
  "a world of changemakers," 9–10
  your journey, 13–14, 258–64
changemaker action, 13–14
  approaches and tactics, 211–26
  art of agency, 194, 195–96, 209
  Baez's words on, 193
  catalyzing change through culture,
    216–17
  the Changemaker Canvas for, 14,
    227–57
  Davis's changemaker action for
    Walmart's paid family leave,
    210–12, 215–26, 262
  dealing with champions, cynics, and
    fence sitters, 212–16, 226
  first firing bullets, then cannonballs,
    194, 197–99
  first steps, 194–201
  from idea to action, 191–209
  identifying a valid idea, 202–4
  intrapreneurship, 199–202
  Klinger's changemaker action to
    nurses' dosage errors at UCSF,
    217–19

lean startup method, 195, 202–6, 208
leveraging resources, 195, 199–202,
  208
logic model, 222
overcoming opposition, 222–26
reframing problems, 195, 208
taking a leap, 195
theory of change model, 219–21,
  279n9
when change is hard, 210–26, 262
Changemaker Canvas (a model for
    change initiatives), 14, 227–57, 263
  asking "what is the change," 235
  determining substantive impact,
    240–41
  form for, 230, 231, 257
  engaging the community, 252–53
  forming coalitions, 253–55, 257
  four S's of change, 238–45
  identifying evangelists, 251–52, 257
  MVP in action, 248
  opportunity (problem identification),
    235–38
  planning a day-to-day team (doers),
    249–51
  scalability, 241–43
  sections of, 230, 231
  starting with why, 233–34, 257
  sustainability, 243
  systems change, 244–45
  vision, 232–35
  what it is, 230
  who to bring on board, 249–55
Changemaker Challenges
  bad leadership traits exercise, 147
  create a new culture, 226
  develop your own vision statement, 104
  fill out the Changemaker Canvas, 257
  identify a five-minute favor, 104
  on leadership style, 187

perform microleadership acts, 168

practice divergent thinking, 62

practice the mirror-and-window concept, 83

put influence superpowers into action, 168

take the Changemaker Index survey, 38

think on an infinite timeline, 104

try the failure exercise, 130

changemaker community, 229

changemaker impact equation, 193–95, 255, 262

Changemaker Index, 30–36, 38

changemaker leadership, 5, 6–9, 13, 232, 256

becoming the leader you wish you had, 169–87

blame and, 67

community engagement and, 252–53

defined, 135, 148

defining principles, 37

empathy and, 114–15

ethical leadership, 90–93

humility and, 65–67, 141, 256, 262

inclusive leadership, 4, 170–76, 256, 262

as an infinite game, 95

lateral leadership, 156–60

McRaven's "make your bed" and, 70–71

leadership styles, 169, 183–86

microleadership, 148–68, 256

reinventing leadership, 133–47

servant leadership, 86–89

six most crucial leadership skills, 136

starting with why, 233–34

team effectiveness and, 176–81

trust as a superpower, 67–77, 141

T-shaped people and, 47

vision and, 98–102

changemaker mindset, 10, 13, 17–38, 83, 95, 255–56, 264

believe in a different way, 21–22, 260

be students always, 37, 105–32

Changemaker Index survey, 38

defining principles, 37

fixed vs. growth mindset, 19–20, 38

go beyond yourself, 37, 84–104, 144

have confidence without attitude, 37, 63–83

innovate at the edges, 22–23

key traits, 21, 37, 260, 261

learned hopefulness, 23–25

"mindset" defined, 18–19

open to collaboration, 64

question the status quo, 37, 39–62, 223, 258

response to failure, 125–26

strong personal vision, 64

student Hana and, 17–18, 23–25, 27, 38, 260

three fundamental building blocks, 21–24

three levers of change and, 26–28

Changemaker of the Week assignment, 28–29

Change.org, 7

Chavez, Cesar, 105, 106

Cherniack, Emily, 88–89, 261

Chesky, Brian, 96–98

Chouinard, Yvon, 50–51, 52

Christensen, Clayton, 202

Chu, Jon, 165–67, 223–24, 262

Chu Yee Ming, Calvin, 30

Cialdini, Robert, 252

Clance, Pauline Rose, 71

climate change, 12, 159, 216–17

Code2040, 26

Coelho, Paulo, 232

Coldplay (music group), 165–67, 223–24

collaboration, 77–82

  alignment of values and, 80–81

  collaboration in action, 80–82

  inclusive leadership and, 175

  process matters, 81–82

  TKI model, 78–79, 179

  working through conflict, 78–80, 82

  See also teams

Collins, Jim, 66–67, 164, 198

community, social change and, 252–53

confidence without attitude, 63–83, 261

  changemaking as a team sport, 77–82

  humility as a strength, 65–67, 82

  trust as a superpower, 67–77, 82

"conformity experiments," 53–54

Conger, Jay, 159

Cook, Tim, 91

Cornerstone OnDemand, 21

corporate social responsibility (CSR), 200

courage, 263–64

Covey, Stephen, 120

  "sharpening the saw," 119

COVID-19 pandemic, 12, 42–43, 61

Crazy Rich Asians (film), 165–67, 262

cultural intelligence, 175

culture and catalyzing change, 216–17, 226

curiosity, 47–50, 62, 260

  diverse array of activities and, 49

  five obstacles to, 48–50

  inclusive leadership and, 174

  leading with your ears and, 146

  modeling, for teams, 179

  practicing a beginner's mind and, 48

  taking time to play, 49–50

  three ways to approach challenges, 48–49

  unstructured time to encourage, 48

Curious (Leslie), 47

Curry, Steph, 156

Davis, Carolyn, 210–12, 215–16, 262

Davis, Damon, 264

Dawkins, Tom, 71, 109–11, 250

DayCape, 234

DC Social Innovation Project, 108

Deloitte, 171–72

"Designing with the Beneficiary" (Cea and Rimington), 253

Dezsö, Cristian, 182

divergent thinking, 44–46, 62, 137

diversity, 182–83, 187

"Do Humble CEOs Matter?" (Ou, Waldman, and Peterson), 65, 174

Dolores Huerta Reader, A (García), 106

Dorsey, Jack, 137

Dropbox, 205

Dudley, Drew, 148–49

Dweck, Carol, 19

Edelman Trust Barometer, 90

Eden Strategy Institute, 30

Edmondson, Amy, 177–78, 179

Ehrlichman, David, 141–42

Einstein, Albert, 235

empathy, 106, 113–18

  "applied empathy," 169

  defined, 113–14

  "The Empathy Exercise," 117–18

  as an influence superpower, 163–64

  overcoming opposition and, 223–24

entrepreneurship, 191, 192

  author's family in Shanghai and, 191–93

  norm entrepreneurship, 216–17, 226, 262

  social entrepreneurs, 228–29, 239–40, 242, 252–53

Equal Justice Initiative (EJI), 40, 56–57

Ericsson telecom, 44

Espinosa, Sid, 94–95
ethical leadership, 90–93
    consumers and brand choice, 90
    Edelman Trust Barometer and, 90
Ethiopia's tree planting, 196, 278n2
"Everyday Leadership" (Dudley), 148–49
"Experimental Evidence for Tipping
        Points in Social Convention"
        (Centola et al.), 139

failure
    entrepreneurial success and, 125
    the failure exercise, 126–29, 275n18
    the privilege of failure, 125–26
    teams and failing forward, 180
Felitti, Vincent J., 203
Finnemore, Martha, 217
"five-minute favor," 89, 104
flexibility, 106, 260, 261
    clear on why, flexible on how, 107–11,
        130
    cognitive, 111–12, 130, 180
    dispositional, 112–13, 130, 255
    emotional, 112, 130, 174
    pivoting and, 107–9
    rapidly changing environments and,
        111–13
    strategic, 112
Floyd, George, 12, 90, 92
Freakonomics Radio, 21
Friedman, Thomas, 11
Frieze, Deborah, 139, 162
Fyre (documentary), 66

García, Mario T., 106
Give and Take (Grant), 89
"Give Black Employees Time to Rest and
        Recover" (King et al.), 119
going beyond yourself, 37, 84–104, 144
    ethical leadership, 90–93

long-term thinking, 93–98
    servant leadership, 86–89
    thinking big, asking why, 102–4
    vision and, 98–102
Goleman, Daniel, 184–86
Good to Great (Collins), 66
Google, 176–77, 186, 254
Google Impact Challenge, 59
Gorman, Amanda, 20
Gottlieb, Hildy, 99
Graham, Darius, 108–9, 261
Grameen Bank, 61
Grant, Adam, 89
Graves, Kelly, 156
Great at Work (Hansen), 77
Greenleaf, Robert, 87
Gulati, Karina, 153
Guo, Jean, 59–60, 141, 163, 241

habit formation, 93
Halloran Philanthropies, 26
Hansen, Morten, 77, 198
Harris, Tristan, 254–55
Harry and Jeanette Weinberg
        Foundation, 109
Harvard Law School, 39
Havanje, Janardhan, 195, 262
Heifetz, Ronald, 156
Hill We Climb, The (Gorman), 20
Hinton, Ray, 56–57
Holland, Sid, 153–54
Hollander, Edwin, 58
Holmes, Elizabeth, 65
Housman, Michael, 21
Houston, Drew, 205
Huerta, Dolores, 105–6, 163–64,
        241
humility, 65–67, 82, 141, 256, 262
    awareness of bias with, 176
    collaboration in action and, 80, 81

humility (*cont.*)
  inclusive leadership and, 174
  influence and, 164–65
  leaders of "great" companies and, 66
  mirror-and-window insight, 66–67,
    83, 164
  networked leadership and, 141
Hummus Bar, Kfar Vitkin, Israel, 241
Hunter, Paige, 152

Ibarra, Herminia, 135–36
IDEO, 47
idiosyncrasy credits, 58–59
Imes, Suzanne, 71
imposter syndrome, 71–72
inclusive leadership, 4, 170–76, 187, 262
  impact of, Deloitte study, 171–72
  "inclusion" defined, 171
  six traits of inclusive leadership,
    174–76
  three least inclusive traits, 172–74
infinite games, 95
influence
  in action: Jon Chu, 165–67, 262
  empathy and, 163–64, 166–67
  influence superpowers, 162–65
  making it safe and, 164–65, 167
  passion, positivity, and, 164, 167
  the power of reciprocity, 161
  relationships and, 162–63, 166
  understanding, 160–61
  vision and, 163, 166
Influence (Cialdini), 252
Ingebritsen, Christine, 216–17
innovation
  CEMEX's Patrimonio Hoy, 199–201
  diversity and increase in, 182–83
  at the edges, 22–23
  identifying a valid idea, 202–4
  "innovation economy," 26

"the innovator's dilemma," 202
  sustainable option for sanitary pads,
    22–23
Innovator's Dilemma, The (Christensen),
    202
"International Norm Dynamics and
    Political Change" (Finnemore and
    Sikkink), 217
intrapreneurship, 199–202

Jiang, Jia, 275n18
Jobs, Steve, 47, 148, 198
Johns Hopkins University, Social
    Innovation Lab, 109
Johnson, Brandi Nicole, 196
Johnson, Lauren Keller, 159
Johnson, Scott D., 145

Kagetsu, Kristin, 22
Kahneman, Daniel, 223
Kalip, Jessica, 30
Katie, Byron, 117
Kelley, David, 47
Kelly, Matthew, 100
Khazei, Alan, 88
Kickstarter, 205
Kisirisa, Muhammad, 229, 256
Kliger, Julie, 218–19, 262
Konexio, 59–60, 141, 163, 241
Korn Ferry, 171–74
Kouzes, James, 98

Lakhani, Kalsoom, 123–24, 126, 128–29
Lally, Phillippa, 93
Lao-tzu, 86
lateral leadership, 156–60
  "the first follower," 157–58
  Pitbull's advice, 160
"Leadership That Gets Results"
    (Goleman), 184–86

Leadership Without Easy Answers
    (Heifetz), 156
Lean Startup, The (Ries), 204
lean startup method, 195, 202–6, 208
    build-measure-learn loop, 205, 206
    minimum viable product (MVP), 205,
      209, 246, 248
    scaling and, 242
    validated learning, 206
Leslie, Ian, 47
LGBTQ+ rights, 91
Lieberman, J. Nina, 46
Linder, Rosie, 113, 242–43
long-term thinking, 93–98, 104
    Airbnb's infinite time horizon, 96–98
    Espinosa's advice, 94–95
    infinite games, 95
    Kinsey study, 93–94
Long View, The (Kelly), 100
Lopez, Aurora, 115–16
Lorde, Audre, 119
Lyons, Rich, 98, 144, 225

Maddon, Joe, 58
"Magic Number of People Needed to
    Create Social Change, The" (Centola
    et al.), 139
Malan, Jocelyn Ling, 95
Martec's law, 12
Martin, Demetri, "Success" graphic, 107
Martinez, Xiuhtezcatl, 159
McCarthy, Matthew, 92, 93
McCracken, Sam, 203–4, 263
McFarland, Billy, 66
McKechnie Klahr, Suzanne, 137–38
McKeown, Greg, 158
McKinsey study, 93–94
McRaven, William H., 70–71
Meadows, Donella, 244, 245
Mette, Joanne, 218

microleadership, 147, 148–68, 256
    alliance building and, 157–59
    changemaker action and, 202
    "the first follower" and, 157–58
    the four keys, 149–53, 155
    influence and, 160–67
    lateral leadership, 158–60
    leading from where you are, 156–58
    opportunities for action, 152–53
    Prince and, 154–56, 262
    seizing leadership moments, 153–54,
      167
    TikToking for change, 154–56
Miller, Christopher, 92
mirror-and-window insight, 66–67, 83, 164
Models of Impact, 241
Moggridge, Bill, 47
Moore, Gordon, 11
Moore's law, 11, 12
"Most Impactful Leaders You've
    Never Heard Of" (Wei-Skillern,
    Ehrlichman, and Sawyer), 141–42
Multipliers (Wiseman), 158
Murphy, Kate, 146

Nakate, Vanessa, 159
networks, 139–42, 147, 162
    Sebastien's composting efforts,
      139–40, 164, 217, 261–62
    social-change movements and, 140–41
    steps to networked leadership, 141–42,
      254
New Politics, 88–89, 261
Nin, Anaïs, 264
NOBL Collective, 212–14
Nook, Erik, 115
norm entrepreneurship, 216–17, 226, 262
"Norm Entrepreneurs: Scandinavia's Role
    in World Politics" (Ingebritsen),
    216–17

Obama, Barack, 105
Ohlgren, Laila, 43–44, 62
"Open Letter to the Airbnb Community About Building a 21st Century Company" (Chesky), 96–98
opportunity (problem identification), 235–38, 244
opposition to change
  anti-persuasion radar, 224–25
  asking for less to overcome opposition, 225
  the endowment effect, 223–24, 225
  status quo bias, 223–24, 225
optimism, 23–25, 112, 214
  learned optimism, 23, 24–25, 260
Ou, Amy, 65, 174

Paluck, Elizabeth Levy, 117
Patagonia, 50–51
Pebble watch, 205
Peltier, Autumn, 159
Perry, Bruce D., 49
personal user manual, 250–51, 280n7
Peterson, Suzanne, 65, 174
Pfister, Jennifer, 154
Portman, Natalie, 71, 72
Posner, Barry, 98
Powers, Laura Weidman, 26, 38, 216
Prince, Sedona, 154–56, 167, 262
"Prosocial Conformity" (Nook et al.), 115
psychological safety, 169–70, 176–81, 186, 262
  tactics for, 179–81
purpose: leading with values, victories, and vision, 142–45, 147

questioning the status quo, 39–62, 223
  Asch conformity experiments, 52, 53–54

  covergent vs. divergent thinking, 45–46
  developing a vision and, 102–3
  dialing up curiosity, 40, 43–50, 62
  five obstacles, 48–50
  reframing a new idea or change initiative, 59
  taking smart risks, 41, 54–60, 261
  three principles, 40–41
  T-shaped people and, 47
  zigging when others zag, 40–41, 50–54, 261

Rael, Ronald, 196
Ransby, Barbara, 140
Reach for Change, 7, 146, 180, 239, 242
Reagan, Ronald, 73
REI, 52, 92
reinventing leadership, 133–47
  bad leadership traits exercise, 137–38
  leading through networks, 139–42, 147
  leading without permission, 135–37, 147
  leading with purpose, 142–45
  leading with your ears, 145–46, 147
  the new leadership playbook, 146–47
"Relationship of Adverse Childhood Experiences to Adult Health, The" (Felitti), 203
resilience, 106, 119–30, 255, 260, 261
  failure and, 125–26
  failure exercise for, 126–29, 275n18
  falling down, getting back up, 122–24
  plan for, 247
  self-care/self-renewal and, 119–22
Richard, Orlando, 182–83
Ries, Eric, 204
Right Management *Flux Report*, 111–13
Rimington, Jess, 253

risk, 54–60
  changemakers and, 54–55
  evaluating decisions for, 55–57
  getting support, 57–59
  protecting against the downside, 74, 82
  psychological safety and, 181, 186
  smart risks, 54–60, 62, 261
risk quotient, 55–60
Rodríguez Aké, Agustin, 229, 256
Roosevelt, Eleanor, 148
Rosenstein, Justin, 254
Ross, David, 182

Saathi company, 22–23
Saksena, Sarika, 258–59
Samuelson, William, 223
Sanchez, Patti, 114
San Fratello, Virginia, 196
Sawyer, David, 141–42
scalability, 241–43
Scholer, Abigail, 59
Schultz, Howard, 71, 72
"Scientific Approach to Entrepreneurial
    Decision Making" (Camuffo et al.),
    125
Seah, Angeline, 30
Seidman, Dov, 107–8
self-care/self-renewal, 119–22, 225
Seligman, Martin, 23, 24
Servant as Leader, The (Greenleaf)
servant leadership, 86–89
  Cherniack and New Politics, 88–89,
    261
  the "five-minute favor," 89, 104
  microleadership and, 151–52
7 Habits of Highly Effective People (Covey),
    120
Shanghai, China, 191–93
Shanghai Jewish Refugees Museum, 192
Sharon, Yuval, 78

Shigeoka, Scott, 80, 227–28, 262–63
Sikkink, Kathryn, 217
Sinek, Simon, 95, 97, 233
Siroya, Shivani, 3–4, 260
Sivers, Derek, 157, 158
"social proof," 252, 257
Solnit, Rebecca, 23
Sota, Luis, 199–201, 262
Southern Center for Human Rights, 39
SpaceX, 100
StartSomeGood, 7, 98–99, 184, 194, 232
  adaptability and, 109–11
  author and lack of self-care, 120
  author learning to lead with trust,
    67–68
  author takes the leap, 207–8
  bias in hiring, 176
  Champion for, 213
  clear on why, flexible on how, 109–11
  cofounder Dawkins's to-do list, 71
  dealing with cynics at, 214
  division of labor at, 250
  fundraising campaigns, 214–15
  "strategic" flexibility and, 112
  taking on too much, too soon, 197
"Status Quo Bias in Decision Making"
    (Samuelson and Zeckhauser), 223
Steele, Ben, 52
Stevenson, Bryan, 39–41, 56–57, 252, 260
"Stop Telling Women They Have
    Imposter Syndrome" (Tulshyan and
    Burey), 71, 72
Stowsky, Jay, 8
students always, 105–32
  empathy and, 106, 113–18
  flexibility and, 106, 107–13
  resilience and, 106, 119–29
Sunstein, Cass, 217
support, idiosyncrasy credits and
    enrolling others, 58–59

sustainability, 243
  "vacation test," 243
Sweden's Barnrättsbyran, 245
"Sweetening the Till" (Strohmetz et al.) 161
systems change, 245–48
  action plan, 246–48
  how to accomplish, 245
  "system" defined, 244

Tala global investment fund, 3–4
teams, 176–83
  absolute unison and, 181
  diversity for, 182–83
  doers for, 249–51
  evangelists for, 251–52
  failing forward and, 180–81
  forming coalitions, 253–55
  at Google, 176–77, 178, 262
  how to frame a challenge for, 179
  modeling behavior and curiosity, 179
  planning a team, 249–55
  psychological safety and, 177–81
  "social proof" and, 252
  strategies for changemakers, 179–81
  what not to do, 172–74
  Zaccaro's cognitive flexibility and, 180
Tervooren, Tyler, 55–56
Tewfik, Basima, 72
Thank You for Being Late (Friedman), 11
"theory of change" model, 219–21, 279n9
Theranos, 65
thinking
  convergent, 44–45
  "design thinking," 48–49
  divergent, 45–46, 62, 137
  long-term, 93–98, 255
  thinking big, asking why, 102–3
Thomas-Kilmann Conflict Mode
    Instrument (TKI model), 78–79,
    179

Thony, Callysta, 30
Thunberg, Greta, 159
Titus, Andrea, 172, 174, 176
Toyoda, Sakichi, 102
transparency, 58, 76, 117
Tribeless, Empathy Box, 63, 82, 142,
    261
Trump, Donald, 170
trust, 67–77
  being hard on ideas but soft on
    people, 77
  earning the trust of others, 75–77
  networked leadership and, 141
  trust-inducing habits, 70–71
  trusting others, 72–75, 82
  trusting ourselves, 70–72
  "trust leap," 68, 69, 73, 74, 75, 77
T-shaped people, 47
Tulshyan, Ruchika, 71
Tversky, Amos, 223
Two Birds Brewing company, 42–43
Tyson, Mike, 107

UCSF Health, San Francisco, 217–19
University of California, Berkeley
  author's class (Becoming a
    Changemaker), 6–9, 13, 30, 31, 116,
    122–23, 159, 264
  author's class: bad leadership traits
    exercise, 137–38
  author's class: "Changemaker of the
    Week" assignment, 27, 28–29
  author's class: "Go fail" assignment,
    127–29, 275n18
  author's class: Sarika's story, 258–59
  author's hiring at, after rejection,
    133–34
  Greater Good Science Center, 113–14
  Haas School of Business, 8, 37, 98,
    133, 143–44, 251

Haas School of Business, initiative on
the role of culture, 225
Hansen at, 77
Nobel Prize winners on faculty, 159
"safe walk" system, MVP for, 248
Stowsky at, 8

values, leading with, 143–44, 147
verynice (design firm), 241
Viktorsson, Pär, 175
vision
articulating your vision, 99–100
Changemaker Canvas method for,
232–35
clear on why, flexible on how and, 107
creating a shared vision, 98–99
DayCape's vision statement, 234
developing your own vision, 101–2, 104
"five whys" of Sakichi Toyoda, 102
as an influence superpower, 163
leading with vision, 143
long-term thinking and, 93–98, 255
NASA's vision, 143, 163
questioning the status quo and, 102–3
SpaceX's and Volvo's visions, 100
thinking big, asking why, 102–3
Volvo, 100

Waldman, David, 65, 174
Wałesa, Lech, 148

Walmart, 210–12, 262
Wei-Skillern, Jane, 141–42
"We've Stopped Trusting Institutions
and Started Trusting Strangers"
(Botsman), 69
What Do You Do with an Idea?
(Yamada), 202–3
"What I Learned from 100 Days of
Rejection" (Jiang, TED talk),
275n18
Wheatley, Margaret, 139, 162
"When Risk Seeking Becomes
a Motivational Necessity"
(Scholer), 59
Wiberg, Hans Jørgen, 151
Wiseman, Liz, 158
Wooden, John, 95
"Work Is a Practice, The" (Katie),
117
World Economic Forum, 59

Yamada, Kobi, 202–3
"Yellow" (song by Coldplay), 165–67
Yi Wong, Gwen, 63–64, 82, 142, 261
YourStory, 22
Yunus, Muhammad, 61, 62, 142

Zaccaro, Steve, 111–13, 180
Zeckhauser, Richard, 223
"zone of genius," 249

About the Author

ALEX BUDAK is a social entrepreneur and a professional faculty member at UC Berkeley Haas, where he created and teaches the transformative course, "Becoming a Changemaker." He previously cofounded StartSomeGood.com and held leadership positions at Reach for Change and Change.org. He teaches, speaks, consults, and advises organizations around the world, with the mission of helping people from all walks of life become changemakers. He's a graduate of Georgetown University and UCLA and received UCLA's recent graduate of the year award. He loves travel adventures, rooting for the underdog, and spending time with his two favorite changemakers: his wife, Rebecca, and their baby son. More at http://alexbudak.com.

Additional Resources

For more tools, resources, and recommendations to support you in your changemaker efforts, visit http://changemaker.us/resources.